POLICE USE OF FORCE THROUGH THE LENS

Police Use of Force Through the Lens provides a comprehensive look at video-recorded use-of-force incidents and how video influences perceptions about the appropriateness of the force used. No other book on the market takes a historical, critical, and contemporary look at how video footage from dash cameras, body-worn cameras, surveillance cameras, or handheld cameras influence how people perceive the appropriateness of force used by law enforcement officers, correctional officers, and security officers.

Supported with academic sources along with practical examples that connect academics to the real world, the book educates readers about the history of cameras in law enforcement, significant events that influenced the proliferation of cameras in law enforcement, how use-of-force incidents are evaluated, how camera factors influence perceptions, and how human factors can impact how officers perceive and recall what occurred during use-of-force incidents.

A thorough discussion of the benefits and disadvantages of cameras—including how camera perspectives can be misleading and incomplete—challenges the presumption of the objectiveness of video and posits a systematic framework to help evaluators or viewers of video-recorded use-of-force incidents arrive at more objective conclusions.

Mike R. Knetzger served as a Wisconsin law enforcement officer for nearly 30 years and retired in 2022 as a patrol sergeant with the Green Bay Police Department (GBPD). Knetzger has earned a doctoral degree in criminal justice management (Colorado Technical University/CTU), a master's degree in public administration (University of Wisconsin – Oshkosh), a bachelor's degree in justice and public policy (Concordia University – Wisconsin), and an associate degree in police science (Waukesha County Technical College – Wisconsin). He is a certified Department of Justice Unified Tactical Trainer/Instructor and Wisconsin Technical College Instructor, and has been teaching part-time for the past 22 years for Northeast Wisconsin Technical College (NWTC). He teaches in the criminal justice program, police academy, and on specialized law enforcement topics, and is affiliated with doctoral-level programs at CTUonline. Knetzger has testified as an expert witness in use-of-force and standard field sobriety cases, and has consulted for police chiefs, plaintiff attorneys, and other law enforcement leaders related to use-of-force, policy and procedure, and other contemporary policing issues.

POLICE USE OF FORCE THROUGH THE LENS

Examining Video-Recorded Incidents

Mike R. Knetzger

NEW YORK AND LONDON

Designed cover image: artas

First published 2025
by Routledge
605 Third Avenue, New York, NY 10158

and by Routledge
4 Park Square, Milton Park, Abingdon, Oxon, OX14 4RN

Routledge is an imprint of the Taylor & Francis Group, an informa business

© 2025 Mike R. Knetzger

The right of Mike R. Knetzger to be identified as author of this work has been asserted in accordance with sections 77 and 78 of the Copyright, Designs and Patents Act 1988.

All rights reserved. No part of this book may be reprinted or reproduced or utilised in any form or by any electronic, mechanical, or other means, now known or hereafter invented, including photocopying and recording, or in any information storage or retrieval system, without permission in writing from the publishers.

Trademark notice: Product or corporate names may be trademarks or registered trademarks, and are used only for identification and explanation without intent to infringe.

ISBN: 9781032886213 (hbk)
ISBN: 9781032873930 (pbk)
ISBN: 9781003538738 (ebk)

DOI: 10.4324/9781003538738

Typeset in Sabon
by Newgen Publishing UK

To the ethical protectors who keep our communities safe – Thank you!

To Lisa, through our many trials and tragedies, we have persevered, and I am blessed to have you by my side.

To mom, I guess the high-school English tutoring helped. Book number six!

CONTENTS

List of Tables and Figures	*x*
About the Author	*xi*
Preface	*xiii*
Introduction	*xvii*

1	Objectively Reasonable Use of Force	1

Tennessee v. Garner (1985) 2
Graham v. Connor (1989) 5
Section 1983 Civil Rights Violations – Excessive Force 9
Objective Reasonableness 11
State Standards and Department Policy and Procedure 15
Use-of-Force Continuums 20
Use-of-Force Policies 22
Use-of-Force Statistics 23

2	The History of Video Cameras in Law Enforcement	29

3	The Advantages and Disadvantages of Cameras in Law Enforcement	38

Dash Cameras – The Limited Research 39
Body-Worn Cameras – A Summary of the
  Use-of-Force Research 44

viii Contents

Video Footage and Officer Performance 45
Video Footage and Officer Accountability 50
Deterrence Theory and Self-Awareness Theory 52
Body-Worn Cameras and Racial Profiling 53
Disadvantages of Body-Worn Cameras in Law
  Enforcement 54
  Costs and Video Management 55
  Camera Footage Review 56
  Camera Footage, Community Relations, and
    Officer Field Activity 57

4 The Camera Perspective   64

Video Recording Length and Clarity 65
Video Footage and Distance 67
Video Angle and Perception 67
Video Footage Steadiness and Field of View 69
Third-Party Recording of Police 71
The Community Briefing 75
Does Video Footage Speak for Itself? 76

5 Camera Footage and Mitigating the Impact of Bias   82

Heuristics: System 1 and System 2 Thinking 82
Impact of Bias on Perceptions of Officer
  Performance and Behavior 86
Hindsight Bias 87
Confirmation Bias 88
Outcome Bias 88
Camera Perspective Bias 89
Mitigating Bias 90

6 Courts and Video-Recorded Use of Force   94

Prosecutorial and Privacy Issues 95
Judicial Acceptance of Video Evidence 96
Contemporary Case Law and Video Evidence 98
  The People v. Dontrae R. Gray (2023) 98
  Baxter v. Roberts (2021) 99
  City of Topeka v. Murdock (2018) 100
  Emmanuel Reyna v. The State of Texas (2017) 100

Contents **ix**

United States v. Kitchenakow (2016) 101
United States v. McKee (2016) 101
Fischer v. State (2008) 102

7 Human Factors, Memory, and Video-Recorded Use
of Force 106

Human Factors and the Use of Force 107
Perceptual Distortions 107
Tunnel Vision and Inattentive Blindness 110
Auditory Exclusion 112
Slow-Motion Time 112
Memory Distortion and Memory Loss 113
Viewing Camera Recordings and Memory 115
Video Recordings and Report Writing 116
*Cameras, Human Factors, and Law Enforcement
  Policy and Procedure 120*
Other Human Factors Research 124

8 Expert Review, Analysis, and Reporting Methods 133

*Qualitative Study – Proper Management of VRUOF
  Incidents 134*
Method – Viewing and Analysis of VRUOF Incidents 138
Watching Video First 140
Reading the Officer's Report First 142
Expert Analysis and Reporting 143
Introduction and Front Matter 144
Case Review or Facts of the Case 144
Analysis 145
Conclusion 145

Appendix A: Law Enforcement Human Factors Research 150
Appendix B: Sample Expert Witness Report 157
Index 173

TABLES AND FIGURES

Tables

1.1	The Graham Factors	14
3.1	Peer-Reviewed Research about BWCs and UOF	46
3.2	Hours of Law Enforcement Video Footage Compared to Professional U.S. Sports	48
7.1	Perceptual Distortion Research Summary	109

Figures

1.1	Sample UOF Continuum	20
1.2	Sample Police Policy Language that Prohibits Profanity	22
3.1	Officer Video Performance Review Procedures	49
7.1	Sample Police Department Policy: Watching Video before Report Writing	116

ABOUT THE AUTHOR

Dr. Mike R. Knetzger served as a Wisconsin law enforcement officer for nearly 30 years and retired in 2022 as a patrol sergeant with the state's Green Bay Police Department (GBPD). Dr. Knetzger spent 10 years on the special weapons and tactics (SWAT) team as a chemical munitions operator, 15 years as a training unit member, and 20 years as a field training officer. Dr. Knetzger is a certified Department of Justice Unified Tactical Trainer/Instructor and Wisconsin Technical College Instructor, and has been teaching part time for the past 22 years at Northeast Wisconsin Technical College (NWTC). He has taught in the NWTC criminal justice program, police academy, and specialized law enforcement topics. Dr. Knetzger also teaches in doctoral-level programs at Colorado Technical University's CTUonline, and regularly serves on dissertation committees. Dr. Knetzger has an associate degree in police science (Waukesha County Technical College – Wisconsin), a bachelor's degree in justice and public policy (Concordia University – Wisconsin), a master's degree in public administration (University of Wisconsin – Oshkosh), and a doctoral degree in criminal justice management (Colorado Technical University). Dr. Knetzger's published dissertation is "A Qualitative Study Exploring Proper Management of Video Recorded Law Enforcement Use of Force Incidents" (Colorado Technical University, 2020).

Dr. Knetzger is a Subject Matter Expert (SME), author, and freelance writer who has written or evaluated over 30 criminal justice courses across the USA. He has authored or co-authored five books: *Investigating High-Tech Crime* (Prentice-Hall, 2008); *True Crime in Titletown, USA: Cold Cases* (Badger Books, 2005); *Careers in Public Safety: Cop or*

xii About the Author

Correctional Officer (Knetzger Consulting, Publishing, & Training, LLC, 2014); *Ashley's Story* (Knetzger Consulting, Publishing, & Training, LLC, 2015); and *Criminal Law* (Words of Wisdom, LLC, 2015). Dr. Knetzger has also written excerpts for published works, including "An Analysis of Outcomes: First Step Act – the Criminal Justice Reform Act of 2018," in Christopher Utecht's *Current Issues in Corrections* (Cognella Academic Publishing, 2021).

To honor the memory of his 18-year-old daughter, Ashley, Dr. Knetzger is an advocate for stronger drunk driving laws in Wisconsin and fostering social change. Dr. Knetzger is a sought-after motivational speaker and speaks regularly to law enforcement groups, members of the military, community and student groups, and others on topics of ethical protector principles, inspiration and motivation, communications skills, and crisis intervention and de-escalation. Dr. Knetzger has also testified as an expert witness in use-of-force and standard field sobriety cases. He has consulted with police chiefs, plaintiff attorneys, and other law enforcement leaders about the use of force, policy and procedure, and other contemporary policing issues. Dr. Knetzger has presented throughout Wisconsin, as well as in Nebraska, New Hampshire, Iowa, Texas, Upper Michigan, and Florida.

Additional information about Dr. Knetzger can be found at his website: https://drmikeknetzger.carrd.co/.

PREFACE

Aside from professional athletes, whose performance is recorded on game day for all to see, law enforcement officers in America comprise the only occupation that submits itself to recording routine duties. The goals of such recording are many: increased transparency, greater trust, fewer complaints and less frequent use of force (UOF), and an objective record of controversial moments. In many instances, video cameras have produced positive outcomes; in other instances, however, footage has been misleading or incomplete, resulting in more questions than answers. Video cameras in law enforcement are not a panacea. Like any equipment worn by an officer in the field, video cameras are merely another tool that must be used appropriately.

When viewed through the appropriate lens, the benefits of such video footage are manifold: more information to determine if actions are appropriate; potential performance improvement; enhanced accountability; as a catalyst for change; and clarification as to why certain techniques, tactics, or force were used. Conversely, misinterpretation of video footage may result in incorrect conclusions having significant consequences, such as unlawful officer termination, inappropriate prosecution, negligent retention, community outcry, or unsubstantiated demands for change. Misinterpreted footage can also have negative consequences for people whose civil rights are violated by excessive force while the footage is incorrectly interpreted in favor of the officer.

Video-recorded-law enforcement use of force (VRUOF) is commonplace, and viral videos reveal an ugly yet sometimes necessary side of law enforcement. No matter how justified, force never looks good. Nearly all

xiv Preface

law enforcement encounters are resolved without force; however, when force is used and viewed on video, it can cause strong emotional responses from viewers. Our perceptions of such force are significantly influenced by personal biases. Advocates of police officers are likely to believe the force is justified; others are likely to believe the force is unnecessary or excessive.

VRUOF reveals a violent side of police work, and the footage is played and replayed by the media, on social media channels, or viewed by the masses via handheld devices. While airing the videos may promote transparency and help show citizens what happened, viewing VRUOF can be either traumatizing or affirming (i.e., influenced by how you feel about policing). Police violence is a part of American culture often sensationalized in movies and television shows. Frequent and fictionalized police UOF can create the inaccurate perception that force is used often, when, in fact, it is not. Police movies, television shows, and viral videos will continue to rule the airwaves simply because we consume them. Police action sells.

For years, I consumed these videos too. From the fictional *CHiPS* to the reality-based and longest running *COPS TV* show, the sights, sounds, excitement, and sometimes shocking footage was alluring. Moreover, a series of adverse childhood events that resulted in a police response exposed me to real police officers: the protectors who brought empathy and peace to a chaotic home environment. My experiences drove me toward police work and strengthened my desire to serve and protect, to help make a difference.

I spent just shy of 30 years (29.9, to be exact) serving as a patrol officer in Wisconsin. I began my career in 1993 with the Town of Brookfield Police Department, where I served as a patrol officer and detective. The dash-camera era was in its infancy and few agencies had them. Dash cameras were most often used to record interactions or gather evidence during traffic stops or performing operating while intoxicated cases. The footage was used for prosecution and training, especially when officers were involved in high-risk encounters. For some reason, dash cameras did not garner the same level of attention that body-worn cameras (BWCs) would.

In 1997, I received a job offer from the Green Bay Police Department (GBPD). I knew little about "Titletown, USA" and quickly discovered the love affair, fanaticism, and worship-like relationship between its National Football League (NFL) team, the Green Bay Packers, and the community. I spent my entire GBPD career in patrol and too often saw the worst in people. I also saw redemption, and quickly realized that all people – regardless of race, socioeconomic status, sexual orientation, or religious belief – desire a safe place to live where they can raise their families and help each generation become more successful.

I spent my last five years of service (2017–2022) as a patrol sergeant and was privileged to lead committed, brave, and dedicated men and women. While the nature of policing the streets did not change much over my three decades of service, agencies themselves became more transparent than ever. BWCs were deployed by the GBPD in 2019. They became a valuable tool to help investigate complaints, more accurately evaluate and report on UOF, gather more evidence in criminal cases, and provide valuable training opportunities.

In addition to policing, I began teaching criminal justice courses at Northeast Wisconsin Technical College (NWTC) in 2000. That same year, I had finished my master's degree in public administration and wanted to help shape the next generation of police officers. Over the next 22 years, I policed at night and taught during the day. I also wrote and published books, articles, and educational material for colleges and universities. In 2017, I received a grant to pursue a doctoral degree in criminal justice management, which allowed me to carry out original research about VRUOF. This original research and findings became the foundation for this book.

My professional, educational, and research background has allowed me to convey informed opinions both in favor of and against police. Within this book, I have made a conscious effort to remain neutral, support perspectives with empirical research or practical examples, and write to a broad audience. Whether you are a police officer, an advocate of police, or someone wary of police – this book is for you. It is my overreaching goal to inform, enlighten, and teach you, the reader, about how BWCs have affected policing in America, especially when UOF incidents are recorded on video.

Wisconsin is unique in that it has the only statewide unified law enforcement officer and correctional officer training curriculum in the U.S. All law enforcement and correctional officers are provided the same recruit-level training and, throughout their career, are exposed to consistent tactical training that helps establish court-defensible and industry-defensible standards. For this reason, many Wisconsin-based examples appear throughout the text; the concepts discussed, however, are relevant nationwide.

Like police work, the narrative is raw at times, and presents a side of policing that may be difficult for some to read. The examples throughout represent the real world and the sometimes ugly side of policing. VRUOF is no different – ugly – and can be informative, but also misleading and incomplete.

Thank you for reading this book. I hope the content will provide valuable insights and, if anything, cause you to pause before passing judgment while watching the next VRUOF incident. First impressions are often wrong.

Dr. Mike R. Knetzger, Green Bay, Wisconsin

INTRODUCTION

"Headquarters, I got one running!" Officer Jones spoke rapidly into his shoulder mic while he ran after the robbery suspect. "Jones needs help," the dispatcher thought, and quickly sent other units to assist. Officer Jones's body-worn camera (BWC), attached to his chest, captured every jarring stride. The "camera guy" riding along struggled to keep up during the foot chase, but provided another point of view. Officer Jones, breathing heavily, caught up to the suspect, lowered his shoulders, and tackled him onto the concrete sidewalk. A civilian saw the tackle and started recording video with their smartphone – a third perspective.

Officer Jones used his body weight to keep the suspect on the ground. "I just have to hold on long enough for my back-up to get here," Jones thought to himself while he yelled, "Stop resisting!" Each time the suspect attempted a push-up to get up and escape, Officer Jones swiped an arm away, forcing the man's chest back onto the ground. At the same time, the man's face hit the concrete. A few times the suspect reached for his waist. "What is he reaching for? A weapon? Evidence? Drugs?" These questions flooded Officer Jones's mind while trying to control the robbery suspect. Like most fear-induced stressful moments, time seemed slow, and Officer Jones perceived that it took his cover officers several minutes to arrive. In fact, they were on scene only 90 seconds after the tackle, and helped handcuff the resistive suspect. A responding supervisor noticed a surveillance camera on a traffic pole had likely captured the tackle and apprehension on video – a fourth perspective.

"Look how the cops beat him!" one bystander yelled as the handcuffed, bloody-faced suspect stood alongside another officer. Another screamed,

"We got this on tape and will take your badge!" Incomplete video footage quickly surfaced on social media. The next day, dozens of protestors lined the sidewalk in front of the police department. "Fire Officer Jones," they chanted. "No justice, no peace!"

Police administration made a proactive and swift response. A review of all video angles revealed no wrongdoing or battering of the suspect's face. In fact, administration concluded Officer Jones used less force than he could have, demonstrating restraint and control during an out-of-control moment. At a press conference, all video angles were shared with the media, along with an explanation of what had occurred. In this case, the multiple video angles helped quell an inaccurate narrative and the peace was kept. Unfortunately, not all law enforcement video-recorded force incidents end this way.

Many law enforcement officers can relate to Officer Jones's incident. The physiological implications of fear-induced stress (e.g., slow motion time, auditory exclusion, or tunnel vision) are very real. The uncertainty, fear, and exhaustion of restraining a dangerous suspect on concrete where the rules only apply to the officer are the norm. The stress experienced by Officer Jones will influence his memory of the incident. Unlike the four different video cameras that captured the event, Officer Jones's brain did not "record" or "recollect" like a camera does. Instead, Officer Jones's memory of the incident, which will be expressed in his report, will be disjointed, out of order, and not contain all the details that were captured on camera, especially if he does not watch his video footage while writing his report. Should Officer Jones be allowed to view his BWC video footage before he writes his report? Or should he write his report first and then watch his BWC video? Should supervisors, reviewers, or arbitrators of fact watch the video footage first or read Officer Jones's report before watching the video? The answers to these questions will influence outcomes.

Video cameras are ubiquitous in contemporary law enforcement. If officers are not recording themselves, they are likely recorded by someone or some other device (e.g., traffic cameras or surveillance cameras). The video footage, when used correctly, can result in more accurate reports related to an officer's perspective at the time of the event or help reviewers arrive at more accurate conclusions. The improper use of video footage can result in inaccurate, false negative or false positive conclusions, negligent retention, or unlawful termination. How video footage is used to determine whether an officer's actions are objectively reasonable will influence accurate judgments, outcomes, or conclusions.

Video cameras also increase transparency, which in turn may improve trust or fuel distrust. Trust is enhanced when officers are recorded treating people with respect and empathy, or with valor under stressful moments that preserve life. In contrast, perceptions of distrust between police and the public occur when video recordings show controversial or unprofessional actions or depict clear incidents of excessive force. Blatant excessive use-of-force (UOF) incidents confirm negative perceptions of the police, especially within minority communities. A lack of trust makes it difficult for officers to carry out their primary mission – to protect and serve. The impact of video transparency will be discussed in more detail later.

The goal of this book is to inform, educate, or enlighten readers about the impact of video footage when officers use force and make difficult, dangerous, and split-second decisions to protect themselves and others. Law enforcement leaders, trainers, officers, and students, along with casual readers, will become more informed about how cameras influence perceptions, memory, and reporting of UOF incidents. Readers will also discover the connection between video-recorded law enforcement use of force (VRUOF) and strong emotional reactions from viewers, which often lead to premature and inaccurate conclusions. Readers must resist the urge to believe what is seen on video because it is often misleading, inaccurate, or incomplete. "Seeing is believing" is not as simple as it sounds; and how we interpret what we see on video is influenced by our biases, knowledge, cultural influences, and interactions with others, including the police. It is my hope that you will keep reading with an open mind, regardless of your perception – in favor of or against – the police.

Contemporary research on policing and video cameras has focused on the law enforcement or policing industry. The research findings have broader implications to anyone who wears a camera or is video recorded while interacting with others. The term "officer" or "officers" used throughout this book applies to police officers, law enforcement officers, deputies, agents, tactical team operators, security officers, community service officers, and others who serve in various capacities.

Today, most officer and citizen interactions are video recorded, which influences perceived outcomes (i.e., justified or excessive force). One camera angle may show the force used is acceptable, while another angle may make it appear excessive. Camera footage is powerful and can cause strong emotions or reactions among viewers. Also, our biases – in favor of or against the police – influence how we perceive officer and citizen interactions. Reviewers who determine whether force is objectively reasonable must recognize the emotional impact of video footage and consciously set aside biases to arrive at an objectively reasonable conclusion. We must also recognize cameras will never capture an officer's perspective. Rather, cameras are "a perspective," and do not suffer from the physiological effects of fear-induced stress that officers often experience

xx Introduction

during high-stress events. These human factors will be explored more later, which can provide valuable insight into officer performance.

Great effort has been taken throughout this book to provide a balance between empirical research, anecdotal examples, and prose that can be appreciated by a broad audience, from law enforcement practitioners and others to the people they protect. As you read, do your best to set aside biases. Consume the content with an open mind and apply the lessons learned to the next viral VRUOF video. Although some may believe that BWCs can resolve all the ills that have plagued law enforcement for decades, they are just another tool that can help gather information during officer and citizen contacts. Like other equipment on an officer's duty belt, the BWC must be used appropriately, from field application to interpretation and analysis of the footage. The mere presence of a camera will not magically reduce force, improve service, or induce cooperation with the police.

People are more likely to believe what they *see* rather than what they read or hear. It is my hope that what you read within these pages will increase and enhance knowledge about the impact of cameras in the law enforcement or security industry. When the next viral VRUOF incident becomes "breaking news," I also hope you will pause before coming to conclusions, and wait for all the reports, evidence, and camera angles to become available before concluding whether or not the force used was appropriate or justified. Video does not necessarily reveal reality, but *our* reality is often influenced or affirmed by what we see.

Before we examine how cameras influence how we perceive officer actions, we will begin with a discussion about objectively reasonable UOF. Although others have written about the landmark cases that have shaped objective reasonableness, we will look at the issue through a slightly different lens. We consider these cases from the perspectives of the officers *and* the people upon whom force has been used. An attempt has been made to explain the constitutional and procedural impact of landmark UOF cases while humanizing all involved.

1

OBJECTIVELY REASONABLE USE OF FORCE

Contrary to what many tend to believe, officer use of force (UOF) is rare, and more than 95 percent of all officer–citizen contacts are resolved with communications skills.[1] Our perceptions about the frequency of force are primarily shaped by our personal experiences, biases, and television. If your perception of policing was shaped by watching the *COPS* television show, then you may inaccurately believe that officers are constantly involved in vehicle pursuits, foot chases, and UOF incidents, or responding to violent crimes in progress. If you grew up in a violent neighborhood with frequent police presence, witnessed excessive force, or were the victim of excessive force, then you likely believe excessive force is common. You may believe that the police are corrupt and what you see on video confirms your worldview. In some instances, force may objectively occur more frequently in higher-crime, more dangerous, and violent environments, although these relationships have been identified as "weak" by some researchers.[2] Our experiences fuel our biases and how we perceive UOF when it unfolds in our presence or on video.

Most law enforcement officers report they spend less than 5 percent of their time responding to violent crimes, rarely use force, and are less often crime fighters and more often involved in resolving order-maintenance calls.[3,4] The mundane aspects of police work are the reality, but they are not what *reality* cop shows air. Reality TV airs what people want to see – the emotionally impacting or adrenaline-driven vehicle pursuits or officers running down a suspect and using a taser to place them in custody. There would be little viewer interest in the "paperwork edition," which would involve hours of report writing after the arrest. When officers use

DOI: 10.4324/9781003538738-1

2 Police Use of Force Through the Lens

force, it must be justified and reasonable to accomplish a lawful objective. The force used must align with department policy and procedure, state standards, and the U.S. Constitution.

We will begin our discussion about UOF by exploring the Constitutional standard. Two seminal U.S. Supreme Court (SCOTUS) cases shaped the application of contemporary UOF: Tennessee v. Garner (1985)[5] and Graham v. Connor (1989).[6] Before Garner, which eliminated automatic use of deadly force in fleeing felon cases, and Graham, which established the objective reasonableness standard, there was broad inconsistency across the United States about what was considered acceptable force. Laws regulating UOF fell under four categories: the Any-Felony Rule, the Defense-of-Life Rule, the Model Penal Code, and the Forcible Felony Rule, which are summarized below:[7]

- The Any-Felony Rule – This allowed officers to use any force necessary to arrest felony suspects and prevent them from fleeing.
- Defense-of-Life Rule – Deadly force was only justified to protect the life of the officer or others.
- The Model Penal Code – This required two conditions to be present to justify deadly force: that the crime committed involved threats or the use of deadly force; and there was substantial risk that the suspect would cause death or great bodily harm if not immediately apprehended.
- The Forcible Felony Rule – This permitted deadly force against suspects who had committed certain "forcible felonies" (e.g., murder, arson, rape, kidnapping, and armed robbery).

The Garner and Graham cases attempted to rectify these inconsistencies and provide clearer rules or guidelines about when force can be used and how to determine whether force used is appropriate. These two cases have been extensively written about and analyzed by scholars and practitioners. Unlike previous writings about these cases, which are mostly filled with legal language, they are written here in a first-person narrative to better humanize all involved. The narratives were formed via an in-depth review of the cases and other sources. After our Constitutional discussion, we will then consider how state laws and department policy and procedure regulate UOF.

Tennessee v. Garner (1985)

On the night of Thursday, October 3, 1974, 15-year-old Edward Garner, an 8th-grader, wandered the streets of Memphis, Tennessee. Was he bored?

A wayward youth? Did he have something to prove? Whatever his reason for breaking and entering a home, it was not worth his life.

Garner smashed his way in through a window. He stepped into the empty single-family residence. His flashlight beam highlighted his path as he wandered through the house. The breaking glass caught the attention of a neighbor, who called the police. (The SCOTUS transcript indicates Garner had a flashlight and broke a window to gain entry.)

Memphis police officers Elton Hymon and Leslie Wright were dispatched to answer a "prowler inside" call. Upon arrival, the officers saw the caller standing on her porch, pointing towards an adjacent residence. "I heard glass breaking," she told the officers, and "someone was breaking in."[8]

Handheld radios were not yet the norm, and Officer Wright returned to the squad car to radio dispatch. Officer Hymon, with 15 months under his belt, approached the victim's house to investigate further, and walked around the back. Did Garner see Officer Hymon? If he did, Garner had a few choices: surrender, hide in the house, or flee. He might have feared arrest and beating by Memphis police, or even death.

It was a tumultuous time in Memphis. Little to no trust existed between the Black community and the Memphis police. Forty-five years later, Officer Hymon said:

> The "N" word was used without hesitation or repercussion and several white officers proudly notched their revolvers for every African-American they had killed ... among many white officers ... there was a practice of a drop gun to place on a shot or killed suspect to justify use of force ... [which] kept a many good officer from going to jail.[7]

Did these unethical and unlawful practices reverberate in the Black community? Did Garner fear a fate similar to other Black people who had been killed or beaten by police?

We will never know why Garner committed this burglary – a property crime – or why he did not surrender. Instead, Garner ran out the back door, which slammed behind him. His take was only ten dollars and a purse.

Officer Hymon saw Garner run across the back yard and yelled, "Police! Halt!" A 6-foot chain link fence stood between Garner and freedom. Officer Hymon's flashlight lit up Garner's frightened face and weaponless hands. Ignoring Officer Hymon's commands, Garner crouched low to start his climb over the fence. Tennessee's fleeing felon law (Statute 40-7-108, 1982) read, "If, after notice of the intention to arrest the defendant, he either flees or forcibly resists, the officer may use all necessary means to effect the arrest." This law could permit Officer Hymon to use any force,

4 Police Use of Force Through the Lens

including deadly force, to apprehend or arrest. Garner would never make his climb to freedom. At that moment, Officer Hymon concluded, "If [he] made it over the fence, he would elude capture."[8] One gunshot echoed through the nighttime air. The 148-grain bullet, traveling at 690 feet per second, pierced the back of Garner's head.

Later that same night, at a local hospital, Garner died on the operating table. Officer Hymon's prayers for Garner's survival were not answered. Upon hearing about Garner's death, Officer Hymon became "unraveled and shaken" to his very core.[8] At the station, he was shaking so badly that his supervisor offered him a shot of Bourbon and counseling. "I refused the counseling, but drank the bourbon immediately," said Officer Hymon.[8]

The ten dollars and purse were found on Garner. Two lives – one ended and another lived knowing what he did – were forever changed. By all accounts, in his police report or testimony, Officer Hymon told the truth – Garner was not armed, which influenced the court's decision. The court struck down fleeing felon laws and developed a new rule precluding lethal force in certain situations:

> [I]f the suspect threatens the officer with a weapon or there is probable cause to believe that he has committed a crime involving the infliction or threatened infliction of serious physical harm, deadly force may be used if necessary to prevent escape, and if, where feasible, some warning has been given.[5]

Today, officers may use deadly force on fleeing suspects only if they pose an imminent threat of serious physical harm (i.e., death or great bodily harm) to the officer or others. The Garner court also recognized that when deadly force is used to stop a person, it is a seizure under the Fourth Amendment. Although the Constitution does not regulate UOF, it does regulate via the Fourth Amendment unreasonable "seizures" of people in deadly force cases. Other standards, such as state peace officer regulations or department policy and procedure, may also stipulate when force (including deadly force) may be used. For a thorough discussion about the Fourth Amendment and UOF, see the law journal article by Stoughton (2021), "How the Fourth Amendment Frustrates the Regulation of Police Violence."

Shortly after the Garner case, another landmark incident unfolded on the streets of North Carolina. Although our next case did not result in death, force used to take a suspect into custody caused serious injury after officers mistook a low blood sugar diabetic event for criminal behavior.

Graham v. Connor (1989)

Prior to the landmark Graham v. Connor decision, the courts used inconsistent methods or analysis when determining whether force to effect an arrest was reasonable or acceptable. Some courts relied upon the Fourth Amendment, others the Fourteenth Amendment (i.e., the State due process clause), and sometimes the Equal Protection Clause. The lack of a consistent judicial standard to determine whether force was properly applied not only made it difficult to analyze these incidents, but there was also (and still is) a lack of consistent force standards for American law enforcement officers. Although the Graham court attempted to set a clear "objectively reasonable" standard, their decision is not without criticism.

Although Graham provides some guidelines to help determine the appropriateness of force, the standard is often inconsistently applied and fails to hold accountable officers who create the need to use force, even if the force used is "reasonable."[9,10] A critical analysis for or against Graham is outside the scope of this work. Unless Graham is overruled, it remains the landmark case that we must rely upon to determine if force used is reasonable or appropriate.

The following narrative was derived from a thorough examination of the Graham v. Connor (1989) SCOTUS transcript and the United States Court of Appeals for the Fourth Circuit transcript (1988). Where appropriate, quotes are supported with in-text citations to indicate the transcript it was obtained from.

Sometime after noon on Monday, November 12, 1984, Dethorne Graham, a diabetic and North Carolina Department of Transportation employee, had been working on rebuilding an automatic transmission. His blood sugar continued to drop while he worked. "I worked a little longer than I should have," Graham thought to himself as his friend, William Berry, joined him. Berry knew about Graham's diabetes and had seen him experience low blood sugar events. Graham simply pointed or gestured. Berry knew Graham needed orange juice, so they climbed into Berry's car.

Graham normally went to his girlfriend's house for help because she knew what to do, but that was too far away. While on West Boulevard, Graham pointed Berry towards "Pilot's Service Station." Berry turned into the lot and stopped about 8 or 9 feet from the glass doors. A Charlotte (N.C.) squad car was parked in front of them. Officer Connor was outside of his squad talking to someone.[11]

Graham hurried into the store. "I can't wait," he thought to himself, when he saw 5 or 6 people at the register. He hurried out of the store and back into Berry's car. "To my girlfriend's house," Graham gestured, pointing in that direction. "Are you all right?" Berry asked. "What did

6 Police Use of Force Through the Lens

you do in the store?"[11] "I didn't do anything," replied Graham as Officer Connor now rolled up behind them. "Skip him. Just keep on to where we're going," Graham suggested when Berry said a police officer was following them. Officer Connor's siren blipped. Now a half-mile from the Pilot store, Berry stopped his car by the curb. Officer Connor walked up along the driver's side door.[11]

"What's wrong with your friend?" Officer Connor asked. Berry replied, "I don't know, but I think he's having a sugar reaction. I don't know what to do for him."[11]

Officer Connor leaned forward and gazed at Graham. "What's wrong with you?" Graham sat silent. "Well, I'm going to have to ... Wait here until I find out what he did at the store," Officer Connor ordered, and walked back to his squad car.[11]

Graham thought to himself, "If he thinks I'm going to sit here in the car while I'm dying to wait for him to find out something when there really is nothing." His blood sugar continued to crash, and Graham's recollection faded. Graham opened his passenger side door and started running around.[11]

When Officer Connor returned to his squad, he saw Graham run twice around Berry's car and then sit down on the curb, near the front bumper. A crowd of onlookers also began to gather and watch the spectacle unfold. The next thing Graham remembers is being on the ground, looking up and seeing a familiar face in the crowd – a woman named Maggie Black, and then Officer Connor.[11]

Berry, scared and unsure of how to help Graham, knelt by him. Officer Connor joined them and also knelt, but didn't say a word. Three other squads arrived and surrounded Berry's car. A large crowd had begun to gather. "Someone, candy, sugar, orange juice or whatever," Berry pleaded to anybody who could help Graham.[11]

One of the cover officers named, Wright, ordered: "Put the handcuffs on him!" Officer Wright pushed Berry out of the way, grabbed Graham, and rolled him face down onto the sidewalk. Graham refused to put his hands behind his back, and thrust them straight above his head. Officers forced his hands behind his back. The handcuffs compressed Graham's wrists, leaving grooves or indentations on his skin. Officer Wright grabbed a handful of Graham's hair while he started to lift him off the ground. A Charlotte Alderman who had also been in the crowd tried to intervene. He put his hand on Officer Wright and said, "No that's not right." Wright continued to pick Graham up.[11]

"They snatched him up off the ground and put him face down on my car," Berry later testified. The force used helped Graham regain some of his senses. "Please look in my wallet!" Graham's pleas for officers to find

Objectively Reasonable Use of Force **7**

his diabetes card were ignored. Each time he lifted his head to talk to officers it was forced or slammed back onto the hood of the car, with a terse "Shut up!"[11]

"Don't tell me to shut up because I am trying to tell you what's wrong with me," Graham replied.[11]

A female officer named Matos quipped, "I've seen a lot of people with sugar diabetes that never acted like this. Ain't nothing wrong with the mother [expletive], but drunk. Lock the son-of-a-bitch up." Berry begged and pleaded: "Please don't lock him up! Just take him home please!"[11]

Four officers carried Graham, horizontally, by his arms and legs, and tossed him headfirst like a bag of potatoes onto the back seat of a squad car. Another officer opened the opposite door and pulled Graham while the other three officers fed him in. During the manhandling, Graham's left shoe fell off, and Berry picked it up. Graham pleaded with officers, "Please give me the orange juice." Officer Matos' retort: "I am not giving you shit."[11]

The Pilot store reported that nothing had occurred. Graham had not committed a crime. The Alderman purchased some orange juice from another store and returned to the scene. He asked, "Can I give him some orange juice?" The police refused, and instead Officer Connor drove Graham home.[11]

"Let me get out myself," Graham demanded as Officer Connor tried to help him out of the squad car. Slowly, he got to his feet. Berry steadied Graham by his left shoulder. Officer Connor propped him up along his right shoulder. The Alderman, who had followed to Graham's house, poured orange juice into his mouth. The handcuffs were removed and Graham fell to the ground. He slowly got himself up again. Berry tried to help put his left shoe on, but Graham's foot pain prevented that. While Graham slowly walked into his house he said, "I think they've broke my foot," which was later verified by an X-ray.[11]

As quickly as the officers had left, they were summoned back to Graham's house. "I want to make a complaint," Graham demanded over the phone to another Charlotte Police Department employee. Officers Wright and Matos were sent back out. Officer Wright, with gun in hand, walked towards the house, and Matos held a blackjack, a leather strap with lead at one end.[11]

"No, that's all right" Berry reassured the officers. "Ain't nothing wrong. Just go ahead on." The officers obliged and drove off.[11]

Berry first took Graham to his primary doctor, who treated his diabetes and told him what happened. After his blood sugar levels were stabilized, Graham was ordered to the hospital. He was treated at Mercy Hospital

8 Police Use of Force Through the Lens

for numerous injuries and hobbled home on crutches. He missed the next five-and-a-half weeks of work. Four years later, during testimony, Graham described his injuries.

> Well, I have to take a shot every day, and I'm right-handed, and that was the arm – I couldn't use it. Just couldn't use it. After being slammed on the hood that day, I didn't realize ringing in my ears right then, but when we was on the way up the street, that's when I realized the ringing in my ear because when that radio came on when he was telling him about the guns that I had, then I realized there was a ringing in my ear, in my right ear. Well, the ringing, it's still there. My shoulder, it was – it got all right after about three or four months. My right hand, both hands were numb. I think the cuffs were too tight. I think they did that. Both hands were numb. I could rake my hand across the back of them and I had no feeling. The right one, the feeling came back in five or six days. The left one, it was about two and a half months before the feeling came in. Before that, when I raked my hand across the back, it was like raking a pencil across the back of it. I couldn't walk because I have a bone disease, and I was under medication before this happened, and after it happened, they had to increase my medication, and the medication that they gave me was so strong.[11]

Graham's case progressed to the United States Supreme Court. The lower courts used the "Glick" test to determine if excessive force had been used in violation of Graham's Constitutional rights. The four Glick factors were derived from the U.S. Supreme Court case of Johnson v. Glick (1973), and were used to determine if officer UOF was excessive in support of section 1983 lawsuits.[12] The Glick factors included:

- The need for the application of the force.
- The relationship between the need and the amount of the force that was used.
- The extent of the injury inflicted.
- Whether the force was applied in a good faith effort to maintain and restore discipline or maliciously and sadistically for the very purpose of causing harm.

Before we apply Glick to the Graham case, some attention to the Section 1983 suits is warranted because they are used today as a premise to file excessive force claims against police.

Section 1983 Civil Rights Violations – Excessive Force

Federal law 42 U.S. Code, Section 1983, provides people with the right to sue state government employees acting "under color of state law" for civil rights violations. Officers working in an official capacity who use force to effect an arrest are considered "under color of law" at the time. In Graham's case, the officers were acting in their official capacity when force was used, which allowed Graham to proceed with a Section 1983 claim.

In addition, when applying force to make an arrest, officers are privileged to use physical methods (e.g., take-downs, punches, kicks, knee strikes), tools (e.g., batons, electronic control devices/ECDs, pepper spray), or deadly force, which otherwise would be considered a criminal act (e.g., battery or homicide). However, privilege is lost when force used is intentionally applied to punish or abuse and is considered "shocking to the conscience." In UOF cases, an officer's actions may be considered "shocking to the conscience" if "it is so egregious, so outrageous, that it may be fairly said to shock the contemporary conscience."[13] Shocking-to-the-conscience cases are rare but sometimes occur. Graham's case was not considered "shocking to the conscience," but a 1997 case out of New York was.

In 1997, New York Police Department (NYPD) officers responded to a disturbance outside a night club. While intervening, Officer Justin Volpe was punched in the face and believed Haitian immigrant Abner Louima was responsible. Louima was arrested for assault and, during the ride to the station, the patrol car stopped in a deserted area, where Louima was beaten by four officers. At the 70th Street precinct, in front of other officers, Louima's pants were pulled down and he was taken to a bathroom, where he was sodomized with a wooden toilet or broom handle, and his teeth were knocked out when the handle was shoved in his mouth. Although Louima's screams were heard by other officers, nobody intervened, and he was placed in a holding cell.[14]

Louima continued to scream from the unbearable pain caused by his perforated bowel and bladder and knocked-out teeth. A few hours later, Louima was taken to a New York hospital, where officers told medical staff that he had been injured while having sex in jail. A Haitian nurse, who took the time to listen to Louima, was told the shocking details about the assault. Furious, the nurse reported it to NYPD internal affairs and the news media.[14] Officer Volpe was convicted and sentenced to 30 years in prison.[14] Several surgeries were needed to repair Louima's injuries, and he would eventually reach a settlement of 8.7 million dollars for this shocking assault.[15]

10 Police Use of Force Through the Lens

The intentional and excessive UOF in this case was clearly an example of behavior that was so egregious, so outrageous, that it shocked the contemporary conscience. The intentional infliction of harm and abuse that Louima experienced was described as the worst case of police abuse and brutality in the history of America.[16] Louima's case also prompted calls for civilians to use video cameras to record the police to deter police brutality and help educate people about their rights.[17] It was not known at the time how effective cameras might be; research on how cameras might prevent unnecessary force or affect the frequency of force would not occur until the proliferation of body-worn cameras (BWCs).

We now turn our attention back to Graham. When applying the Glick test to the Graham case, the lower courts considered the evidence in the light most favorable to Graham and concluded the following:

- Graham was having an insulin reaction and was in such a state of agitation that his witness, Berry, asked Officer Connor to help catch him.
- The amount of force used included handcuffing Graham, which even one of his own witnesses testified was appropriate under the circumstances.
- There was no discernable injury inflicted on Graham. It is true that his foot was broken during the scuffle with the police. However, there is absolutely no evidence that the police inflicted any injury on Graham.
- It is quite evident that the force applied was a good faith effort to maintain or restore order in the face of a potentially explosive situation, and was not applied maliciously or sadistically for the very purpose of causing harm.

Clearly dissatisfied with the lower court's decision, Graham appealed, and his case was eventually accepted by the U.S. Supreme Court. The Supreme Court vacated the lower court decisions and remanded the case back for analysis under new standards. The justices rejected the Glick test in favor of a new "objective reasonableness" standard. Glick was rejected by the court because of the subjective requirement to consider whether the force used was done "maliciously or sadistically for the very purpose of causing harm." Determining some sort of malicious or sadistic intent was a subjective consideration, which has no bearing on whether a particular seizure is unreasonable under the Fourth Amendment. Therefore, even if an officer had some sort of malicious intent when using force, if the force used was appropriate or justified under the circumstances, then their underlying motivation does not matter. The Graham court sought to take a more objective approach, although the justices did not provide much guidance on how to apply the new standards. At the same time, the court admitted that "the test of reasonableness under the Fourth Amendment is not capable of precise definition or mechanical application."[6]

Objective Reasonableness

> "Hindsight is not only clearer than perception-in-the-moment but also unfair to those who actually lived through the moment."
> – Edwin S. Schneidman

The "reasonableness" of force, according to the Graham court, requires avoiding the "20/20 vision of hindsight," or hindsight bias, by paying careful attention to the facts and circumstances of each case. This admonition against hindsight bias does not mean we should not review officer performance. Video-recorded use of force (VRUOF) provides us with an opportunity to review, learn from, and improve performance, and video footage should be used proactively in this manner. However, hindsight bias cannot creep into the analysis, and we must only consider the officers' subjective perceptions and observations based upon the information that was known or perceived to them at the time.

Facts and circumstances include the severity of the offense, whether the suspect poses an immediate threat to the safety of officers or others, and whether the person is actively resisting arrest or attempting to evade arrest by flight. The Graham court opined that, to help determine if the force used to affect a seizure is reasonable under the Fourth Amendment requires a careful balancing of the nature and quality of the intrusion on the individual's Fourth Amendment interest against the countervailing governmental interests at stake. The type of offense – whether it be infraction, ordinance violation, misdemeanor, or felony – must be part of the analysis. Lower levels of force would be reasonable or expected when enforcing minor violations versus dangerous felonies where higher levels of force may be used. The severity of *all offenses* in a scenario must also be considered. For example, an incident may begin with investigating a curfew offense or other ordinance violation, but escalate to a physical assault, or felony battery on an officer, by the suspect.

The facts and circumstances within each case must also be viewed from the perspective of a "reasonable officer on the scene," while recognizing that officers make "split-second judgments" in "circumstances that are tense, uncertain, and rapidly evolving." The court did not provide insight into what a "reasonable officer" is. Questions such as the following were

12 Police Use of Force Through the Lens

not posed or considered by the court to help clarify or identify what makes a reasonable officer and their actions reasonable at the time force is used:

- Which qualities, traits, or attributes does a reasonable officer possess?
- How do officers' training, education, and experience influence their perception of reasonableness?
- What if a more experienced officer viewed the scenario as less intense, uncertain, and rapidly evolving than a less experienced officer?
- What about the officer's previous experience with the person?
- How do department policies and procedures influence what a reasonable officer would do?
- How does the number of subjects as well as their age, sex, size, and relative strength compare with the officer involved?
- How do industry or state UOF standards influence what a reasonable officer would do?
- How do local customs or culture influence reasonable officer actions?

A lack of consistent training across the nation further clouds the "reasonable officer" standard. The length and type of law enforcement training varies. On average, American law enforcement academies are between 650 and 1075 hours with varied curricula, including UOF standards.[18] In contrast, Canadian officers receive more than 1000 hours of training, England more than 2000 hours, Australia more than 3000 hours, and Finland 5500 hours.[19] The curricula in these other countries are also consistent, much like the unified training offered to Wisconsin officers. Consistent training, standards, and criteria for using force would help evaluators determine if the force used by the reasonable officer is justified or appropriate. However, providing officers with more education or training does not necessarily reduce the frequency of force used or enhance the legitimacy, or reasonableness, of force used.

Some states require some college education to become a police officer, while others mandate only a high school diploma. Whether college-educated or not, we ask these same men and women, after police academy training, to make important constitutional decisions about when to use force – and how much. Are we doing a disservice to American officers by not increasing minimum standards or requiring more training or education? Are there strong connections between college education and officer performance? The research in this area is inconclusive. In four studies, researchers discovered that officers with at least a bachelor's degree used force less than counterparts with less education.[20,21,22,23] In contrast, others have found no correlation between education level and frequency of force.[24,25] If college education is not a decisive factor, then what about more training?

Researchers have discovered positive connections between certain training methods and improved force outcomes. Officers who were exposed to an "international performance resilience and efficiency program" (iREP), which taught participants to better regulate arousal and reduce psychological threat perception, made more accurate force decisions compared to others who did not have the training.[26] In Chicago, over 1000 officers were exposed to a months-long pilot training program called situational decision-making (Sit-D).[27] The training featured small class sizes and employed a mix of lectures, scenario-based video simulation, and peer discussion to increase engagement. The purpose of the scenario-based simulation training was to "teach situational awareness, continuous assessment, and emotional regulation," while also helping officers recognize situations where they may be likely to use cognitive shortcuts (i.e., those based upon past experiences) to make force decisions. Multiple scenarios provided officers with opportunities to consider their decision-making, scene assessment, and critical thinking before applying the skills on the streets. The scenarios were followed by in-depth peer discussion about their assumptions and how they influenced decisions and outcomes. A randomized controlled trial about the impact of Sit-D revealed that trained officers were 23 percent less likely to use non-lethal force and 23 percent less likely to make discretionary arrests for minor offenses (e.g., disorderly conduct, obstructing an officer).[27]

The Sit-D training program appears to align with the recommendation of Baldwin et al. (2022) that law enforcement training should focus on scene assessment, including recognizing threat cues, improving competence with intervention options, enhancing de-escalation skills, and maintaining a tactical advantage (i.e., time, distance, cover, and concealment).[28] Greater training in and emphasis on these areas may result in improved overall officer performance, with reductions in the UOF.

These limited examples allow us to surmise that it may not necessarily be the *number* of training hours officers receive, but rather the *type* of training that will help improve force outcomes and better inform the reasonable officer standard. More research beyond a laboratory setting about the impact of training and force frequency or accurate force decision-making is needed.

Reasonableness is also determined by the *known* facts and circumstances of each case at the time of the event, while realizing that officers often make split-second judgments in circumstances that are tense, uncertain, or rapidly evolving. When analyzing a force incident, if the hypothetical

14 Police Use of Force Through the Lens

reasonable officer at the scene would have believed using the force was necessary, the court will then likely deem the force reasonable.

The court emphasized that an overriding function of the Fourth Amendment is to protect personal privacy and dignity against unwarranted police intrusion. These Graham factors do not provide bright-line rules about the type of force and how much should be used in certain circumstances. It would be unreasonable for the court to surmise all possible scenarios where force might be used. Rather, the guidelines or "Graham Factors" provide evaluators with some criteria that should be considered when determining if force used is reasonable and justified. The court did not clearly define the criteria or provide practical examples. The "Graham Factors" have evolved over time, and their meaning and application are outlined in Table 1.1.

There have been calls for a revision of the objective reasonableness standard to a "necessary force" standard to justify the use of deadly force. California became the first state to create a necessary force standard, and partially discarded Graham's objective reasonableness standard when

TABLE 1.1 The Graham Factors

Graham Factors	Meaning and Application (i.e., criteria)
20/20 vision of hindsight prohibited	Only the facts and circumstances known to officers at the moment force was used are relevant to the analysis
Reasonable officer at the scene	What would a reasonable, well-trained officer who was *aware* of the facts and circumstances at the time force was used have done in the situation?
Totality of the facts and circumstances of each case	What is the severity of the offense? Did the person pose an immediate threat to the safety of officers or others? Did the person actively resist arrest or attempt to evade arrest by flight?
Nature of the offense and intrusion on individual Fourth Amendment interest	Consider the nature of the underlying offense, the individual's Fourth Amendment interest to be free of unnecessary governmental intrusion, and the government interest in enforcing the law violation
Split-second judgments in circumstances that are tense, uncertain, and rapidly evolving	Consideration must be given to intensity, uncertainty, and how rapidly an incident evolved

evaluating deadly force incidents. However, the California legislature did not include a definition of what "necessary" means and left that up to the courts.[29] California Penal Code Section 835a states: "a peace officer is justified in using deadly force upon another person only when the officer reasonably believes, based on the totality of the circumstances, that such force is necessary."[30] The penal code also recognizes that decisions to use force shall be evaluated from the perspective of a reasonable officer based upon the totality of the circumstances at the time of the force incident, rather than with the benefit of hindsight. Although the penal code appears to forbid hindsight when determining if force is justified, the "necessary" force clause implies that reasonableness will be influenced by outcomes. The objective reasonableness standard is not intended to be an analysis of the incident after it occurred, and the circumstances *not* known to the officer at the time force was used must not be part of the evaluation.

If we create an environment where outcomes inform the "necessary" standard, then instances where officers had mistaken, albeit reasonable, beliefs could be held liable or even imprisoned for their mistakes. For example, over a two-year period studied by *The Washington Post*, 86 people brandishing guns that looked real were killed by police.[31] Published images of the fake or facsimile guns appeared real; and, if pointed at police, would likely cause a reasonable officer to believe they were going to be shot, and respond with deadly force. The outcome – a person holding a fake gun shot by police – under a "necessary force" doctrine would be deemed unnecessary. Had these guns not been fake and the officers hesitated, they would likely have exposed themselves to serious injury or death.

The objectively reasonable versus necessary force debate will continue, and there are no easy answers. Further exploring this issue is beyond the scope of this work. To reduce errors and adverse outcomes, the industry should be committed to providing empirical and evidence-based training, proactively using video to improve performance and outcomes, providing less-lethal force options that reduce risk to officers and suspects, and promoting policing cultures that emphasize de-escalation and recognize that they are policing people and not problems. Next, we will discuss how state standards and department policy and procedure influence the objectively reasonable force analysis.

State Standards and Department Policy and Procedure

Another challenge with determining whether force used is justified is a lack of national UOF standards. There are nearly 18,000 law enforcement agencies in America, and only one state in the nation, Wisconsin, has unified tactical standards for all officers across the state – which are consistent from the academy to instructors, and to all certified law enforcement officers. The unique Wisconsin unified tactics system includes consistent statewide standards for Defensive and Arrest Tactics (DAAT), Professional Communications Skills (PCS), Vehicle Contacts, Firearms, Emergency Vehicle Operations (EVOC), and Tactical Response. These uniform tactical standards are grounded in communications skills. The DAAT manual states:

> Wisconsin's system of Defensive and Arrest Tactics is defined as a system of verbalization skills coupled with physical alternatives. This definition reflects the goal of obtaining voluntary compliance. Achieving your objective by verbal persuasion is always preferable to having to use physical intervention.[32]

The effective use of communications skills can help resolve conflict and prevent the need for force or escalation of force.[33] The nature of an officer's communications skills is an accurate predictor of whether force will be used and how much.[34] As stated earlier, some studies have shown that college-educated officers tend to communicate more effectively, promote de-escalation, and use force less frequently to gain compliance.[35,36] Officers who are rude, condescending, profane, disrespectful, and who lack empathy are more likely to escalate the communication environment and be involved in force incidents. Negative perceptions of the police are also likely when profanity is used during UOF incidents and the force used is often perceived as excessive.[37] UOF systems grounded in professional communications skills should help encourage policing that focuses on de-escalation, voluntary compliance, and less frequency of force.

Gaining voluntary compliance with professional communications skills is not a new concept. Sir Robert Peel (1788–1850), considered the father of modern policing, supported the use of communications skills instead of force to induce public cooperation. Peel authored nine policing principles. The following excerpts address using force and advocating for professional communications.[38]

- To seek and preserve public favor, not by pandering to public opinion, but by constantly demonstrating absolute impartial service to law, in complete independence of policy, and without regard to the justice or injustice of the substance of individual laws, by ready offering of individual service and friendship to all members of the public without regard to their wealth or social standing, by ready exercise of courtesy, and friendly good humor, and by ready offering of individual sacrifice in protecting and preserving life.

Objectively Reasonable Use of Force **17**

- To use physical force only when the exercise of persuasion, advice, and warning, is found to be insufficient to obtain public cooperation to an extent necessary to secure observance of the law or to restore order, and to use only the minimum degree of physical force which is necessary on any particular occasion for achieving a police objective.

Well ahead of his time, Peel advocated for the use of effective communications skills to resolve conflict and embraced the power of humor. Officers who use appropriate humor are more effective at resolving conflict and inducing cooperation.[39] If force was necessary, much like force options today, Peel proposed that only the amount of force used to accomplish a lawful objective was appropriate.

Decades after Peel, in the 1950s, authors of police textbooks such as *The Practical Patrolman* (1959) also preferred the use of communications skills instead of physical force. Communications skills are not just the words used by officers, but also their presence or how they appear in uniform. Presence and dialogue are well correlated, and an officer must "look the part."

> Most patrolmen begin their careers in fine physical condition. But some lose their trimness after several years on the job. The pot-bellied, red-nosed patrolman is a thing of the past (if, indeed, he ever existed at all). To win the respect of the public and his superiors, the modern officer must look well in his uniform ... He must be in good physical condition and present a clean and neat appearance ... He has to look the part.[40]

Officers who "walked the beat" were adept at using their communications skills to build trusted relationships with the public, which also helped promote cooperation. Policing became less personal as walking the beat was replaced by the squad car and radio systems to more effectively patrol sprawling cities during the post-World War II era. Additionally, the civil rights era of the 1950s and 1960s was marred by many examples of police quelling demonstrations with physical force, fire hoses, and police K-9s (dogs), which fueled distrust between police and minority populations. These tumultuous times would eventually force law enforcement agencies to change how they policed communities. A return to Peelian principles, it was believed, would help promote police–community relationships and encourage cooperation to help reduce crime.[41]

The community policing era of the 1980s was guided by Peel's principles, but also greatly influenced by the work of an academic-turned-cop. Little did an English professor and accomplished martial artist-turned-police officer know how his ideas would help improve police conflict resolution

18 Police Use of Force Through the Lens

and communications skills. George Thompson (1942–2011), co-author of *Verbal Judo: The Gentle Art of Persuasion* (1993), became a police officer when he tired of teaching and wanted to do something he felt more meaningful. Early in his policing career, Thompson found himself inducing cooperation with physical force, which was not a problem for this skilled martial artist and black belt in Judo and Taekwondo. However he eventually questioned his methods and believed there must be a better way. Thompson's expert knowledge, along with much trial and error in his street-based laboratory, helped him discover what became his Verbal Judo system. His concepts would eventually be taught to more than a million people in the public and private sector.[42]

Beginning in the early 1980s, training in Verbal Judo taught officers to use communications skills to resolve conflict more effectively with less frequent UOF. Thompson's teachings were widely embraced and adopted by many in the law enforcement sector. He advocated a basic approach for all citizen contacts, which included a professional introduction, an explanation for the contact, and a fair resolution. Thompson believed, and discovered on the streets, that any time citizens were approached by officers they might wonder, "Why the heck is this officer talking to me?" When an officer explains the reason for a contact rather than merely inquiring, "Do you know why I am stopping you?", that "reason" becomes less an issue of contention and immediately reduces conflict during the interaction. Thompson taught other methods, including the effective use of humor, deflecting verbal insults, and providing people with options versus orders before taking action. His book is still in print today and has also been embraced by business and industry.[42]

Today, we can find BWC video examples of officers using Verbal Judo tactics and others who do not. A 2024 California law now requires law enforcement officers to tell drivers why they were stopped instead of asking, "Do you know why I stopped you?"[43] While some law enforcement officials believe this law is strict, Thompson advocated for this same approach decades ago. Verbal Judo concepts are simple to learn and can easily be transferred from the classroom to the streets.[44]

In contrast, poor communications skills, including the use of profanity, tend to increase conflict and frequency of force. What an officer says when force is being used can also influence perceived reasonableness. For example, a 2017 study asked two sets of participants to view the same force encounter: one encounter included the officer using profanity while striking a person with a baton; and in the other scenario, the same force was used but the officer did not use profanity. The mere addition of profanity increased viewer perception that the force used was unreasonable. In addition, the profane officer was perceived as less competent.[37] Profanity can also negatively affect agency perception, which can ripple through a community.

Although other states have standardized recruit curricula, the unified Wisconsin standards follow officers from the police academy and throughout their careers. Only training consistent with the uniform standards is recognized by the Wisconsin Training & Standards Bureau. The uniform tactical training is delivered by certified Department of Justice, Training and Standards Instructors. An instructor from Green Bay, Wisconsin, could travel more than 100 miles south to Racine and deliver any part of the uniform curriculum. Other states lacking such uniformity do not provide consistent tactics training to all their officers, especially post-academy. In states without uniformity, neighboring agencies may use different defensive tactics or carry different force options (e.g., batons, pepper spray, ECDs). One agency might use Krav Maga as their physical tactics system; another might use Pressure Point Control Tactics (PPCT) or a generic "Defensive Tactics" course, while some even carry nunchucks.[45] The criteria for employing certain tactics may also vary or even be non-existent, further complicating the reasonable officer analysis. Training focused only on applying a particular tactic, rather than on decision-making and criteria for using a tactic, will fail to improve force outcomes.

Applying uniform standards like Wisconsin's can help evaluate UOF cases and better identify what a reasonable officer would do in UOF incidents. But implementing uniform UOF standards across America is unlikely. It is a nation with a constitution that promotes state autonomy or "home rule" and limits federal powers. States set up their own governments, determining how they police, and cannot be forced to enforce federal law or adopt federal UOF standards. Further, American culture is diverse, with varying perceptions of acceptable policing.

Although there are no community standards about reasonable force, agencies must be cognizant of how community members perceive interactions between the police and the public, including how force is used. A certain level of acceptable force used in one community may be considered excessive in another. The community perception will not influence objective reasonableness from a constitutional position. However, citizen review boards staffed by community members can conduct inquiries about UOF complaints and draft findings or recommendations to police administrators accordingly. Force may be constitutionally reasonable but deemed unreasonable from a community perspective or as a violation of policy and procedure.

If a Graham analysis reveals that force is excessive and a Fourth Amendment violation, plaintiffs (i.e., victims of the excessive force) may receive monetary relief or "justice" when an offending officer is found guilty. In addition to Graham, other procedural approaches may hold officers accountable and determine if force is justified. Internal department investigations can consider if violations of policy or procedure or state standards occurred during a force incident. It might be determined, for example, that force used by an officer was constitutionally acceptable but a violation of department policy or procedure. Any policy violations will expose officers to department sanctions, up to and including termination.

These three areas of analysis – Constitutional, department policy and procedure, and state standards – can help ensure force applied is reasonable, identify instances of unreasonable force, offer performance improvement opportunities for officers, and assist juries with determining the appropriateness of actions. Any force deemed excessive or inconsistent with policy and procedure or established standards may support plaintiff claims and lead to justice or monetary settlements.

Use-of-Force Continuums

The Garner (1985) and Graham (1989) era also influenced the development of UOF continuums to assist officers in learning and applying proper and reasonable force (Figure 1.1). UOF continuums are widely used and attempt to match the proper level of force with personal behavior. For example, if a person exhibits assaultive behavior (i.e., attempting to fight with fists), the officer may respond with a non-lethal weapon, such as an

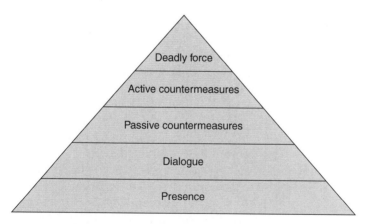

FIGURE 1.1 Sample UOF Continuum

Source: Author

electronic control device. If the ECD is not effective, the officer may then respond by escalating to a higher level of force in a sequential fashion.

Force continuums create the inaccurate impression that officers must progress through each step, which is often not possible during rapidly unfolding and deadly incidents.[46] For example, if an officer were suddenly faced with a deadly threat, it would be unreasonable for them to try all lesser options before using deadly force. Real-world application of continuums requires flexibility, adaptability, and application to rapidly unfolding or stressful scenarios. Researchers such as Longridge et al. (2023) and Alpert (2015) have affirmed that force encounters are often complex and chaotic, requiring split-second decisions, contrary to the impression simplified force continuums may create.[33, 47]

Presence is the lowest level of force. An officer in full uniform brings legal authority to every scene. Sometimes mere presence can resolve conflict or even prevent crime. Dialogue, or the ability to resolve conflict with communications skills, is the most used level of force.[39] Passive countermeasures are also called "soft skills" and are used when officers experience passive resistance (e.g., an officer grabs a noncompliant person, feels physical resistance, and decentralizes them to the ground). Electronic control devices or the use of oleoresin capsicum (OC spray, commonly known as pepper spray) are often considered passive countermeasures. Physical strikes or baton strikes are active countermeasures used to overcome violent resistance (e.g., a person threatens to or physically assaults an officer). The intentional use of a firearm or other instrument to prevent great bodily harm or death to the officer or another person constitutes deadly force, the highest level of force. Force is not a 50/50 proposition; officers can be one step above the threat they face while ensuring any force used is not excessive – an often delicate balancing act.

Any time officers use force, especially deadly force, they must articulate that the person (against whom the force was used) had a weapon, intent, and ability to carry out the threat. For example, if an officer responded to investigate a man with a large knife sitting on his porch and threatening to kill people walking on the sidewalk in front of the house, deadly force is not automatically justified. The officer may discover the man is elderly and restricted to a wheelchair, but has a large samurai sword, and says to the officer, "Take one more step closer and I will slice you with my sword." The officer likely has other options, such as distance, to avoid being harmed because, although the man may have a weapon and express intent, he cannot deliver on it. However, if the man should suddenly pick up a rifle and point it at the officer, deadly force would likely be justified.

Some states, such as Wisconsin, abandoned force continuums and replaced them with an "Interventions Options" system that provides

22 Police Use of Force Through the Lens

officers with a range of options versus the perceived sequential fashion.[32] The Wisconsin model recognizes that UOF encounters are dynamic, and allows for officers to apply a range of objectively reasonable options to accomplish lawful objectives.

Use-of-Force Policies

In addition to force continuums or options guidelines, it is also imperative for law enforcement agencies to have clear policies. UOF policies must recognize, articulate, and provide guidance related to imminence, necessity, and proportionality of force. These factors should be balanced with the nature of the offense and the governmental interest enforcing the particular law violation. These policies can be more restrictive than state or constitutional standards. For example, if an officer were to use unprofessional or inappropriate communications skills in violation of policy that escalated a contact, which results in force used to make an arrest, the officer could be disciplined for the policy violation (Figure 1.2). The officer's pre-seizure conduct (use of poor communications skills) is irrelevant to the constitutional standard about reasonableness of force.[48] Even if an officer provoked a confrontation, the force used may still be considered objectively reasonable.[49] However, the provocative actions may be a violation of state standards or department policy and procedure, which provides agencies or plaintiff attorneys with other means to hold officers accountable for their actions. It is therefore essential for officers to ensure any force used is constitutional and aligns with state standards as well as department policies or procedures.

Determining objective reasonableness is a challenging endeavor for the courts, police leaders, experts, trainers, and civilian review boards. Video footage of police UOF incidents can further complicate this important issue. There are no established industry standards or methods to help evaluators use video footage to arrive at the most accurate conclusions.

Green Bay (WI) Police Department, Green Bay PD Policy Manual

Policy 320 – Standards of Conduct

Section 320.6.9(j): Use of obscene, indecent, profane, or derogatory language while on duty or in uniform [is prohibited].

FIGURE 1.2 Sample Police Policy Language that Prohibits Profanity

Source: City of Green Bay (2024). Green Bay Police Department. Green Bay PD Policy Manual. https://greenbaywi.gov/DocumentCenter/View/12322/Green-Bay-PD-Policy-Manual---April-2024

VRUOF events provide more information for evaluators to consider. These recordings may better inform, sometimes mislead, or confirm what viewers believe about the police. How the video footage is used to determine objective reasonableness is critical. We will explore appropriate methods later. For now, it is important to consider video footage as merely another piece of the objectively reasonable puzzle. We now briefly turn our attention to the frequency of force used by American law enforcement officers.

Further discussion about determining objective reasonableness can be found in the book *Evaluating Police Uses of Force* by Stoughton, Noble, and Alpert (2020).

Use-of-Force Statistics

An extensive examination of force used by American law enforcement officers is outside the scope of this work, so we will briefly discuss American UOF statistics and relate the conversation back to VRUOF incidents.

While law enforcement UOF in America is infrequent, there is a lack of consistent measurement and national data on how often force is used.[50] Further complicating accurate measurement is the lack of a national standard regarding what constitutes a UOF incident.[50] Some agencies may consider an officer yelling at someone to gain compliance a force incident, while others may not. Other agencies would consider an officer pointing a duty weapon at a person a documented force incident, while others would not. An accepted academic definition describes UOF as any law enforcement officer behavior that intentionally threatens, attempts, or inflicts physical harm on another to accomplish a lawful objective.[51]

Empirical research on the frequency of force demonstrates that most encounters between citizens and officers are resolved without force.[52] Nearly every study on the frequency of officer UOF reports that the application of force is infrequent.[53] An examination of UOF studies in peer-reviewed journals between 1995 and 2013 also revealed that force is rare, but more likely when suspects are male, intoxicated, and offer resistance.[54] Of 49.2 million police contacts in 2022, force was threatened or used in less than 2 percent of those encounters.[55] If force is used, it is more likely to take the form of low-level shoving or empty-hand control.[55] Additionally, the use of deadly force (resulting in death) is rarer still and applied in only 0.0003 percent of police–citizen contacts.[52]

Researchers have reached contrasting findings when examining the relationship between BWCs and the frequency of force during police–citizen encounters and complaints. Some studies have demonstrated a relationship between BWCs and reductions in UOF and citizen complaints.

24 Police Use of Force Through the Lens

For example, Jennings et al. (2015) attributed BWCs to a 53.4 percent reduction in UOF complaints and a 65.4 percent reduction in external complaints when compared to officers who did not wear BWCs.[56] Similarly, Hedberg et al. (2017) reported that the presence of a BWC reduced the likelihood of complaints against an officer by about 62 percent.[57] Ariel et al. (2016), discovered that the use of BWCs dramatically reduced complaints against police officers.[58] A contrasting and significant study of officers in Washington DC comprising a robust treatment and control population revealed no difference in UOF and citizen complaints between officers who wore BWCs and those who did not.[59] A Canadian pilot study revealed that BWCs had no statistically significant effect on officer force or citizen complaints.[60] Although most studies demonstrate that BWCs appear to have a civilizing effect and can alter officer and citizen behaviors, the contrasting studies highlight the need for continued research in this area.

Regardless of its frequency, when force is used during a police–citizen contact it can negatively affect perceptions of the police, especially within at-risk communities. VRUOF events can further these negative perceptions and confirm what people in at-risk communities believe about police encounters. While White people are more likely to express support for an officer's decision to use force, Black people are less likely to express support and more likely to resent it.[61] Force incidents captured on video can create strong emotional reactions among viewers, civilians and law enforcement officers alike.[62] All officer–citizen contacts begin with presence and communications skills, which together successfully resolve most incidents without force – an ideal outcome.[63] Camera footage can capture the beginning, middle, and end of an incident. For this reason, and others discussed thus far, it is critical for law enforcement leaders, officers, citizens, policy makers, the media, and the courts to have a deeper understanding of how cameras can influence outcomes and perspectives.

Cameras in law enforcement are not a new phenomenon, and early pioneers have influenced how cameras are used today. Next, we will examine the history of video cameras in law enforcement and explore how the evolution of their use has affected American policing and populations.

References

1. Office of Justice Programs (2022, Nov. 18). U.S. residents contact with police was lower in 2020 than 2018. U.S. Department of Justice, Office of Justice Programs. https://bjs.ojp.gov/sites/g/files/xyckuh236/files/media/document/cbpp20_pr.pdf

Objectively Reasonable Use of Force **25**

2. Lee, H., Vaughn, M. S., & Lim, H. (2014). The impact of neighborhood crime levels on police use of force: An examination at micro and meso levels. Journal of Criminal Justice, 42(6), 491–499. https://doi.org/10.1016/j.jcrim jus.2014.09.003

3. Garner, J. H., Hickman, M. J., Malega, R. W., & Maxwell, C. D. (2018). Progress toward national estimates of police use of force. PloS ONE, 13(2), e0192932. https://doi.org/10.1371/journal.pone.0192932

4. Vitale, A. S. (2020, June 26). Five myths about policing. Washington Post. https://www.washingtonpost.com/outlook/five-myths/five-myths-about-policing/2020/06/25/65a92bde-b004-11ea-8758-bfd1d045525a_story.html

5. Tennessee v. Garner, 471 U.S. 1 (1985)

6. Graham v. Connor et al., 490 U.S. 386 (1989)

7. Tennenbaum, A. N. (1994). The influence of the Garner decision on police use of deadly force. Journal of Criminal Law and Criminology, 85(1), 241–260

8. Lasimba, L. & Gray, M. (2019, Feb. 22). Elton Hymon: An unsung hero. https://tri-statedefender.com/elton-hymon-an-unsung-hero/02/22/

9. Ross, D. L. (2002). An Assessment of Graham v. Connor, ten years later. Policing: An International Journal of Police Strategies & Management, 25(2). https://doi.org/10.1108/13639510210429383

10. Soghomonian, A. (2024). Rethinking hindsight: The failed interpretation of Graham v. Connor. NYU Review of Law & Social Change, 47(55). https://socialchangenyu.com/wp-content/uploads/2024/03/7-Soghomonian.pdf

11. Dethorn Graham, Petitioner v. M. S. Connor, et al., Respondents, No. 87-6571, October Term 1988. http://users.soc.umn.edu/~samaha/cases/graham_v_connor_tria_%20record.html

12. Johnson v. Glick, 481 F.2d 1028 (1973)

13. County of Sacramento v. Lewis, 523 U.S. 833 (1998)

14. Spectrum News Staff (2023, June 13). Ex-officer convicted in Abner Louima attack released from federal prison early. Spectrum News NY 1. https://ny1.com/nyc/all-boroughs/news/2023/06/13/justin-volpe-prison-early-release-abner-louima#:~:text=Volpe%20was%20sentenced%20to%2030,the%20face%20during%20a%20brawl

15. ABC News (2001, July 12). Louima to receive $8.7M in torture suit. ABC News. https://abcnews.go.com/US/story?id=92902&page=1

16. Rubenstein, S. (2002, Feb. 8). Transcript: Abner Louima attorney press conference. https://www.cnn.com/2002/LAW/02/28/rubenstein.louima.pres ser/index.html

17. Tyre, P. (1997, Oct. 3). Black Panthers focus cameras on police abuse. http://www.cnn.com/US/9710/03/black.panthers/index.html

18. U.S. Department of Justice (2021). State and Local Law Enforcement Training Academies, 2013. https://bjs.ojp.gov/sites/g/files/xyckuh236/files/media/document/slleta13_3.pdf

19. Horton, J. (2021, May 17). How US police training compares with the rest of the world. https://www.bbc.com/news/world-us-canada-56834733

20. Donner, C. M., Maskaly, J., Piquero, A. R., & Jennings, W. G. (2017). Quick on the draw: assessing the relationship between low self-control and officer-involved police shootings. Police Quarterly, 20(2), 213–234

21. McElvain, J. P., & Kposowa, A. J. (2008). Police officer characteristics and the likelihood of using deadly force. Criminal Justice & Behavior, 35(4), 505–521

22. Paoline, E. A., & Terrill, W. (2007). Police education, experience, and the use of force. Criminal Justice and Behavior, 34(2), 179–196

23. Rydberg, J., & Terrill, W. (2010). The effect of higher education on police behavior. Police Quarterly, 13(1), 92–120

24. Ingram, J. R., Terrill, W., & Paoline, E. (2018). Police culture and officer behavior: Application of a multi-level framework. Criminology, 56(4), 780–811

25. Paoline, E. A., Terrill, W., & Somers, L. J. (2021). Police officer use of force mindset and street-level behavior. Police Quarterly, 24(4), 547–577

26. Andersen, J. P., & Gustafsberg, H. (2016). A training method to improve police use of force decision making: A randomized controlled trial. SAGE Open, 6(2). https://doi.org/10.1177/2158244016638708

27. University of Chicago Crime Lab (2024). Situational decision-making (Sit-D). https://crimelab.uchicago.edu/projects/situational-decision-making/

28. Baldwin, S., Bennell, C., Blaskovits, B., Brown, A., Jenkins, B., Lawrence, C., McGale, H., Semple, T., & Andersen, J. P. (2022). A reasonable officer: Examining the relationships among stress, training, and performance in a highly realistic lethal force scenario. Frontiers in Psychology, 12. https://www.frontiersin.org/journals/psychology/articles/10.3389/fpsyg.2021.759132/full

29. San Francisco Police Department (SFPD) (2020). Modifications to California's Use of Force Standard (AB 392); SFPD Department Notice. https://www.sanfranciscopolice.org/sites/default/files/Documents/2020-03/SFPDNotice20.011.20200304.pdf

30. California Legislative Information Code Section (2020). Chapter 5. Arrest by whom and How Made, 835a. https://leginfo.legislature.ca.gov/faces/codes_displaySection.xhtml?sectionNum=835a.&lawCode=PEN

31. Sullivan, J., Jenkins, J., & Tate, J. (2016, Dec. 18). In two years, police killed 86 people brandishing guns that look real – but aren't. Washington Post. https://www.washingtonpost.com/investigations/in-two-years-police-killed-86-people-brandishing-guns-that-look-real—but-arent/2016/12/18/ec005c3a-b025-11e6-be1c-8cec35b1ad25_story.html

32. Wisconsin Department of Justice, Law Enforcement Standards Board (2023). Defensive and arrest tactics: A training guide for law enforcement officers. Madison, WI

33. Longridge, R., Chapman, B., Bennell, C., Clarke, D. D., & Keatley, D. (2023). Behaviour sequence analysis of police body-worn camera footage. Journal of Police and Criminal Psychology, 38(2), 255–262. https://doi.org/10.1007/s11896-020-09393-z

34. Fridell, L., & Binder, A. (1992). Police officer decision-making in potentially violent confrontations. Journal of Criminal Justice, 20, 385–399

35. Chapman, C. (2012). Use of force in minority communities is related to police education, age, experience, and ethnicity. Police Practice and Research, 13(5), 421–436. doi: 10.1080/15614263.2011.596711

36. Manis, J., Archbold, C. A., and Hassell, K. D. (2008). Exploring the impact of police officer education level on allegations of police misconduct. International Journal of Police Science and Management, 10(4), 509–523. doi: 10.1350/ijps.2008.10.4.102

37. Patton, C. L., Asken, M., Fremouw, W. J., & Bemis, R. (2017). The influence of profanity on public perception of excessive force. Journal of Police and Criminal Psychology, 32, 340–357. doi: 10.1007/s11896-017-9226-0

38. Law Enforcement Action Partnership (n.d.). Sir Robert Peel's policing principals. https://lawenforcementactionpartnership.org/peel-policing-principles/

39. Skinns, L., Rice, L., Sprawson, A., & Wooff, A. (2017). Police legitimacy in context: An exploration of "soft" power in police custody in England. Policing: An International Journal, 40(3), 601–613. https://doi.org/10.1108/PIJPSM-06-2016-0077

40. Gilston, D. H., & Podell, L. (1959). The practical patrolman. Springfield, IL: C. C. Thomas

41. Lewis, M.A. (2011, Dec. 1). Peel's Legacy. FBI Law Enforcement Bulletin. https://leb.fbi.gov/articles/perspective/perspective-peels-legacy

42. Verbal Judo Institute (n.d.). Tribute: Dr. George Thompson, Ph.D. https://verbaljudo.com/george-thompson/

43. Khan, N. (2024, Jan. 31). Police can no longer ask 'do you know why i pulled you over?' in California – here's why. KQED. https://www.kqed.org/news/11974283/police-can-no-longer-ask-do-you-know-why-i-pulled-you-over-in-california-heres-why

44. Giacomantonio, C., Goodwin, S., & Carmichael, G. (2019). Learning to de-escalate: evaluating the behavioural impact of Verbal Judo training on police constables. Police Practice and Research, 21(4), 401–417. https://doi.org/10.1080/15614263.2019.1589472

45. Schmelzer, E. (2023, Feb. 10). Denver sheriff deputy suspended for breaking inmate's wrist with nunchucks. Denver Post. https://www.denverpost.com/2023/01/10/denver-sheriff-nunchucks-broken-wrist/

46. Police Executive Research Forum (2016). Guiding principles on use of force. https://www.policeforum.org/assets/30%20guiding%20principles.pdf

47. Alpert, G. P. (2015). Police use of force. In: Wright, J. D., editor. International encyclopedia of the social & behavioral sciences. Second Edition. Amsterdam: Elsevier, pp. 255–259. https://doi.org/10.1016/B978-0-08-097086-8.45073-7

48. Carter v. Buscher, 973 F.2d 1328 (7th Cir. 1992)

49. Cnty. of L.A. v. Mendez, 137 S. Ct. 1539, 198 L. Ed. 2d 52 (2017)

50. Hollis, M. E. (2018). Measurement issues in police use of force: A state-of-the-art review. Policing, 41(6), 844–858.

51. Bolger, P. C. (2014). Just following orders: A meta-analysis of the correlates of American police officer use of force decisions. American Journal of Criminal Justice, 40, 466–492. doi: 10.1007/s12103-014-9278-y.

52. Johnson, R. R. (2016). Dispelling the myths surrounding police use of lethal force. Retrieved from https://www.dolanconsultinggroup.com/wpcontent/uploads/2016/07/Dispelling_the_Myths_July18.pdf

53. Atherley, L. T., & Hickman, M. J. (2014). Controlling use of force: Identifying police use of excessive force through analysis of administrative records. Policing: A Journal of Policy and Practice, 8(2), 123–134. doi: 10.1093/police/pau003.

54. Klahm, C., & Tillyer, R. (2010). Understanding police use of force: A review of the evidence. Southwest Journal of Criminal Justice, 7(2), 214–239.

55. Tapp, S. N., & Davis, E. J. (2024). Contacts between police and the public, 2022. U.S. Department of Justice, Bureau of Justice Statistics. https://bjs.ojp.gov/document/cbpp22.pdf

56. Jennings, W. G., Lynch, M. D., & Fridell, L. A. (2015). Evaluating the impact of police officer body-worn cameras (BWCs) on response-to-resistance and serious external complaints: Evidence from the Orlando police department (OPD) experience utilizing a randomized controlled experiment. Journal of Criminal Justice, 43(6), 480–486. doi:10.1016/j.jcrimjus.2015.10.003

57. Hedberg, E. C., Katz, C. M., & Choate, D. E. (2017). Body-worn cameras and citizen interactions with police officers: Estimating plausible effects given varying compliance levels. Justice Quarterly, 34(4), 627–651. doi: 10.1080/07418825.2016.1198825

58. Ariel, B., Sutherland, A., Henstock, D., Young, J., Drover, P., Sykes, J., Megicks, S., & Henderson, R. (2016). "Contagious accountability": A global multisite randomized controlled trial on the effect of police body-worn cameras on citizen complaints against the police. Criminal Justice and Behavior, 44(2). doi: 10.1177/0093854816668218

59. Yokum, D., Ravishankar, A., & Coppock, A. (2017). Evaluating the effects of policy body-worn cameras: A randomized controlled trial. The Lab @ DC Working Paper. https://bwc.thelab.dc.gov/TheLabDC_MPD_BWC_Working_Paper_10.20.17.pdf

60. Edmonton Police Service (2015). Body worn video: Considering the evidence. Retrieved from https://www.edmontonpolice.ca/News/BWV

61. Carter, J. S., & Corra, M. (2016). Racial resentment and attitudes toward the use of force by police: An over-time trend analysis. Sociological Inquiry, 86(4), 492–511. doi: 10.111/soin.12136.

62. Boivin, R., Gendron, A., Faubert, C., & Poulin, B. (2017). The body-worn camera perspective bias. Journal of Experimental Criminology, 13(1), 125–142.

63. Harrell, E., & Davis, E. (2020). Contacts between police and the public, 2018: Statistical tables. U.S. Department of Justice, Bureau of Justice Statistics. Washington, DC

2

THE HISTORY OF VIDEO CAMERAS IN LAW ENFORCEMENT

The use of video cameras in law enforcement is not a new concept. The first documented use of a camera in a squad car was reported in a 1939 issue of *Modern Mechanix* magazine.[1] In that year, Officer R. H. Galbraith of the California Highway Patrol used a motion picture camera mounted on his dashboard to film traffic law violators and create a visual record for later use in court.[1] A year later, in 1940, a *Los Angeles Times* news story reported that a 35mm camera was being used to record traffic violators through a hole cut in a police vehicle roof.[1] These creative early adopters were ahead of their time. Eventually, dash camera video would become commonplace, but not until decades later.

In 1968, a *Popular Mechanics* magazine reporter went on a ride-along with Connecticut State Police Sergeant Nelson Hurlburt and wrote about dash cameras being used in two squad cars to record traffic violations, including impaired driving.[2] Police believed the camera footage influenced driver behavior and acceptance of wrongdoing when shown the video, and near certainty of conviction in court.[2] The reporter witnessed a variety of traffic violations, including an impaired driving incident. An oncoming speeding white convertible driving like "a jet strafing a highway" drove into Sgt. Hurlburt's lane. Sgt. Hurlburt braked, evaded, did a full 180, and went after the motorist. Sgt. Hurlburt narrated into the microphone hanging from his neck, "Southbound in pursuit ... white convertible ... ran me off the road ... clock one mile ... clock two ... doing 84 ... 94 ... I'm stopping him."[2]

Next, the camera filmed the driver stumbling out of the convertible and staggering to Sgt. Hurlburt's squad car. The driver claimed he was "cold

DOI: 10.4324/9781003538738-2

30 Police Use of Force Through the Lens

sober" while staring blankly, "goggle-eyed," at the video as the footage was played for him. "I must be stoned," admitted the driver, who was then arrested. The potential impact of this video footage in court was described as follows:

> For men of Hurlburt's skill and experience, arresting a killer-drunk is almost routine. But it's never easy to convince a judge and jury that this "upstanding, sober citizen here in court with us today" (complete with neat haircut, a freshly pressed suit) could be a potential killer. That's where TV comes in. This guy will deny everything tomorrow ... He's still so stiff he'll even forget the TV. But wait'll his lawyer sees it. (Fales, 1968, p. 204)[2]

We cannot say for certain why the efforts of these pioneers did not catch on until years later. We can assume cumbersome camera sizes, separate screens, lack of wireless microphone technology, different criminal justice and policing philosophies, and less nationwide emphasis on the enforcement of impaired driving all played a role. Advancements in technology, such as the more compact Betamax and VHS tape, along with the advocacy efforts of campaigners such as Mothers Against Drunk Driving (MADD), launched the dash camera movement into American policing.[3] In the early 1980s dash cam recordings were considered the "most effective method" to gather evidence of impaired driving and help ensure drunk driving convictions.[4]

Officers also saw the potential value of dash cam footage and began recording themselves with dash-mounted VHS cameras. Some officers, like retired Police Officer Bob Surgenor (of Berea, Ohio), mounted his own camera on the passenger seat of a squad car, secured to the frame of an old child seat.[5] Although proactive and ahead of his time, using a personal camera to capture police evidence was not a recommended practice, then or now. Officer Surgenor's creativity, however, resulted in hundreds of hours of video footage, from high-speed chases to impaired driver arrests, armed robbery suspect apprehensions, and other police-related cases.

In 1988, Surgenor became the first police officer to record a high-speed chase.[5] Not only did the footage record the dangerous chase of armed robbery suspects, but it also captured the excited, humorous, and sometimes inappropriate color commentary. The 13-minute chase began on busy Berea city streets, went into oncoming traffic, through crowded intersections, and eventually onto a freeway. Segments of Officer Surgenor's video and audio are described below, including direct quotes that may be offensive to some readers.

"Come on, come on, you piece of shit," Officer Surgenor yelled, encouraging his squad car to catch up to the large, light-blue four-door that had sped onto the freeway on-ramp, pulling farther away. Other marked squads joined the chase, which would sometimes exceed 100 miles per hour. At these speeds, the squad cars were likely "outrunning" their sirens, making it difficult for motorists ahead to hear them until the squad cars were directly behind. As expected, some motorists in front of oncoming squad cars did not move over or yield.

"Move, get out of the way dildo!" Officer Surgenor quipped at a car in the left lane that did not move right. Moments later Surgenor, giddy, said, "All right, all right, yahoo, a roadblock!" Other squads ahead of the chase had set up a roadblock near an off-ramp. The suspect had four options: stop, drive into the roadblock, go around it, or exit the freeway. The vehicle darted right, hit the back end of a squad car, drove around the roadblock, maneuvered left, nearly hit the exit sign, and continued down the freeway. "Holy shit, holy shit!" Officer Surgenor exclaimed as he skidded and nearly crashed into the same sign, following the suspects' jagged path.

Officer Surgenor and several other squads stayed in the chase, including the damaged car with the now-open trunk. Minutes later, a moving roadblock forced the fleeing vehicle onto the center median. "Box him in, that's it, that's it, that a boy, that a boy, that's it, all right, all right, good deal, good deal," said Officer Surgenor, encouraging the successful maneuver. The camera continued to roll while steam bellowed from Officer Surgenor's squad car hood and the two suspects were taken into custody.

Any casual viewer of Officer Surgenor's pursuit watches with interest, awe, or excitement, and is often amazed or shocked that people do such foolish things. Others may perceive Officer Surgenor's utterances as inappropriate, vulgar, or unprofessional, while others understand his comments were made under stress. Experienced officers may watch with similar interest, but also analyze the tactics, decision-making, and legal issues involved. To others, Officer Surgenor's comments are just part of the "gallows humor" of police work. Much could be gleaned from this groundbreaking video footage – from officer performance, policy or procedure adherence to perceived professionalism, emergency driving skills, officer tactics, radio communications skills, or use-of-force (UOF) decisions. At the time, video was not embraced for these reasons, but mainly for evidentiary purposes or entertainment value. The high entertainment value partially explains the draw of reality-based police TV shows, which are among the most popular. Little did Officer Surgenor know that he may have helped usher in a new TV era. A year later, on March 11, 1989, *COPS* debuted and has become one of the longest-running television shows in the United States.[6]

32 Police Use of Force Through the Lens

Dash-mounted cameras were often an ally of the police and would help officers secure convictions with powerful video evidence. Other footage could help justify why force was used or reveal excessive force and hold officers accountable. Similar cameras in the hands of citizens allowed them to be video vigilantes or practitioners of sousveillance (i.e., third-party recorders of interactions between the police and the public). Sousveillance captured the March 3, 1991 beating of African American Rodney King by police officers in Los Angeles, California.

Shortly after midnight, citizen witness George Holliday was awakened by a traffic stop outside his house. Holliday grabbed his new Sony video camera and stood on his balcony to film the interaction between Rodney King and Los Angeles Police Department (LAPD) officers. What he recorded would eventually be sold to media outlets, shown to the world, and fuel five days of rioting in Los Angeles. Looting and burning caused millions in property damage. More than 60 people, mostly in South Central Los Angeles, died by shootings and other violence, and 2383 were injured. The "L.A. Uprisings" became the largest civil disturbance in American history.[7]

Just before Holliday pushed the record button, King had led the police on a high-speed chase. Once stopped, King was ordered out of his car. He charged at officers, a segment not shown on video, which may have justified some level of initial force. For the next 15 minutes, LAPD officers kicked and beat King, struck him 56 times with wooden batons, and used a stun gun. Officer team-tactics, such as swarming and controlling, may have been a more effective approach. Instead, they battered and beat King into submission. King suffered a skull fracture, broken bones and teeth, and permanent brain damage. The footage confirmed what minority communities believed – that excessive police violence was the norm. Although the footage was compelling, it alone was not enough to convict the officers of excessive force; they were acquitted. A few hours later, the city burned.[8]

The Rodney King footage, although compelling, did not *speak for itself*, and was embedded in context by the prosecution and defense. Frame by frame, the defense used police experts to identify and explain King's potentially dangerous movements, which were used to justify the force. Officers involved testified why they *believed* King was dangerous and potentially violent, human perceptions that could not be captured by the video footage. The officers' perceptions were an experienced reality that could not be viewed through the lens of a camera. The lack of video clarity, which contained "blurry and ambiguous images," cast doubt on its value as reality. Slow-motion replay of the videos was also used, which created the impression that officers had more time to act or used reasoned and well thought-out decisions in response to King's aggression. These alternative

The History of Video Cameras in Law Enforcement **33**

and incomplete views created a different reality, much like incomplete or segmented contemporary footage aired by mass media or via social media that often creates inaccurate perceptions or conclusions. The alternative reality was enough to sway the jury, which comprised ten white, one Hispanic, and one Asian-American juror.[9]

The prosecution relied heavily on the video footage, which showed obviously excessive force – or so they assumed. The prosecution took a contrasting approach and broke down the same video to explain the excessive force. Relying on video footage alone to explain reality was an insufficient legal and procedural tactic. The same video footage would support King's lawsuit against the City of Los Angeles. King prevailed in his federal Section 1983 lawsuit and was awarded $3.8 million.[10] King's case inspired others to video record the police, and today sousveillance is a norm.

About 90 days before the King incident, dash cam footage recorded the tragic death of Constable Darrell Lunsford of Garrison County, Texas. Constable Lunsford's death was the first ever law enforcement officer line-of-duty death recorded by a dash camera.[11] The video footage helped identify and convict the three men responsible.

On January 23, 1991, at about 1:20 a.m., Constable Lunsford stopped a suspicious vehicle on U.S. Highway 59 near Garrison. The white 1981 Oldsmobile Cutlass with Maine license plates was occupied by three men who were transporting 30 pounds of marijuana in the trunk, on their way to Chicago from Houston. Constable Lunsford, an experienced drug interdiction officer, handled the traffic stop on his own. The driver claimed to have a driver's license but did not have it with him. For reasons we will never know, Lunsford's suspicion grew, so he asked the driver if he could search the trunk.

The driver and a passenger joined Lunsford at the open trunk. The odor of marijuana was immediately apparent; but, before Lunsford could confiscate it, the men attacked. Moments before the attack, Lunsford's microphone recorded the men, who spoke Spanish and discussed how they were going to attack. Lunsford primarily spoke English, and probably did not understand or hear what the attackers were planning to do. Then one tackled low, the other high, and dragged Lunsford to the ground. The third man exited the Cutlass and joined the attack. Lunsford was kicked, beaten, stabbed, and shot with his own gun. His lifeless body was dragged off the road into the ditch. The killers hurried back into the Cutlass and sped off.

Just before Lunsford's murder, another officer, Deputy Don Welch, had driven by the traffic stop. A few minutes later, Deputy Welch saw the Cutlass speed past him and wondered if Lunsford was okay. Welch returned to Lunsford's location. His squad car was still there, and Lunsford's lifeless

34 Police Use of Force Through the Lens

body was found in the ditch. The dash cam was still recording, and the camera's VHS tape contained the last moments of Lunsford's life. The "very sharp, very detailed" footage, for its day, was used to obtain complete descriptions of the three killers, which were viewed by hundreds of officers and deputies who joined the manhunt. Within a week, all three men were arrested, and eventually charged and convicted of Lunsford's murder.[12]

Not only did this video footage help ensure justice was served, but it also became an officer-safety training film that was viewed by officers across the country. Within these tragedies are valuable lessons that can save the lives of other officers. The lack of a cover officer, the importance of appropriate officer–subject factors (i.e., enough officers present to safely monitor the number of people), and not searching cars alone were often identified errors in Lunsford's case. It is fair to say that Lunsford's tragedy improved officer safety and tactics, and saved other officers' lives.

When camera technology became miniaturized, the body-worn camera (BWC) era began. BWCs were first field tested in the United Kingdom in 2005.[13] In 2013, the Rialto, California Police Department became the first agency in the United States to implement a BWC program.[14] The Rialto police, led by Chief Tony Farrar, Ph.D., also participated in the first peer-reviewed published study about the impact of BWCs, which revealed that the use of BWCs was associated with reductions in UOF and fewer officer complaints.[15] Since the Rialto study, other researchers have discovered the manifold benefits of BWCs, including the ability to alter officer and civilian behaviors. Beyond this, BWCs also help allow agencies to:

- enhance training;
- exonerate officers accused of policy violations;
- reduce time spent investigating complaints;
- improve Fourth Amendment compliance and criminal prosecution;
- improve report writing;
- enhance officer recollection;
- reduce police UOF; and
- reduce officer-involved shootings.[16]

These findings are not without criticism, however, and will be discussed in more detail later.

Although these are promising benefits of BWCs, they have become an often misunderstood and misleading "gold standard." There is a societal expectation that officers will wear them, and a misguided belief that they will solve any problem encountered during a police–citizen encounter. Today the public, the media, academics, and the courts expect video footage of police–citizen interactions. Surprisingly, not all United States law enforcement agencies deploy dash cameras or BWCs. A 2018 Bureau of Justice Statistics (BJS) report revealed that 47 percent of general-purpose law enforcement agencies (e.g., municipal, county, regional police departments, most sheriff's departments, and highway patrol agencies) and 80 percent of large police departments (i.e., those serving 100,000 persons or more) deploy BWCs.[17] Regarding only dash cameras, at least 70 percent of police agencies have them in their squad cars.[18] Overseas, a 2017 survey in the United Kingdom revealed that 60,000 BWCs are deployed by UK law enforcement agencies.[19] Worldwide, it is estimated that there are 1.5 million BWCs in use.[20]

Many of the current BWC systems include a dash camera component, but the literature does not clearly delineate the use of one or both. The deployment of BWCs or dash cameras is expected to continually increase and may one day be mandated across the country. Agencies that do not deploy cameras may be perceived as lacking transparency and missing valuable opportunities to collect evidence that can assist with prosecution, promote accountability, and more accurately sustain or dismiss allegations of wrongdoing. A lack of transparency can also raise concerns about the legitimacy of UOF investigations, increase tension among community members, and fuel protest or riots.

Although the use of cameras can be quite effective in law enforcement, it will not magically improve policing. Video footage can be quite valuable, but at the same time also misleading, incomplete, or misinterpreted. Examining the advantages and disadvantages of cameras in law enforcement can reveal why some agencies do not deploy them, or why others unquestionably embrace them. We will discuss this next.

References

1. DePalma, J. (2015). Caught on camera: The history of the police dashcam. NBC News. Retrieved from https://www.nbcnews.com/feature/long-story-short/video/caught-on-camera-the-history-of-the-police-dashcam-54870 8419951
2. Fales, E. D. (1968). Watch it! You're on trooper TV! Popular Mechanics. Retrieved from https://books.google.com/books?id=G9QDAAAAM BAJ&pg=PA84-IA3&lpg=PA84-IA3&dq=%22Watch+it+you%27re+ on+trooper+TV%22+popular+mechanics&source=bl&ots=Hy3ez_O 6LE&sig=6AsW515C-kDa85g6wnds_9dHnCM&hl=en&sa=X&ved= 2ahUKEwj0u7uA4JrdAhXBna0KHeR4CO0Q6AEwAnoECAgQAQ#v= onepage&q=%22Watch%20it%20you're%20on%20trooper%20 TV%22%20popular%20mechanics&f=false
3. Nash, A. C., & Scarberry, J. L. (2014). Let's have a look at the footage. Law Enforcement Technology. Retrieved from https://www.officer.com/on-the-str eet/body-cameras/article/11302594/lets-have-a-look-at-the-footage

4. U.S. Department of Justice (2004). The impact of video evidence on modern policing. Retrieved from http://www.theiacp.org/Portals/0/pdfs/WhatsNew/IACP%20In-Car%20Camera%20Report%202004.pdf
5. Live Police Pursuits (2020, Apr. 19). First ever recorded high-speed pursuit of a stolen vehicle in 1988 [Video]. YouTube. https://www.youtube.com/watch?v=KZE6krdTvD0
6. This Day in History (1989, March 11). "Cops" makes TV debut. https://www.history.com/this-day-in-history/cops-makes-tv-debut#:~:text=On%20March%2011%2C%201989%2C%20Cops,off%20the%20air%20in%202020
7. Feuerherd, P. (2018, Feb. 28). Why didn't the Rodney King video lead to conviction? JSTOR Daily. https://daily.jstor.org/why-rodney-king-video-conviction/
8. Krbechek, A. S., & Bates, K. G. (2017, Apr. 26). When LA erupted in anger: A look back at the Rodney King Riots. NPR. https://www.npr.org/2017/04/26/524744989/when-la-erupted-in-anger-a-look-back-at-the-rodney-king-riots
9. Kim, S. (2016). Alternative truths: The construction of narratives in the Rodney King trial. Elements, 12(2). https://ejournals.bc.edu/index.php/elements/article/view/9453/8517
10. Mitchell, J. L., & Hubler, S. (1994, Apr. 20). Rodney King gets award of $3.8 million. Los Angeles Times. https://www.latimes.com/local/california/la-me-king-award-19940420-story.html
11. Smith, D. (2012, Sept. 6). Reality training: Lunsford incident. Police1. https://www.police1.com/officer-down/videos/reality-training-lunsford-incident-U3vlZnVpdJBDxnbU/
12. New York Times (1991, Jan. 25). Special: Constable's death seen on videotape. https://www.nytimes.com/1991/01/25/us/constable-s-death-seen-on-videotape.html
13. Suss., J., Raushel, A., Armijo, A., & White, B. (2018). Design considerations in the proliferation of police body-worn cameras. *Ergonomics in Design*, 26(3), 17–22. doi: 10.1177/1064804618757686.
14. Amira, D. (2013, Aug. 16). Rialto police chief: Body-worn cop cameras were far from a "nightmare." Daily Intelligencer. Retrieved from http://nymag.com/daily/intelligencer/2013/08/nypd-cameras-rialto-farrar-bloomberg.html
15. Ariel, B., Farrar, W. A., & Sutherland, A. (2015). The effect of police body-worn cameras on use of force and citizens' complaints against the police: A randomized controlled trial. Journal of Quantitative Criminology, 31(3), 509–535. doi: http://dx.doi.org/10.1007/s10940-014-9236-3
16. Williams, M. C., Weil, N., Rasich, E. A., Ludwig, J., Chang, H., & Egrari, S. (2021). Body-worn cameras in policing: Benefits and costs. University of Chicago Working Paper No. 2021-38. https://bfi.uchicago.edu/wp-content/uploads/2021/04/BFI_WP_2021-38.pdf
17. Hyland, S. S. (2018). Body worn cameras in law enforcement agencies, 2016. U.S. Department of Justice. Retrieved from https://www.bjs.gov/content/pub/pdf/bwclea16.pdf

18. Reaves, B. A. (2015). Local police departments, 2013: Equipment and technology. U.S. Department of Justice, Bureau of Justice Statistics. Retrieved from https://www.bjs.gov/content/pub/pdf/lpd13et.pdf
19. Home Office (2017) Home Office consults on using body-worn video for police interviews. London: Home Office. Available at https://www.gov.uk/government/news/home-office-consults-on-using-body-worn-video-for-police-interviews
20. Bowling, B., & Iyer, S. (2019). Automated policing: The case of body-worn video. International Journal of Law in Context, 15, 140–161, doi: 10.1017/S1744552319000089

3

THE ADVANTAGES AND DISADVANTAGES OF CAMERAS IN LAW ENFORCEMENT

Cameras in policing will not increase officer–community trust, which can only be achieved by building trusted and sincere relationships. Body-worn cameras (BWCs) became mainstream in 2014. Since then, American confidence in the police has declined from a high of 57 percent (great deal, quite a lot of trust) to 43 percent in 2023.[1] However we cannot empirically say there is causation between greater use of BWCs (i.e., increased transparency) and decreased confidence in police, merely that *using* BWCs will not increase citizen confidence. However, recordings showing officers using unprofessional language, engaging in unethical behavior, or using excessive force will negatively affect citizen perceptions. Interpersonal communication is a critical component, and often the best tool an officer can use to resolve conflict. How officers communicate with people tends to influence perceptions of respectfulness, fairness, politeness, professionalism, and compliance.[2,3]

Video recordings of officer–citizen interactions provide yet another perspective of an incident but may not always reveal what really happened. In this chapter, we will explore the advantages and disadvantages of video cameras in law enforcement. Too often, video alone is accepted as "truth," although it can be misleading, incomplete, or inconsistent with what the officer experienced or perceived during an incident. We will also explore more proactive uses of video footage to help improve performance, which could result in fewer errors, greater constitutional compliance, and better outcomes. First, we will focus our discussion on dash cameras and then turn our attention to BWCs.

DOI: 10.4324/9781003538738-3

Dash Cameras – The Limited Research

Although valuable, squad car dash cameras capture a limited view of officer–citizen interactions. Footage is constrained to the view through a windshield, which is useful during impaired driving cases or other traffic enforcement incidents, but less useful in any incident that occurs off camera. When outside of camera range, a wireless microphone may capture officer–citizen interactions, providing some context about what has occurred. Although audio alone can be informative, it lacks other nuances, such as body language or facial expressions, which can change or impact meaning.

In the 1980s, campaigners Mothers Against Drunk Driving (MADD) were strong proponents of dash cameras. Although there was little research to support the claim, the group's members believed that camera footage would improve impaired driving enforcement and increase the number of convictions.[4] The cameras were used primarily to record prisoner transports, traffic matters, impaired driving behavior, and standard field sobriety tests, which helped support convictions.[4] Dash camera views were limited to incidents that occurred around and within squad cars in the public domain. The BWCs enhanced the view of police work to include virtually any interaction with the public: suspects, victims, witnesses, and complainants. This raised concerns among privacy advocates. These perceived police intrusions into the lives of others, along with the potential impact of BWCs, may be motivating factors for the expansive research continuing in this area. However, empirical research about the impact of dash cameras is still lacking as they never garnered the same attention as BWCs from researchers. Why? Likely because the dash camera was less intrusive and recorded footage in what would be considered public spaces. BWCs, however, can record anywhere, expanding Fourth Amendment and privacy implications.

There is a lack of documentation in the literature about dating the United States dash camera and BWC eras. The research for this book revealed that the dash camera era (1980s–2013) began in the early 1980s, when they were advocated and partially funded by MADD to capture evidence in impaired driving cases. In 2000, the U.S. Department of Justice Community Oriented Policing Services (COPS) office helped proliferate the use of dash cameras via $21 million in grant funds to help police agencies purchase over 5000 cameras.[4] This era would continue until the early 2010s, when agencies slowly began adopting BWCs.

The beginning of the BWC era (2013–present) aligns with the first published study about their use and impact, in 2013, when the Rialto (CA) Police Department became the first to rigorously study and report on the potential impact of BWCs. Two years later, the U.S. Department of

Justice announced that $20 million in funding was available to help local and tribal law enforcement agencies establish BWC programs.[5] Before the Rialto study, only one other robust study about the impact of cameras in law enforcement had been published – the International Association of Chiefs of Police (IACP) report *The Impact of Video Evidence on Modern Policing*,[4] which we will discuss next.

The IACP report included findings from a study of 21 state police departments that used dash cameras. The report expressed support for dash camera footage in impaired driving cases, while also noting that defense attorneys could benefit when footage showed their clients were apparently not impaired. Dash camera footage could also provide exculpatory evidence, which added to the fairness of adversarial criminal court processes. Other benefits included enhanced officer safety and performance, agency accountability, reduced liability, simplified incident review, and improved police–community relationships. Dash camera footage also allowed for more efficient prosecution, provided officer training opportunities, reduced frivolous lawsuits, and increased homeland security.

Before we continue our discussion about the dash camera study, it is worth noting the distinct difference between dash cameras and BWCs: the field of view. Dash cameras provide a limited view of police–citizen interactions. The footage typically captures officer and civilian actions within the frame, which tends to help provide a more accurate picture and neutral perception of the interaction. BWC footage focuses primarily on the citizen, and viewers tend to give more deference or credibility to the person wearing the camera.[6] If an officer did something not captured by the BWC that served to escalate the interaction and resulted in a force incident, viewers are more likely to believe the officer's perspective of the event.[6]

Viewers also tend to over-attribute causation to a given stimulus (i.e., the person within the camera frame) when it is salient or the focus of their attention.[6] Officer actions are typically missed or not in the BWC view, while they may be present in the dash camera view. These missed actions contribute to an incomplete picture of the event. The dash camera view or a third-party recording of an interaction helps create a more neutral perspective when both officer and civilian actions are captured in the frame. BWCs are not a replacement for dash cameras, but are yet another tool or view that can help provide a more complete picture. BWCs and dash cameras tend to produce better results in concert with each other. While these differences would not be discerned until years after the dash camera study, the results of that study foreshadowed the potential benefits of BWCs. We now turn our attention to the study conducted by the International Association of Chiefs of Police.

The IACP researchers also reported that the presence of a dash camera enhanced courtesy (i.e., officer communications skills). Other researchers report that the use of dash cameras promotes police accountability, accurately documents motorists' consent to a police search of their vehicle, and provides a response to widespread allegations of racial profiling.[7] A closer look at the study results provides a more complete picture of these perceived benefits.

The IACP researchers used written surveys and qualitative interviews with 3680 officers and supervisors to gather data about their lived experiences with the use of dash cameras. The report articulated the findings summarized under the following categories:

- **Officer Safety** – About one-third of the officers surveyed believed dash cameras increased officer safety, most often in retrospect when the video was used to self-critique performance. "Many officers" reported that making an announcement that a camera was present during tense situations helped promote de-escalation 48 percent of the time. Nearly two-thirds of respondents reported the dash camera had no impact on their safety, while 3 percent believed it hampered their safety because they were more concerned about putting themselves at the best camera angle versus a more advantageous officer safety position.
- **Agency Liability and Internal Control** – Dash cameras showed a significant positive impact upon adjudicating complaints, with 93 percent reporting the footage helped exonerate the officer versus 5 percent of complaints being sustained with the footage. In addition, supervisors reported that, about 50 percent of the time when a complainant was made aware that the interaction with the officer was recorded, the citizen withdrew the complaint. Less time was also spent investigating complaints, and fewer were referred to internal affairs investigators because first-line supervisors were able to resolve them with the assistance of video footage. Interestingly, 89 percent of the officers reported that camera presence had no effect on their decision to use force in a situation. The potential impact upon use of force (UOF) frequency was not explored in the study. Determining the impact upon agency liability was difficult to measure, but anecdotal examples were reported (e.g., camera footage helped settle cases in lieu of trial, saving ligation time and helping mitigate liability).
- **Training** – There was a lack of consistent training on the use of dash cameras prior to field use. The report highlighted the importance of providing officers with dash camera training that encompassed pertinent laws, rules of evidence, department policies and procedures, and operation of the equipment. The report also revealed the value of

video footage for self-critique and new officer training by reviewing performance through the "objective eye of the camera immediately after an event occurs." The finding about use of video for training is insightful, but did not seem to garner further attention from the industry or researchers on how to best carry it out.

- **Community Perception** – Researchers collected survey results from 900 citizens in 18 states where dash cameras were in use. They discovered that 94 percent of citizens approved of the use of cameras and the majority (71 percent) believed they should be advised when they are being recorded. The citizens also reported that camera presence would alter their driving behavior (51 percent), make them less likely to file a complaint (48 percent), or more likely to file a complaint (34 percent). There was a common misperception that *all* squads had cameras, and that the camera followed officers along like a movie camera. The findings supported the importance of educating the public and jurors about cameras, including their limitations, so they do not have unreasonable expectations.
- **Judicial Process** – Through a collaborative effort with the National District Attorney's Association (NDAA), the researchers explored the use of video footage by prosecutors within the judicial system. Feedback from 148 prosecutors revealed that 91 percent had used video footage in court to obtain more guilty pleas prior to trial; 58 percent reported reduced time spent in court, and 41 percent reported increased preparation time. Common prosecutor problems associated with dash camera video included: camera limitations (e.g., cameras do not see, feel, or smell as humans do); field of view; poor audio or video quality; obtaining copies from law enforcement; lack of equipment or skill to play footage in court; obtaining copies for defense attorneys; explaining contradictions between an officer's report, testimony, and video; and chain of custody.
- **Officer Performance and Police Professionalism** – The majority of officers surveyed reported that dash camera presence did not alter their performance, while 20 percent reported that camera presence improved their professionalism and communications skills. Improvements in professionalism and courtesy were associated with fewer citizen complaints. However, when officers perceived that their video footage was periodically reviewed by supervisors, they were more likely to focus on improving their courtesy. There also appeared to be a positive reciprocal relationship between officer and citizen courtesy when a camera was present. Due to the lack of data, researchers were unable to appropriately measure the impact of dash cameras on complaint frequency. The researchers surmised that camera presence may help

reduce complaints, or that complaint reduction might be influenced by improved courtesy. Officers also reported that camera presence influenced their discretion, and they were more likely to take enforcement action. Increased enforcement action could result in more complaints.

- **Agency Policies, Procedures, and Protocols** – The report recommended that all agencies with dash cameras implement policies that outline camera use (e.g., when to turn it on or off), video tape security and access, and storage and retention. The initial study and follow-up a year later revealed that, of the 21 agencies studied, all but one had implemented dash camera policies and procedures. Policy compliance appeared to be influenced by how officers perceived the video footage would be used. Policy compliance was more likely when officers perceived it would not be used primarily to single out officers or discipline them for minor infractions, which could be better handled via training. Ensuring officers were part of policy development and that they received training about dash camera use (e.g., they must be activated during all traffic stops, police pursuits, or citizen contacts) helped improve policy compliance.
- **Leadership** – Although the dash camera provided supervisors with the opportunity to go on a "virtual ride along" with their officers, the report emphasized the importance of not using camera footage review to replace field supervision or the important interpersonal relationships with the people in their charge. Regular review of video footage was highlighted to help serve as "an early warning of an officer experiencing problems that should be addressed." Early intervention may help prevent more serious adverse outcomes, such as excessive force, and help protect against agency liability.
- **Homeland Security** – Three years removed from the September 11 attacks, the researchers considered how dash camera footage might be used to help identify potential threats to homeland security. The footage could be used to gather intelligence by comparing video images or audio to existing voice samples or images of known or suspected terrorists. Video date and time stamps could also place a suspect or vehicle near strategic targets or at the scene of a terrorist attack. The 1995 bombing at the Oklahoma City Murrah federal building was offered as an example, although the evidentiary images of perpetrator Timothy McVeigh's Ryder truck were captured via a video camera positioned at an apartment complex. The footage showed the Ryder truck near the building shortly before the explosion. The researchers also surmised that video footage could be transmitted to central locations such as fusion centers and compared with intelligence records to help identify known terrorists, allowing for intercession before attacks occur.

44 Police Use of Force Through the Lens

Challenges cited with dash camera implementation were many: unreliable microphones; time-consuming acquisition processes; excessive down time for system issues; the absence of infrastructure for the management, storage, and handling of recorded footage; cameras being used by supervisors to monitor officers; lack of training; and absence of written camera policies and procedures. Similar challenges would also surface during the BWC era; these are discussed later.

The dash camera, it was believed, also helped improve the accuracy of officer reports. Officers were encouraged to view their dash cam videos to assist in report writing and to compare written reports with video records to ensure accuracy, which remains a contemporary and controversial issue. Watching video footage before writing a report will help guarantee that video and reports match, which is less concerning when detail versus perception is the primary focus. For example, when documenting the clues that a driver exhibited during standard field sobriety tests, these details are necessary for accuracy and completeness. In contrast, when writing a report about a UOF incident, emphasis is on officer perception, which can be unduly influenced by video footage. The issues concerning watching video footage before report writing will be explored in more detail later.

The IACP study offered insight into the potential benefits of dash cameras but did not become the impetus for further research. The findings merited additional inquiry, which might have affirmed initial findings, exposed shortcomings, or influenced the legitimacy of dash cam use. As White (2014) reported, between 2007 and 2013, there was limited research about the impact of cameras on law enforcement.[8] White examined five early studies about the impact of BWCs, which echoed some aspects of the IACP report.[8] Intense academic and industry focus on cameras in law enforcement would not occur until the beginning of the BWC era (2013). The more extensive scope of BWC research further examined, advanced, and even contradicted the early dash camera findings.

Body-Worn Cameras – A Summary of the Use-of-Force Research

Although the Rialto Police Department study (2013) is recognized as the first published study about the impact of BWCs in the United States, the agency's was not the overall first. In 2007, the United Kingdom Police and Crime Standards Directorate (PCSD) published *Guidance for the Police Use of Body-Worn Video Devices*.[9] The guidance within that report was supported by the findings from the "Plymouth Head Camera Project," which included qualitative and quantitative analysis of 3054 recordings. Key findings highlighted improved, more accurate evidence; less officer time spent gathering verbal statements that were recorded versus written in their field notes; increased numbers of guilty pleas and less time spent handling citizen complaints; and improved UOF justification and documentation. The potential benefits of BWCs to the appropriateness of force were based upon one incident where a taser was used to subdue a man with a knife, and additional research in this area was encouraged. (Note: Unlike United States law enforcement officers, only specially trained and designated UK officers carry firearms.)

Since the Rialto study (2013), other researchers have discovered that BWCs can alter officer and civilian behaviors, enhance training, exonerate officers accused of policy violations, and reduce time spent investigating complaints. Further, they may improve Fourth Amendment compliance and criminal prosecution, improve report writing, enhance officer recollection, demonstrate that officers are being held accountable, and reduce citizen complaints and UOF.[10,11,12,13] BWCs also tend to influence proactive policing. Officers who support the use of BWCs may engage in more proactive policing, while those who oppose BWCs may engage in less proactive policing.[14] Although reduced citizen complaints and frequency of law enforcement UOF have been reported by some BWC studies, others have reported no differences after BWC implementation.[10] To further complicate this analysis, the reductions in force incidents after BWC implementation may diminish over time. A 2020 paper reported that the number of force incidents reached pre-BWC implementation frequency after three years, and that the impact of BWCs on officer behavior tends to weaken over time.[15] Table 3.1 provides a snapshot of published peer-reviewed studies about BWCs and UOF.

Video Footage and Officer Performance

Body-worn cameras can enhance transparency and provide additional perspectives not offered by dash cameras. Transparency is necessary for law enforcement given the great power granted to them. BWCs provide more information to help determine whether police–citizen interactions are appropriate, and become another check and balance for discretionary power within a society that embraces freedom and prefers less governmental coercion. These are all promising attributes of BWCs and, when used appropriately, they can be a valuable tool to help improve policing.

While it is promising that BWCs can improve outcomes, they are not typically used to help improve officer performance. Video is often reviewed by supervisors to check for policy compliance, in response to complaints, or after UOF incidents. Failing to use BWC footage to help identify deficient performance or to improve performance is a missed opportunity

46 Police Use of Force Through the Lens

TABLE 3.1 Peer-Reviewed Research about BWCs and UOF

Year	Title	Authors	Methodology	Findings
2015	The effect of police body-worn cameras on use of force and citizens' complaints against the police: A randomized controlled trial	Ariel et al.[16]	Randomized controlled trial	Officers assigned to wear BWCs were less likely to use force
2015	Evaluating the impact of police officer body-worn cameras (BWCs) on response-to-resistance and serious external complaints: Evidence from the Orlando Police Department (OPD) experience utilizing a randomized controlled experiment	Jennings et al.[17]	Randomized controlled trial	Officers assigned to BWCs had fewer UOF complaints than officers without BWCs
2016	Report: increases in police use of force in the presence of body-worn cameras are driven by officer discretion:Aprotocol-based subgroup analysis of ten randomized experiments	Ariel et al.[18]	Multisite randomized controlled trials	Officers with minimal camera *on* discretion and high rates of camera *on* compliance used force less
2018	The effects of body-worn cameras on police activity and police-citizen encounters: A randomizedcontrolled trial	Braga et al.[14]	Randomized controlled trial	Officers with BWCs were less likely to use force compared to those without BWCs
2019	Evaluating the effects of policy body-worn cameras: A randomizedcontrolled trial	Yokum et al.[19]	Randomized controlled trial	The use of BWCs did not show an increase or decrease in UOF (null findings)

The Advantages and Disadvantages of Cameras in Law Enforcement **47**

TABLE 3.1 (Continued)

Year	Title	Authors	Methodology	Findings
2020	When no one is watching: evaluating the impact of body-worn cameras on use of force incidents	Koslicki et al.[15]	Interrupted time series analysis	The frequency of force reached pre-BWC implementation after three years
2021	The distribution of police use of force across patrol and specialty units: A case study in BWC impact	Gaub et al.[20]	Quantitative analysis of randomized controlled trial data	BWCs had no impact on UOF frequency among patrol officers, specialty unit officers
2022	A randomized controlled trial of the impact of body-worn activation on the outcomes of individual incidents	Huff et al.[21]	Randomized controlled trial	Officers wearing BWCs were more likely to use force than officers without BWC, but the differences were substantially small

to enhance service delivery, avoid negative police–community interactions, or identify training needs. Unfortunately, the use of camera footage for officer training is one of the most understudied areas of BWC research.[22]

U.S. law enforcement agencies generate more hours of video footage than all major league sports combined (see Table 3.2). While major league sports video footage is used to help improve athlete performance, law enforcement agencies do not similarly use camera footage to improve officer performance. Limited research suggests that expert video review improves cognitive decision-making and performance when faced with similar environments or incidents that align with the video training. Tennis players who watched selected images of their deficient performance, conducted self-analysis, and received expert feedback improved their cognitive decision-making.[23] Video feedback has improved the performance of collegiate divers.[24] Video review can also improve recall of performance, develop understanding of performance, encourage self-critique, and improve confidence.[25] Improved officer outcomes may occur when video footage is used to help improve performance and service delivery.

TABLE 3.2 Hours of Law Enforcement Video Footage Compared to Professional U.S. Sports

Sport	# of Teams	# Games Per Yr.	Avg. Length of Game (minutes)	Minutes of Video Recording
National Football League	32	17 (272)	192	52,224
Major League Baseball	30	162 (4860)	160	777,600
National Basketball Association	30	82 (2460)	150	369,000
National Hockey League	32	82 (2624)	150	393,600
			Total Minutes	1,592,424

Number of Law Enforcement Officers in U.S.	Hours worked per year, per officer	Total hours worked per year	Total minutes per year	Half-time video recording
560,000*	2080 (40 hrs. per week)	1,164,800,000	69,888,000,000	34,944,000,000

Notes: Although most BWCs are "always on," if we presume half of their shift is video recorded, then U.S. law enforcement officers would generate more than 34 billion minutes of video footage. The average length of each professional sports game is based upon 2024 Internet queries.

* According to the U.S. Census Bureau, the country has approximately 700,000 law enforcement officers. Nearly 80 percent use BWCs, which would equate to approximately 560,000 officers.

Source: United States Census Bureau (2023, May 14). National Police Week: May 14–20, 2023. https://www.census.gov/newsroom/stories/police-week.html.

Video review with the goal of improving officer performance, discovering training shortcomings, and improving service delivery should become an established best practice. Supervisors or trainers dedicated to performance, not discipline, and who are trained to use appropriate video performance analysis methods, may help improve officer field performance and decision-making, especially with regard to what force to use and how much. A 2022 pilot study revealed that a BWC video training program reduced officer performance errors by 25 percent and helped identify training gaps.[26] It was made clear to the officers involved in the program that it would be focused

The Advantages and Disadvantages of Cameras in Law Enforcement **49**

on improving performance, not used for discipline, which improved trust, cooperation, and communication between officers and supervisors.[26] These video review sessions also provide opportunities for officers to reflect on their own actions and discover ways to improve their performance.

The supervisors or trainers administering the video training must be experienced, respected, trusted, and recognized as experts. These reviewers should not represent internal affairs divisions, which are primarily focused on discipline versus officer performance. Officer performance programs must be solely focused on performance that is consistent with best practices, established criteria, or key performance indicators. Performance criteria should be published and provided to officers being evaluated. Similar video-analysis steps that were used to improve tennis player performance could be used for officer video review (Figure 3.1).

Another method to support this training approach could be the application of Systemic Social Event Modeling (SSEM) advocated by Makin et al. (2021).[27] The SSEM model provides a method for viewing video footage to help identify key events that may have influenced outcomes. The method involves watching and re-watching footage and coding for the presence and frequency of variables related to the reason for the review. For example, in a UOF incident, the reviewer might identify profanity, officer–subject factors, officer–citizen demographics, and citizen resistance as "codes" that may have influenced the application of force.

Step 1 – Watch Selected BWC or Dash Camera Footage
- Officer and trainer watch the full video to be analyzed.
- Allow a moment for the officer to recall the incident.
- Watch specific segments of video related to improving performance or highlight exceptional performance.

Step 2 – Officer Self-Analysis
- Allow the officer to self-assess their performance compared to key performance indicators or criteria.

Step 3 – Combined Analysis, Officer-Trainer or Supervisor
- Trainer or supervisor provides analysis of performance with the officer.
- Trainer questions or prompts to solicit officer explanation or deeper self-analysis include: *"What were you thinking at this point?" "Why did you do what you did?" "How do you see yourself doing this the next time?"*
- Identify desired performance and provide appropriate feedback or strategies to attain the desired performance.
- Reinforce positive aspects of the officer's performance.

FIGURE 3.1 Officer Video Performance Review Procedures

Other factors to consider are causality (e.g., one event causes another), correlation (e.g., factors associated with an outcome but not necessarily a cause), documentation (e.g., the type of camera, where worn, camera angle), and interpretation (e.g., how an officer reacted to changes in citizen emotional state or actions). This method can help viewers identify positive or negative key points within video footage that may merit additional attention or help explain outcomes. For a more in-depth discussion of SSEM, review the research article by Makin et al. (2021), which is listed at the end of the chapter.

Performance-based video review can be hampered by time constraints, workloads, lack of supervisor staffing, and sheer volume of video. For example, sergeants responsible for seven officers who each generate an average of 120 minutes of video per shift (840 total minutes from all seven officers per shift, 4200 minutes per five-day work week, or 70 hours of footage) would be tasked with reviewing footage and identifying performance enhancement opportunities in addition to their other responsibilities. Other technologies, such as artificial intelligence (AI), may be a solution to this problem. For example, AI software programs can be integrated into an existing BWC program and used to flag video footage that contains behaviors indicative of poor performance.[28] Natural language systems (NLS) – used to detect non-compliance, profanity, insults, or threats – can flag videos with these unprofessional and escalating behaviors, notify supervisors for review, and provide opportunities for coaching and performance improvement.[29] NLS systems can also identify, highlight, and encourage acceptable or exemplary behaviors to promote positive performance and outcomes.

Creating a culture of high performance may also help improve cognitive awareness of camera presence, and in turn positively alter officer performance. Not using video to enhance or improve officer performance is also a disservice to the people they are sworn to protect. Cameras alone are not a solution, and merely wearing them does not guarantee improved office performance. Camera footage should be used proactively, not reactively, to improve field performance. A proactive performance-based approach may also help improve negative perceptions of police when they are recorded performing in keeping with expectations.

Video Footage and Officer Accountability

Video footage can also reveal corruption and help hold officers accountable. The footage can be used by internal affairs investigators, administrative review boards, police and fire commission members during disciplinary hearings, and plaintiff attorneys during civil suits to hold officers accountable for unethical and illegal behaviors under color of law. In these cases, the cameras serve as a virtual watchdog to catch corrupt cops. A few examples follow.

In 2018, a Florida deputy suspected of frequently planting drug evidence was recorded via BWC apparently holding the methamphetamine in his hand before initiating the search, and then "finding it" in the defendant's truck. In response to a complaint, the agency investigated and terminated the deputy, and 119 of the deputy's other drug arrests were dismissed by the courts.[30] The deputy was eventually tried and convicted of racketeering, official misconduct, fabricating evidence, false imprisonment, and possession of controlled substances and drug paraphernalia.[31]

In 2017, a Baltimore police officer recorded himself planting drug evidence.[32] Apparently, he was not aware of the 30-second buffer that existed on the camera, which recorded 30 seconds back from when the BWC was activated. Most BWCs are always recording, absent sound, and, when activated by the user, the recorded footage of the previous 30 seconds becomes part of the record. In other instances, officers may forget or may not be "aware" their cameras are still recording, and capture inappropriate, unethical, or illegal behaviors. The camera can be a silent observer, body of oversight, and check and balance to police power, while also protecting officers from false accusations of wrongdoing.

Also in 2017, an officer in Farmington, New Mexico, was shown in a social media image standing over a man who was lying on the ground in a parking lot. The photo caption read, "Only in Farmington. Farmington police bears down native American while cuffed." The post implied inappropriate or excessive force. The BWC footage revealed that, during the arrest of an intoxicated man, the man fell and hit his head and the officer had attempted to catch him. The officer was also shown asking the man if he was okay and requesting medical assistance. The video cleared the officer of any wrongdoing.[33] In 2018, a woman in Grapevine, Texas, alleged she had been sexually assaulted by a state trooper during a traffic stop. The woman claimed the trooper offered to let her go in exchange for sexual favors and, when she refused, sexually assaulted her. The BWC footage directly conflicted with her allegations and the trooper was exonerated.[34]

These are just a few examples and others can be found online. Video footage in these cases eliminates the "he said, she said" or "he said, he said" versions of events, and provides more information to help determine the veracity of accusations.

Deterrence Theory and Self-Awareness Theory

Cameras may also influence or alter police and civilian behavior. The extensively researched theories of deterrence and self-awareness are often used to explain why cameras, especially BWCs, can alter the behavior of officers and civilians.[35] Deterrence theory posits that, where there is a high likelihood of apprehension, severe punishment, and certain or swift punishment, behavior will likely be positively modified.[35] The presence of a camera increases the perception that police misconduct or inappropriate citizen behaviors will be recorded and, in turn, creates a deterrent effect.[35] Self-awareness theory examines the impact upon behavior when people know they are being observed. Research has shown that, when officers or civilians are aware they are being recorded, they will alter their behavior in socially acceptable ways.[35,36] In the presence of BWCs or other cameras, where deterrence theory or self-awareness theory is in action, it can positively influence behavior of all participants, a significant benefit.

Although there is strong support for the ability of BWCs to alter behavior, self-awareness theory and deterrence theory have limitations. When an officer first wears a BWC, self-awareness of the new device is high, and it is more likely to alter behavior. Over time and with frequent use, the officer may eventually become habituated to the BWC, which can lessen self-awareness and minimize the impact upon behavior, especially when involved in an emotionally driven incident.[19]

When emotionally affected by what someone says or does, officers are more likely to say or do something they will later regret, even when they are aware of a recording BWC. For example, in a YouTube video with 4.4 million views, a Springfield, Illinois police officer filmed himself battering a 19-year-old man. The footage began with a cordial and professional exchange between the officer and a female complainant, the young man's mother. The situation escalated when the 19-year-old interjected and told the officer how to do his job. The officer's demeanor quickly changed and, amid a string of profanities, challenged the man to a fight while acknowledging the recording BWC when the officer said, "You see that red dot? It's on. It's on. It's on with your scary ass!" Minutes later, the officer shoved and punched the man's head and face multiple times and didn't arrest him.[37] The footage captured a public servant quickly becoming a defendant who would lose his job and be convicted of official misconduct and battery.[38]

Although other examples of officers wearing BWCs and using excessive force or engaging in unethical behavior can be found online, they do not represent most ethical, brave, and honest officers who exhibit positive

The Advantages and Disadvantages of Cameras in Law Enforcement   **53**

behaviors, and any unethical behavior is often minor (e.g., accepting gratuities, sleeping on duty, unnecessarily speeding).[39]

Body-Worn Cameras and Racial Profiling

Researchers and practitioners have hoped that dash cameras and BWCs would expose, reduce, or eliminate racial profiling. Racial profiling occurs when law enforcement officers stop, interdict, detain, arrest, or search people when the contact or stop is solely based upon race or ethnic status.[40] Some outside of law enforcement believe that racial profiling is common, while others within law enforcement believe that BWCs will demonstrate that racial profiling does not occur.[41] A complete analysis about the impact of dash cameras or BWCs upon racial profiling is outside the scope of this work and readers are encouraged to dig deeper into empirical studies about this important issue. A brief exploration follows.

In 2013, in response to concerns about "indirect racial profiling," a Manhattan, New York, judge ordered officers from the NYPD to wear BWCs.[42] Since then, the NYPD has spent $36 million for a federal monitor to ensure racial profiling does not occur, an allegation the NYPD denies.[43] The NYPD position is that officers normally stop people based upon descriptions provided by callers or victims, while plaintiff lawyers cite BWC examples of officers stopping and searching people without suspicion or arresting Black and Hispanic drivers 80 percent more than white drivers.[43,44] Regardless of perspective, a BWC may reveal questionable police actions or examples of racial profiling, but the camera itself will not completely prevent it. The ability of BWCs to reduce any racial or ethnic policing disparities appears to be overstated.[45]

Officers wearing BWCs must ensure they are lawfully stopping people regardless of race, based upon suspected or actual criminal behavior, and taking appropriate enforcement action with discretion. When dash cameras or BWCs uncover instances of racial profiling, the footage can be used for appropriate supervisor intervention (e.g., training or discipline), as support for potential litigation, or as a consideration by the criminal courts to influence justice outcomes (e.g., refusal to issue a criminal complaint, dismiss a case, resolve a case).

Eberhardt (2016) analyzed stop data and BWC footage for the Oakland, California Police Department (OPD) and discovered that OPD officers stopped, searched, handcuffed, and arrested more African American than white people.[46] Eberhardt's findings were significant even after considering neighborhood crime rates, demographics, and officer race, gender, and experience. In another study, researchers used tollbooth camera images to identify the race of speeding drivers and the frequency at which they were stopped by law enforcement.[47] The authors discovered that speeding African American drivers were stopped on a par with the percentage of African American drivers, and police were acting in an unbiased manner. Several years later, researchers used a similar "direct observation" approach across nine locations within a particular geographic area to determine whether racial profiling was occurring.[48] Across five locations there were no differences between the race of motorists stopped and observed, and in three locations Black motorists were stopped less frequently than non-Black motorists. But in one location Black motorists were stopped more frequently than non-Black motorists. Readers are encouraged to review the literature review by McCabe et al. (2021), which contains a thorough examination of the racial profiling research with mixed results.[48]

Like the findings about the impact of dash cameras and BWCs upon racial profiling, the ability of video recordings to reduce racial disparities about UOF is uncertain. Although more attention has been given to how BWCs reveal the frequency of force and race, the findings are often inconsistent, and researchers have yet to determine the impact of BWCs in this area.[48] However, a video recording of police using force can help mediate conflicting perspectives, and is often viewed as a powerful tool to more accurately determine what occurred. When there is a racial mismatch (e.g., the officer is white and the person is African American, or the officer is African American and the person is Hispanic), people often perceive further investigation is necessary to determine what happened.[49] However, irrespective of race, people perceive that when the force incident is video recorded, it is less likely that an internal investigation is necessary to determine what occurred.[49] Consistent with comments earlier in this work, the camera footage is perceived as a source of a more objective reality. This in turn can help stakeholders make better judgments about the appropriateness of force, increase transparency, and, when necessary, hold officers accountable.

Disadvantages of Body-Worn Cameras in Law Enforcement

Although the potential advantages of BWCs are voluminous, some disadvantages exist. BWCs can be expensive to deploy, and require significant, secure storage space and rigorous review. Further, they may decrease the quality of police–community interactions. Citizens may be less willing to talk on camera, and officers may be less willing to interact with the public. BWCs also have the potential to invade privacy and inaccurately sway jury deliberations.

Costs and Video Management

Costs for BWC programs, especially in larger agencies, can run to millions of dollars. While the purchase of BWCs is often affordable, video storage fees can be four times the cost of cameras. For example, a 2018 Police Executive Research Forum (PERF) study revealed that the most expensive large agency BWC program cost $1,334,717 for cameras and $4 million to store the video footage.[50] Video storage fees do not span the life of the BWC program and must be renewed every few years. A 2021 State of Maryland study estimated the average cost to equip an officer with a BWC was $2445 per year, which included video storage costs.[51] To reduce costs, some agencies store video footage on their own servers or other cloud-based systems, but soon realize how quickly available storage space is consumed by saved files. Further, these self-storage agencies must manage the data with existing personnel or hire dedicated personnel who are responsible for data integrity, appropriate redaction to fulfill open records requests, and assurance that video records attach to reports or are routed to appropriate governmental entities (e.g., prosecutors' offices, police and fire commissions, civilian oversight boards).

Agencies that attempt to manage their own camera data may be perceived as having fewer layers of accountability than third-party storage options that track downloads, edits, views, and deletions. Unfortunately, there are examples of internal management incidents where video has "disappeared" or been heavily edited, which negatively impacts data integrity or confirms what some believe about corrupt policing. In Nashville, Tennessee, a civilian employee redacted officer and civilian profanity from BWC footage.[52] Regardless of motive, these edits changed the way the BWC footage was perceived. The edits also covered up violations of the Metropolitan Nashville Police Departmental Manual (2022) policy on "Department and Personal Appearance" (Policy 4.20(J)), which prohibits indecent or profane language while interacting with the public.[53] Video redactions directed by law, such as blurring out juveniles, are appropriate and necessary, but anything more is inappropriate.

More expensive, third-party storage via encrypted "cloud" applications is secure, readily available, and requires less administrative burden. Third-party storage also eliminates the burden of ensuring adequate storage space is available. A large police department with 250 officers will produce an average of 76,000 videos per year, which would consume about 30 terabytes of data.[54,55] Eliminating the need for data storage management allows personnel to focus on fulfilling open records requests and making legally required redactions.

Agencies that require BWCs to be "always on" for the duration of a shift will also require more storage space. BWCs that are "always on" or continuously recording a 30-second or 1-minute buffer can improve integrity and capture corruption, as in Baltimore, but may also violate officer privacy rights. An "always on" BWC may record personal, embarrassing, or irrelevant comments or situations. In response, agencies often prohibit officers from wearing BWCs in private areas such as locker rooms or bathrooms. Capturing footage in areas where expectations of privacy are high may expose municipalities to liability. For example, in Round Lake, Illinois, officers filed a $10 million federal lawsuit against the agency and village when it was discovered the BWCs were always recording and saving the footage. Over an eight-and-a-half-month period, officers were recorded using the bathroom as well as while changing clothes, which exposed their genitalia to camera view.[56]

Camera Footage Review

Most agencies do not have dedicated BWC compliance and review staff; camera footage review is an additional duty assigned to supervisors. Regular review of camera footage is necessary to ensure policy compliance and constitutional policing. Review may also identify training needs, aid officer performance review, uncover officer misconduct, or highlight proper or exemplary performance. Officers should also be encouraged to review their own camera footage to self-assess performance and correct unsafe tactics or questionable behaviors. All of this takes time beyond the demands of police work and supervision.

Camera footage review may occur randomly or regularly, such as once per shift. For example, the Chicago, Illinois, Police Department requires watch lieutenants to view one BWC recording daily to ensure officers are using the cameras properly and following policies and procedures.[57] One random video review is a small sample compared to the number of Chicago officers on patrol and the hours of video footage produced each shift. The time required for review and/or lack of additional staffing committed to conduct multiple video reviews per shift are likely prohibitive factors.

The video length, the nature of the incident being reviewed, and the reason for the review all influence the time needed for review. Agencies must be committed to regular review of camera footage. Supervisory review for policy compliance should also be separate from a dedicated performance review system or process as discussed above. These dedicated review systems require extra time and personnel, both of which are scarce within most police agencies.

Camera Footage, Community Relations, and Officer Field Activity

Body-worn cameras may decrease outcomes of officer–community interactions, especially when citizens are less willing to talk on camera. Citizens who do not wish to have their statements recorded are less likely to provide useful information, such as eyewitness accounts of an incident. Officers wearing BWCs may also be less likely to gather intelligence from informants who are unwilling to talk on camera or who request anonymity. To address this potential problem, BWC policies should allow officers to deactivate their camera while speaking with a reluctant complainant, witness, or victim.

BWCs may reduce officer self-initiated field activity, such as stops of suspicious people (e.g., Terry Stops, when an officer detains someone briefly because they reasonably believe they are involved in criminal activity), or help ensure Fourth Amendment compliance when stops occur. Some may welcome such a reduction, while others believe less proactive policing will lead to more crime. Other officers report that wearing a BWC makes them more "robotic" in their citizen interactions, feeling that more street-based or informal communications may help build rapport.[58] An officer using profanity to build rapport with a known gang member may be perceived as unprofessional by some, or skilled by others when the "street-based" slang helps induce cooperation. These same recordings from the streets will eventually make it to the courtroom and influence juror perception.

Much like the "CSI effect" – where jurors tend to expect the existence of forensic evidence in every criminal case,[59] – jurors may also expect video will always be present, clearly resolve disputed facts, or help determine if force used is reasonable. In a 2020 study, researchers examined how BWC footage influenced mock juror perceptions of a UOF incident. The footage alone, versus a transcript of the incident or a summary of the facts, had the most influence on how the mock jurors perceived the force used to remove a driver from a vehicle. The use of a taser, loud commands, and emotions captured on camera tended to sway perceptions more powerfully than the written record or a verbal summary of the event.[60] No longer is the officer's word or testimony accepted as truth. Rather, it is surmised that jurors expect testimony to be supported by or confirmed with BWC footage.

Although BWCs have become a societal expectation, they can also be perceived as another example of government overreach, especially when they are recording in private, Fourth Amendment-protected areas. BWCs in public do not pose a Fourth Amendment conflict. However, when recording in a home, BWCs may be used to support "plain view" observations that are "seen" on camera later during a frame-by-frame analysis and not actually observed by the officer. Might the plain view camera footage then be used to justify further intrusion or support a search warrant? In contrast, the same footage could be used to ensure constitutional compliance. Courts or police administrators could review the video footage to determine whether police complied with the Fourth Amendment.

From a human performance perspective, BWCs do not *feel* tactile threats that officers may experience and react to, which may prompt force. Officers may not necessarily see what the camera recorded, or what was recorded may not be recollected by the officer. Officers may over-rely on BWCs, such as relying on camera memory versus paying attention and taking notes, which will negatively affect recollection. Further, BWCs are only one perspective and do not include officer body language or actions, which may influence citizen behavior. Human factors and camera footage will be discussed in more detail later.

When used properly, video footage provides opportunities for increased transparency, accountability, policy compliance, improved service, and more thorough accounts of officer–citizen interactions, especially when force is used. At the same time, video footage may have a limited impact on force reduction over time. Camera systems can also be expensive to deploy, require rigorous review to ensure policy compliance or help improve performance, and may decrease the quality of police–community interactions when citizens are less willing to talk on camera. Further, their use may invade privacy and inaccurately sway jury deliberations. Recognizing the advantages and disadvantages of cameras in law enforcement provides insight into expected, potential, and realistic outcomes of their use in the field.

Today, video footage of officer–citizen encounters provides us with more information to help determine what occurred. If force is used, video footage can better inform the objectively reasonable analysis. Although useful, the video must be viewed with caution, especially when it has recorded officers involved in making split-second decisions during dangerous and rapidly evolving events. Several camera factors can influence how we, the viewer, perceive what has occurred on video. These camera factors will be discussed next.

References

1. Gallup (2023). Confidence in Institutions. https://news.gallup.com/poll/1597/confidence-institutions.aspx
2. Voight, R., Camp, N. P., Prabhakaran, V., Hamilton, W. L., Hetey, R. C., Griffiths, C. M., Jurgens, Jurafsky, D., & Eberhardt, J. L. (2017). Language

The Advantages and Disadvantages of Cameras in Law Enforcement **59**

from police body camera footage shows racial disparities in officer respect. PNAS, 114(25), 6521–6526. https://doi.org/10.1073/pnas.1702413114

3. Barker, V., Giles, H., Hajek, C., Ota, H., Noels, K., Lim, T., & Somera, L. (2008). Police-civilian interaction, compliance, accommodation, and trust in an intergroup context: International data. Journal of International and Intercultural Communication, 1(2), 93–112. http://dx.doi.org/10.1080/17513050801891986

4. International Association of Chiefs of Police (IACP) (2002). Impact of video evidence on modern policing research and best practices from the IACP study on in-car cameras. Retrieved from https://www.bja.gov/bwc/pdfs/IACPIn-CarCameraReport.pdf.

5. U.S. Department of Justice (2015, May 1). Justice Department announces $20 million in funding to support body worn camera pilot program. https://www.justice.gov/opa/pr/justice-department-announces-20-million-funding-support-body-worn-camera-pilot-program

6. Lassiter, D. G., Ware, L. J. Ratcliff, J. J., & Irvin, C. R. (2009). Evidence of the camera perspective bias in authentic videotaped interrogations: Implications for emerging reform in the criminal justice system. Legal and Criminological Psychology. 14, 157–170. doi: 10.1348/135532508X284293

7. Turner, B. L., Caruso, E. M., Dilich, M. A., & Roese, N. J. (2018). Body camera footage leads to lower judgements of intent than dash camera footage. PNAS, 116(4), 1201–1206. doi: 10.1073/pnas.1805928116

8. White, M. (2014). Police officer body-worn cameras: Assessing the evidence. Washington DC. Office of Community Policing Services. https://bja.ojp.gov/sites/g/files/xyckuh186/files/bwc/pdfs/diagnosticcenter_policeofficerbody-worncameras.pdf

9. United Kingdom Police and Crime Standards Directorate (PCSD) (2007). Guidance for the police use of body-worn video devices. https://library.college.police.uk/docs/homeoffice/guidance-body-worn-devices.pdf

10. Stoughton, S. W. (2018). Police body-worn cameras. North Carolina Law Review, 96, 1362–1424. Retrieved from http://amjudges.org/pdfs/2018%20Annual%20Meeting/Police-Body-Worn-Cameras.pdf

11. U.S. Department of Justice (2004). The impact of video evidence on modern policing. Retrieved from http://www.theiacp.org/Portals/0/pdfs/WhatsNew/IACP%20In-Car%20Camera%20Report%202004.pdf

12. The Century Council (n.d.). Hardcore drunk driving: Law enforcement guide. Retrieved from https://www.responsibility.org/wp-content/uploads/HCDD_LawEnforcementGuide.pdf

13. Dawes, D., Heegaard, W. Brave, M. Paetow, G., Weston, B., & Ho, J. (2016). Body-worn cameras improve law enforcement officer report writing accuracy. Journal of Law Enforcement, 4(6). Retrieved from: http://jghcs.info/index.php/l/article/viewFile/410/355

14. Braga, A. A., Sousa, W. H., Coldren, J. R., & Rodriguez, D. (2018). The effects of body-worn cameras on police activity and police-citizen encounters: A randomized controlled trial. Journal of Criminal Law & Criminology, 108(3), 511–538.

15. Koslicki, W. M., Makin, D. A., & Willits, D. (2020). When no one is watching: Evaluating the impact of body-worn cameras on use of force incidents. Policing & Society, 30(5), 569–582. https://doi.org/10.1080/10439463.2019.1576672

16. Ariel, B., Farrar, W. A., & Sutherland, A. (2015). The effect of police body-worn cameras on use of force and citizens' complaints against the police: A randomized controlled trial. Journal of Quantitative Criminology, 31(3), 509–535. https://doi.org/10.1007/s10940-014-9236-3

17. Jennings, W. G., Lynch, M. D., & Fridell, L. A. (2015). Evaluating the impact of police officer body-worn cameras (BWCs) on response-to-resistance and serious external complaints: Evidence from the Orlando Police Department (OPD) experience utilizing a randomized controlled experiment. Journal of Criminal Justice, 43(6), 480. https://doi.org/10.1016/j.jcrimjus.2015.10.003

18. Ariel, B., Sutherland, A., Henstock, D., Young, J., Drover, P., Sykes, J., Megicks, S., & Henderson, R. (2016). Report: Increases in police use of force in the presence of body-worn cameras are driven by officer discretion: a protocol-based subgroup analysis of ten randomized experiments. Journal of Experimental Criminology, 12, Article 3. https://doi.org/10.1007/s11292-016-9261-3

19. Yokum, D., Ravishankar, A., & Coppock, A. (2019). A randomized controlled trial evaluating the effects of police body-worn cameras. PNAS, 116(21), 10329–10332. https://doi.org/10.1073/pnas.1814773116

20. Gaub, J. E., Todak, N., & White, M. D. (2021). The distribution of police use of force across patrol and specialty units: A case study in BWC impact. Journal of Experimental Criminology, 17(4), 545–561. https://doi.org/10.1007/s11292-020-09429-8

21. Huff, J., Katz, C. M., & Hedberg, E. C. (2022). A randomized controlled trial of the impact of body-worn camera activation on the outcomes of individual incidents. Journal of Experimental Criminology, 18(2), 247–272. https://doi.org/10.1007/s11292-020-09448-5

22. White, M. D., & Malm, A. (2020). Cops, cameras, and crisis: The potential and the perils of police body-worn cameras. New York University Press.

23. García-González, L., M, P. M., Moreno, A., Gil, A., & del Villar, F. (2013). Effectiveness of a video-feedback and questioning programme to develop cognitive expertise in sport. PLoS One, 8(12). https://doi.org/10.1371/journal.pone.0082270

24. Chen, F. (2015). The use of video feedback to enhance performance in collegiate divers. Southern Illinois University – Carbondale Research Paper. https://opensiuc.lib.siu.edu/cgi/viewcontent.cgi?article=2273&context=gs_rp

25. Nicholls, S. B., James, N., Bryant, E., & Wells, J. (2019). The implementation of performance analysis and feedback within Olympic sport: The performance analyst's perspective. International Journal of Sports Science & Coaching, 14(1), 63–71. https://doi.org/10.1177/1747954118808081

26. Elkins, F. C. (2022). Better performance through body-worn camera footage review. Community Policing Dispatch, 15(8). https://cops.usdoj.gov/html/dispatch/08-2022/body_camera_footage.html

The Advantages and Disadvantages of Cameras in Law Enforcement **61**

27. Makin, D. A., Willits, D. W., & Brooks, R. (2021). Systematic social event modeling: A methodology for analyzing body-worn camera footage. International Journal of Social Research Methodology, 24(2), 163–176. https://doi.org/10.1080/13645579.2020.1766775

28. Farooq, U. (2024, Feb. 2). Police departments are turning to AI to sift through millions of hours of unreviewed body-cam footage. ProPublica. https://www.propublica.org/article/police-body-cameras-video-ai-law-enforcement

29. [KingsCrowd]. (2023, July 20). How Truleo is revolutionizing policing with AI | Inside startup investing [Video]. YouTube. https://www.youtube.com/watch?v=7-mc8B-_Edk

30. Quandt, K. R. (2019, June 17). Floridians Are suing a cop fired for planting drugs in their vehicles. The Appeal. https://theappeal.org/floridians-are-suing-a-cop-fired-for-planting-drugs-in-their-vehicles/

31. Burlew, J. (2021, May 18). Former Deputy Zachary Wester convicted on drug planting charges, taken to jail in handcuffs. Tallahassee Democrat. https://www.tallahassee.com/story/news/local/2021/05/18/zachary-wester-verdict-update-trial-drug-planting-case-court-jury-guilty-not/5143472001/

32. Chappell, B. (2017, June 20). Baltimore police caught planting drugs in body-cam footage, public defender says. NPR. https://www.npr.org/sections/thetwo-way/2017/07/20/538279258/baltimore-police-caught-planting-drugs-in-body-cam-footage-public-defender-says

33. Grover, H. (2017, Feb. 2). Body camera footage clears officer's name. Farmington Daily Times. https://www.daily-times.com/story/news/local/farmington/2017/02/02/body-camera-footage-clears-officers-name/97401294/

34. Branham, D. (2018, May 25). False rape allegation during DUI stop shows how body cams can bulletproof arrests. Dallas Morning News. https://www.dallasnews.com/news/2018/05/25/false-rape-allegation-during-dwi-stop-shows-how-body-cams-can-bulletproof-arrests/

35. Ariel, B., Sutherland, A., Henstock, D., Young, J., & Sosinski, G. (2017). The deterrence spectrum: Explaining why police body-worn cameras "work" or "backfire" in aggressive police-public encounters. Policing: A Journal of Policy and Practice, 1–21. doi: 10.1093/police/paw051

36. Ariel, B., Sutherland, A., Henstock, D., Young, J., Drover, P., Sykes, J., Megicks, S., & Henderson, R. (2018). Paradoxical effects of self-awareness of being observed: Testing the effect of police body-worn cameras on assaults and aggression against officers. Journal of Experimental Criminology, 14, 19–47. https://doi.org/10.1007/s11292-017-9311-5

37. Police Activity (2017, Mar. 21). Bodycam shows Springfield police officer fighting with teenager [Video]. YouTube. https://www.youtube.com/watch?v=95oB0Uj2nvo&rco=1

38. WICS/WRSP Staff (2019, Aug. 22). Former Springfield officer guilty of felony misconduct. https://newschannel20.com/news/local/former-springfield-officer-guilty-of-official-misconduct

39. Simpson, C. R., & Kirk, D. S. (2023). Is police misconduct contagious? Non-trivial null findings from Dallas, Texas. Journal of Quantitative Criminology, 39(2), 425–463. https://doi.org/10.1007/s10940-021-09532-7

40. Connecticut General Statutes (2024). Sec. 54-l. Short Title: Alvin W. Penn Racial Profiling Prohibition Act. (Connecticut General Statutes, 2024)

41. Glasbeek, A., Alam, M., & Roots, K. (2020). Seeing and not-seeing: Race and body-worn cameras in Canada. Surveillance & Society, 18(3), 328–342. https://www.proquest.com/openview/f48143176b57163d1c6fbe046c9f9d96/1?pq-origsite=gscholar&cbl=396354

42. Goldstein, J. (2013, Aug. 13). Judge rejects New York's stop-and-frisk policy. New York Times. http://www.nytimes.com/2013/08/13/nyregion/stop-and-frisk-practice-violated-rights-judgerules.html?_r=0.

43. Parascandola, R. (2024). NYPD monitor tracking stop and frisk abuses has cost $36 million. https://www.flcourier.com/news/nypd-monitor-tracking-stop-and-frisk-abuses-has-cost-36-million/article_d44c7062-24ce-11ef-abb0-43172fb12a19.html

44. CBSNewYork/AP (2013, May. 20). Months-long stop-and-frisk trial wrapping up. https://www.cbsnews.com/newyork/news/months-long-stop-and-frisk-trial-wrapping-up/

45. Huff, J. (2022). Do body-worn cameras reduce disparities in police behavior in minority communities? Evidence of nuanced influences across Black and Hispanic neighborhoods. Criminology & Public Policy, 21(3), 671–711. https://doi.org/10.1111/1745-9133.12590

46. Eberhardt, J. L. (2016). Strategies for change: Research initiatives and recommendations to improve police-community relations in Oakland. Stanford University, SQARQ: Social Psychological Answers to Real-world Question

47. Lange, J. E., Johnson, M. B., & Voas, R. B. (2005). Testing the racial profiling hypothesis for seemingly disparate traffic stops on the New Jersey Turnpike. Justice Quarterly, 22(2), 193–223. https://doi.org/10.1080/07418820500088952

48. McCabe, J. E., Kaminski, R. J., & Boehme, H. M. (2021). Racial profiling and CT motor vehicle stops: An observational study in three towns. Police Practice and Research, 22(6), 1567–1584.

49. Wright, J., & Gaozhao, D. (2024). Body-worn cameras and representation: What matters when evaluating police use of force? Public Administration Review, 84(6), 1117–1133. https://doi.org/10.1111/puar.13746

50. Police Executive Research Forum (PERF) (2018). Cost and benefits of body-worn camera deployments. https://www.policeforum.org/assets/BWCCostBenefit.pdf

51. Crowe, M., & Lauer, E. (2021). Cost analysis of police body-worn cameras in Maryland. Energetics Technology Center. https://www.etcmd.com/sites/default/files/content/BWC%20Study%20Final%20V%203%20%281%29.pdf

52. LaMere, M. (2022, Aug. 15). COB Calls for more action following Metro Police staffer deleting profanity from body cam. Fox17 – WZTV Nashville. https://fox17.com/news/local/cob-calls-for-more-action-following-metro-police-staffer-deleting-profanity-from-body-cam

The Advantages and Disadvantages of Cameras in Law Enforcement **63**

53. Metropolitan Nashville Police Dept. (2022). Departmental manual. https://www.nashville.gov/sites/default/files/2022-09/MNPDManual.pdf?ct=1663761963

54. Miller, L. Toliver, J., & Police Executive Research Forum (2014). Implementing a body-worn camera program: Recommendations and lessons learned. https://www.justice.gov/iso/opa/resources/472014912134715246869.pdf

55. Newcombe, T. (2015, Sept. 4). Body worn camera data storage: The gorilla in the room. Government Technology. https://www.govtech.com/dc/articles/body-worn-camera-data-storage-the-gorilla-in-the-room.html

56. Goudie, C., Markoff, B., & Tressel, C. (2016, July 14). Officers file lawsuit after body cams record them non-stop. ABC 7 Eyewitness News. https://abc7chicago.com/federal-lawsuit-body-cams-police-round-lake-park/1399056/

57. City of Chicago, Office of Inspector General (2019). Evaluation of the Chicago Police Department's random reviews of body-worn camera recordings. https://igchicago.org/wp-content/uploads/2019/07/CPDs-Random-Reviews-of-Body-Worn-Camera-Recordings.pdf

58. Taylor, E., & Lee, M. (2019). Points of view: Arrestees' perspectives on police body-worn cameras and their perceived impact on police-citizen interactions. British Journal of Criminology, 59(4), 958–978. https://doi.org/10.1093/bjc/ https://bja.ojp.gov/sites/g/files/xyckuh186/files/media/document/points-of-view-arrestees-perspectives-on-police-bwc-and-perceived-impact-on-police-citizen-interaction.pdf

59. Shelton, D. E. (2008). The "CSI effect": Does it really exist? National Institute of Justice Journal, 259. https://nij.ojp.gov/topics/articles/csi-effect-does-it-really-exist

60. Saulnier, A., Burke, K. C., & Bottoms, B. L. (2020). New research shows jurors are influenced by body-worn camera footage. Blue Line: Canada's Law Enforcement Magazine. https://www.blueline.ca/new-research-shows-jurors-are-influenced-by-body-worn-camera-footage/

4
THE CAMERA PERSPECTIVE

Video-recorded interactions between the public and the police provide yet another perspective of an event. Video footage cannot replace testimony or an officer's report, but can provide additional information, context, or perspectives to determine most accurately what happened. Unlike the perspective of the Supreme Court of the United States (SCOTUS), video recordings do not speak for themselves.

The camera cannot not "see" as the human eye does; and nor can the human eye capture all that a camera can. Cameras are merely static observers of an event from a single point of view and are not adversely affected by stress or fear associated with force incidents. Absent some sort of mechanical failure, cameras will record everything within the field of view and create a permanent record of the event. The field of view is what the camera lens can capture while stationary (i.e., not panning or being turned by the wearer). The recorded footage may not be consistent with what an officer saw or experienced, and can create contrasts between what an officer reports and what is recorded. Inconsistencies between video footage and officers' reports are to be expected unless they consistently watch or review their video while writing reports, which is unlikely. Several camera factors influence how we perceive, interpret, remember, or recollect what occurred.

Contrary to common belief, video, in and of itself, is not an objective, certain, and unambiguous display or view of reality.[1] Many aspects of video recordings – such as the length, clarity, distance, angle, steadiness, scope, field of view, and lighting of the footage – affect what the video means or tells us.[1] Whether or not a partial or complete sequence has been

DOI: 10.4324/9781003538738-4

captured will also affect the meaning of the video. Frame rate is another important factor that can affect perception of video images. A discussion of these camera factors follows.

Video Recording Length and Clarity

The length of a video, or the length of a police–citizen interaction before force is used, can affect perceptions. According to Vierordt's law, people tend to underestimate long durations of time and overestimate short durations.[2] If there is a short duration between the time of the contact and the use of force (UOF), one may perceive that the officer had little time to act; one may also conclude that the officer did not take the necessary time to de-escalate the incident through effective communication skills or patience. In contrast, if an officer was involved in a long, drawn-out event that suddenly required force (e.g., the suspect quickly pointed a weapon at the officer), some may believe other alternatives were available because of the extended time before the force was used. Runtime displays within video frames can help viewers more accurately discern the duration of a video and provide insight into the time it took for an officer to respond or act. But these runtime displays cannot be used to determine how long it took for the officer to internally perceive or become aware of the threat. First recognizing a threat before reacting to it takes additional processing time.

Video camera clarity is influenced by the number of frames per second (fps) and camera resolution. Most body-worn camera (BWC) video resolution is between 720 and 1080 pixels, with a minimum recommended resolution of 640×480 pixels.[3] The more pixels in a frame, the clearer the image. Any video below 720 pixels may become grainy, lack clarity, and miss important details. The recommended minimum for BWCs is 25 frames per second, although 30 fps provides clear and smooth video.[4] A frame rate below 25 fps creates motion blur or "jumpy" video that can cause a viewer to miss important action, such as quick assaultive behavior or the use of a weapon.[4] The impact of "jumpy" video was highlighted in a 2020 video-recorded use-of-force (VRUOF) incident in Ottawa, Canada.

Ottawa officers were involved in the arrest of a man who had been involved in an assault. The force used was captured by a surveillance camera. Unfortunately, during the arrest the man died (i.e., an in-custody death). When played back, the surveillance camera footage made it appear as though the officers had violently slammed the man onto the concrete, and his head appeared to snap forward onto the surface. The video was used, in part, to criminally charge the officers with manslaughter. The footage was also released to the media, which caused a public outcry.

66 Police Use of Force Through the Lens

A forensic video examiner analyzed the Ottawa surveillance video and discovered that, during the process of downloading the video, at least one frame had been dropped, which caused the video to "jump" or "accelerate" and make action appear faster or more violent than it had been. A similar experience may occur with lower fps video footage. When downloaded properly, the video told a different story, and showed the officers lowering the man to the ground, controlling his rate of descent, and applying handcuffs. The accurate version of the video helped clear the officers of all charges.[5]

How video footage is saved may also alter the original recording. For example, if the footage is compressed to save server space, the compression process may cause frames or images to be dropped and give the illusion of action not consistent with what actually occurred.[6]

In contrast, slow-motion viewing of VRUOF incidents may help improve clarity of rapid and intense events, but cause viewers to believe officers' actions are more intentional or that they had more time to act. For example, a 2016 study of people viewing a murder or broadcast replays of violent contact in professional football in slow motion showed that they perceived the acts as more intentional.[7] Slow-motion replay also causes viewers to perceive that displayed actions lasted longer than they actually did.[7] A slow-motion intentionality bias was observed, even when a time-lapsed counter showed the actual amount of time that had passed during the slow-motion replay. Watching the action at regular speed and in slow motion mitigated the bias but did not eliminate it.[7] Slow-motion replay must therefore be used with caution, especially when making judgments about intent, as it can create a distorted sense of perception and reaction times.[8]

The human eye does not contain pixels, but rather filters images through rods and cones. What is "seen" is influenced by human experiences as the brain interprets the image(s). More simply, one looks with the eyes and sees with the brain. This process takes time. There is always a time lag between seeing something and interpreting its meaning. This phenomenon is known as the "flash-lag" effect, which influences how we perceive the position of objects in motion.[9] In a study by Wojtach et al. (2008), participants inaccurately reported the position of a moving object because of the time it took for them to "see" the object with their eyes and interpret its location with their brain.[9] Cameras and the footage they produce are not affected by this "flash-lag" effect. Just because camera footage shows certain suspect actions at a given time does not mean the officer saw or interpreted the movement at the same time. Therefore, we should expect contrasts between camera and human perception, especially as related to movement.

The Camera Perspective **67**

These complexities of information processing are not unique to law enforcement officers. Pilots, for example, are also sometimes required to make decisions under pressure. The Federal Aviation Administration (FAA) provides pilots with a simple model about human information processing. A pilot must first sense a problem, perceive it as such, decide how to solve the problem, and finally implement that decision.[10] This process takes time and, if pilots are not paying attention or do not perceive a problem (although one may be present), they will miss it. Cognitive errors, which are part of the human condition, are attributed to most aviation accidents.[11] This may, in some cases, also help explain officer errors.

Regardless of the environment, the camera is merely a static observer, and possesses 20/20 vision with clarity and acuity that exceeds the human eye, especially when attempting to focus on multiple items at varying distances. For example, if the human eye is looking at something close by, it would have difficulty also seeing printed text that is beyond or behind the closer object.[12] Further, when officers pay attention to one thing, especially an imminent threat, there is a lack of focus on other things in the immediate environment.[12] The camera, however, can focus on multiple things simultaneously and remains unaffected by the stress of the incident. The camera is a casual observer with no concern for what the footage "means." The camera will continue to "see" clearly within a field of view far greater than the human field of view, especially under stress. The more stress and perceived threat officers experience, the narrower their field of view (FOV).[12]

Video Footage and Distance

Camera footage influences how we perceive distance. A wide-angle lens, such as the 120–170-degree lenses often used in BWCs, can make people seem closer than they actually are. In contrast, a narrow field of view can make a person seem further away. These distance distortions can create misperceptions about officer actions, especially regarding reaction time. A wide-angle lens will make an armed person appear to be further away, which may cause a viewer to believe the officer had more time to react. A narrow-angle lens would make the armed person look closer and create the perception the officer had less time to react.[13]

Video Angle and Perception

Camera angles also affect what we see and how we perceive actions. One camera angle may show force that appears reasonable while another angle suggests it is unreasonable. For example, a chest-mounted camera will

68 Police Use of Force Through the Lens

not capture what is occurring below when worn by an officer who is in an upright kneeling position stabilizing a person on the ground with the assistance of other officers. If officers were yelling "Stop resisting" while attempting to control the person, force used to overcome the presumed resistance may be perceived as reasonable. However, another angle may reveal the force is clearly unreasonable when the person is seen surrendering while being beaten. A similar incident occurred in Florida during the 2014 arrest of Derrick Price.[14]

Price, a wanted drug dealer, was being chased by Marion County deputies, one of whom was wearing a chest-mounted BWC. The BWC footage recorded deputies yelling at Price to "Stop resisting" and "Get your hands behind your back!", and showed the upper backs and shoulders of the deputies apparently using force to arrest him. Like other BWC UOF cases, the lens did not capture the entire encounter. The BWC angle did not reveal the level of resistance, if any, by Price. Another camera angle, from a surveillance camera mounted on the building adjacent to the parking lot where the arrest occurred, showed another perspective. Price can be seen running into the parking lot while being chased by an unmarked pick-up truck. Price looks over his shoulder at the truck barreling towards him, throws his hands up into the universal sign of surrender, and lies on the ground. Price sprawled himself out, on his stomach, like an X. The truck comes to a quick stop, five deputies quickly pounce on Price, and the beating begins. Deputies repeatedly punched, kicked, and kneed Price's head, neck, shoulder, and torso.

The surveillance footage, from an overhead angle, revealed a different perspective. The audio, which also influences what we believe, sounded like Price was resisting. "Stop resisting" and "Get your hands behind your back" are commands officers are trained to use when they encounter resistance. These commands alone would likely cause an experienced reviewer to believe Price had resisted arrest. The video footage told a different story. Had the surveillance footage not been available, this excessive force incident was unlikely to have been discovered. Four deputies pleaded guilty to violating Price's rights. A fifth pleaded not guilty and was acquitted by jury. All five were terminated.[15] Sadly, the video footage became another strike against positive police–community relationships and yet more affirmation for the minority community of what they believe occurs regularly during police encounters.

This incident affirms how important it is for reviewers to seek out multiple camera angles of any force incident, including from dash cameras, surveillance cameras, traffic cameras, or civilians recording police activity. The third-party recording of the police, or sousveillance, will be discussed later in this chapter. Multiple camera angles can help provide a more accurate portrayal of what occurred during VRUOF incidents and allow for a more balanced perspective.

A more balanced perspective, influenced by multiple camera angles and a thorough review can therefore help ensure conclusions are procedurally fair. Bailey et al. (2021) conducted a study to see if the BWC perspective of an event influenced perceptions of procedural justice based upon citizen skin color.[16] Procedural justice posits that personal impressions of legal authority (e.g., the police) are influenced by their perceived fairness, equitability, and application of procedures to arrive at conclusions or decisions.[17] Bailey et al.'s study discovered that viewers perceived the force used to be more procedurally just, in favor of the officer, when force was used against a dark-skinned citizen. In contrast, the lowest evaluations of procedural justice occurred when the force was used against light-skinned citizens. This study also provides insight into biased viewing of VRUOF incidents, which will be addressed in more depth later.

Video Footage Steadiness and Field of View

BWCs can create what Stoughton (2018) describes as "deceptive intensity," where incidents appear more violent than they actually are.[13] BWCs create jarring images when the officers wearing them run or are involved in close encounters. The jumping or jarring footage can then create the impression that force used or resistance experienced is greater than what actually occurred. Although not a scientific study, Stoughton demonstrated this deceptive intensity while wearing a BWC and engaging in a "violent" dance with another role player. The camera footage makes it appear that Stoughton is being assaulted, but another angle from a third-party observer reveals the dance.[18] The field of view and camera angle do matter.

The BWC field of view is wider than the one the human eye can clearly perceive, especially when an individual is under stress. The useful field of view is defined as the visual field area over which information can be acquired in a brief glance without head or eye movement.[19] The human useful field of view is within 60 degrees (a 30-degree radius to either side from the center of a person's face).[19] Experiments related to speed of processing information within the useful field of view have revealed that more errors occur when people are under stress.[20] In contrast, BWC manufacturers often report fields of view of 120 to 170 degrees, although one study revealed it to be less, 72 to 114 degrees.[21] Although there are variations in the BWC field-of-view data, the cameras still have a wider view than a human can see without turning the head.

Human peripheral vision detects motion, and, when perceived, it draws attention to what caused the motion. We must turn our head to clearly see

70 Police Use of Force Through the Lens

what caused the motion in our peripheral vision, while the BWC clearly "sees" it all. The more stress an officer experiences, the more narrow the useful field of view.[19] Recall that the effective field of view of a video camera, which never experiences the stress of using force, is wider than that of the human eye. As a result, officers will sometimes see something not captured on camera. Conversely, the camera will record something the officer did not see. This may complicate the reasonable officer analysis because, although video footage may have recorded the entire event, the officer may not have perceived or been aware of certain details that influence perceptions of reasonableness.[22]

Since humans are a diurnal species (i.e., awake during the daytime), we tend to see well during daylight hours. Daylight BWC and dash cam footage also produces clear footage. During the nighttime, however, BWCs and dash cameras with night vision or infrared capabilities create images and footage that exceed human night vision abilities. Humans can only see well in the dark when there is a light source (e.g., starlight, moonlight, flashlight). Without a light source, it can take 10 to 30 minutes for the eyes to become adapted to low-light environments. Once adapted, only black-and-white (no color) vision is possible.[23] Artificial light, such as flashlights, will illuminate the low-light environment and allow officers to see what the light is focused on with less visual acuity outside the cone of light. More errors also occur in low-light environments, especially when making tactical or force decisions that require concentration or cognitive effort.[22]

Cameras with low-light and night-vision capabilities can capture footage that is clearer than the human eye can see under similar conditions. In low-light conditions, the cameras can immediately adjust and provide a clear image, while it takes time for the human eye to completely adjust. Low-light environments can make it more difficult for officers to see and respond to suspect actions or objects suspects may be holding. Under such circumstances, while the actions or objects are clear in the camera footage, officer response is likely to be delayed and objects may be undetected or misinterpreted. The low-light and night-vision footage of force incidents may create a clearer picture of the event than the officers were able to see; this may result in unfair judgments or conclusions about their actions.[23] Just because an action was captured on video at night does not necessarily mean the officer also saw it.

Finally, partial or complete footage may influence how we interpret the appropriateness of actions. BWCs often fail to capture an entire force incident and may not record or "see" dangerous actions that influenced police response.[24] In the Murray et al. (2024) study, the BWC only captured 66 percent of the critical incidents studied, including when the suspect retrieved or fired a weapon.[24] The vantage point or camera angle and what it records or misses can tell a misleading story. Partial or incomplete footage will miss parts of the police–citizen interaction, which can influence the meaning of the recording. Every interaction has a beginning, middle, and end. Footage that does not capture the beginning will not provide insight into the reason for the contact, how the officer initially used communication skills, and what may have led up to force being used. Footage that only captures the end, such as a deadly force encounter, may not show suspect actions that justify the force (e.g., pointing a weapon at an officer). The camera angle or distance away may fail to capture the dangerous actions.

These limitations, and other camera factors discussed, confirm that BWCs cannot be relied upon to create an objective truth about what happened. Rather, they are merely another tool that can provide more information to help reviewers more accurately determine if force used is objectively reasonable. The camera limitations discussed must be part of the objective reasonableness analysis. Some agencies, such as the Greendale, Wisconsin, Police Department, have recognized similar camera limitations within department policy. Greendale Police Department Policy 9.03 states:

> The Department recognizes that cameras can't always capture everything that is seen by the officer or that happens at a scene but can act as a tool to help explain an event. Sometimes the cameras are unintentionally obstructed, on a fixed mount, or may not have enough frames per second to capture what the human eye saw or perceived.[25]

BWCs offer a first-person perspective of an incident with a focus on the civilian. Dash cameras, which often capture the officer and civilian encounter in the frame, offer a more neutral view of the interactions. Any action that occurs outside the view of the dash camera will be less informative, although it may still capture sound. A civilian witness recording the incident with a camera or, more commonly today, a handheld device may help fill this void. Third-party recording of the police, known in academic circles as sousveillance, can offer yet another view, which can reveal action from another angle that may not be captured by other means.

Third-Party Recording of Police

The ubiquitous presence of mobile phones, surveillance cameras, home security cameras, and traffic cameras allows for sousveillance, or the third-party recording of interactions between the police and the public. One of the best-known examples is the beating of Rodney King at the hands of Los Angeles police officers in 1991, which exposed a side of police work familiar to minority communities. The recording served as confirmation of its existence.[26]

Whether through a VHS handheld recorder, digital camera, or the more common smartphone, sousveillance is a way to police the police and provide another check and balance to police power. The third-party filming of force encounters provides yet another perspective, and sometimes reveals inappropriate force (e.g., Rodney King and Walter Scott).

A casual review of viral videos lawfully recorded by citizens where officers inappropriately interact with citizens demonstrates a need for better officer training in this area. Additionally, in surveys related to the prevalence of sousveillance, officers report they are very aware of but not fond of it. This may have an impact upon their performance, whether perceived or actual.[27,28,29] An officer may perceive sousveillance as a threat (i.e., when inappropriate actions are captured) or an ally to support their actions.[30] Sousveillance recordings can also create positive and negative perceptions of officers. Recordings of force incidents tend to create negative perceptions, while positive encounters (i.e., showing respectful, non-violent, and professional resolutions) are associated with positive perceptions.[31] Some believe that sousveillance explains, in part, why fewer people want to be police officers, while others hope it will help moderate police behavior and promote more professional policing.[32] If officers believe it is likely that citizen video footage of them will be aired to the masses via social media or other digital platforms, the more likely they are to internalize that possibility and alter their behavior.[32]

Sousveillance is blatantly carried out by First Amendment auditors. These auditors often "test" the law enforcement response to protected First Amendment activities, namely recording officers while working and ultimately posting the content to social media or video websites. The inappropriate detention or illegal arrest of First Amendment auditors has occurred across the U.S. For example, a Colorado man standing on a public sidewalk and filming marked police cars in a station parking lot was unlawfully detained and later received a $41,000 settlement.[33] A Wisconsin man was unlawfully grabbed and detained by police after filming the police department building from a public sidewalk.[34] The City of Boston paid a $170,000 settlement to a man who had filmed, from a public place, Boston police officers while they arrested a teenager.[35]

Although SCOTUS has not affirmed the legality of sousveillance, some lower courts have, thereby providing valuable guidance and insight into the often contentious issue. In ACLU v. Alvarez (2012), the appeals court affirmed that, "Audio recording (of the police) is entitled for First Amendment protection."[36] Earlier, in Glik v. Cunniffe (2011), the justices articulated: "Is there a constitutionally protected right to videotape police carrying out their duties in public? Basic First Amendment principles, along with case law from this and other circuits, answer the question unambiguously in the affirmative."[37] Although these court decisions only apply to the Seventh and First circuits, respectively, they provide insight into how other circuits or even SCOTUS may view the issue. Although the civilian recording of officers is permitted, it is not without some restrictions.

In Alvarez, the justices recognized that video recording of the law enforcement officers is not without some reasonable exceptions and gave deference to officer safety, the integrity of crime scenes, and the confidentiality of investigations. The justices opined:

> It goes without saying that the police make take all reasonable steps to maintain safety and control, secure crime scenes and accident sites, and protect the integrity of and confidentiality of investigations. While an officer surely cannot issue a "move on" order to a person because he is recording, the police may order bystanders to disperse for reasons related to public safety and order, and other legitimate law-enforcement needs … Nothing we have said here immunizes behavior that obstructs or interferes with effective law-enforcement or the protection of public safety.[36]

Department policy or procedures must clearly outline how officers are to interact with First Amendment auditors or others video recording police actions. Policy and procedures should align with state, federal, or constitutional law and include the following content:

- Civilians may record officers from any public place or private place where they have a legal right to be present.
- While recording, civilians may not interfere with law enforcement activity.
- Examples of interference include witness or suspect tampering, inciting others to violate the law, being too close to officers so as to create a clear safety hazard or being too close and interfering with officer and victim, witness, or suspect communication.

Officers must be trained in the proper response to First Amendment auditors or civilian recording of the police. Merely telling citizens they cannot record or attempting to take their camera is not appropriate. Officers must articulate why a civilian cannot record (e.g., because they are interfering with law enforcement activity, pose an officer safety risk, or are not legally present) and provide a reasonable explanation before acting. If the civilian recorder is interfering with a witness, victim, or suspect, it may be easier to relocate the witness, victim, or suspect versus attempting to interact with or ordering the civilian to stop. Violating the First Amendment rights of civilians recording the police may expose the officer or agency to civil liability and is sure to result in poor social media exposure.

Surveillance videos and traffic cameras may also capture the interactions of force encounters and provide yet another perspective for reviewers to consider. Like any video record, surveillance footage filmed from various angles can provide different perspectives of a force event, similar to sousveillance. Various camera angles of an event can enhance contextual data of the incident.[20] The value of these other perspectives became apparent in the Derrick Price case, which was discussed earlier. The Price case supports the concerns expressed by Stoughton (2018)[13] related to the claim that video recordings "speak for themselves," while research demonstrates otherwise. A reviewer who merely accepts the video record at face value is likely to arrive at inaccurate conclusions or perceptions regarding force.

The use of BWCs, when compared with the more limited views of dash cameras used to capture police–citizen interactions in the public domain, raises important privacy concerns. These concerns include when BWCs should be activated, who should be recorded, and how to convey notification. Some of these issues are regulated by law, while others are researched practices that can inform and assist in identifying best practices expressed in policy. For example, Wisconsin State Statute 968.31(2)(b) grants law enforcement the authority to record communications between two (or more) people when one person has given consent.[38] The person giving consent includes the person who is recording the activity; no announcement or notification of a recording to others present is necessary. Although no announcement is necessary, in some instances it may be beneficial to make an announcement, while in others it should be avoided.

A camera that is visibly present (versus one recording surreptitiously) along with a verbal notification tends to create an environment of "contagious accountability" for all present that certain ground rules are in play, and civilized behavior is more likely.[39,40] The verbal notification tends to internalize or remind all present, including the officer, that a camera is recording.[40] Further, this awareness tends to improve perceptions of procedural justice (i.e., outcomes), the lawfulness of police actions, and citizen compliance.[41] These announcements support an environment of "contagious accountability" for civilians and officers that "civilized" communications are expected. However, during incidents where escalation of aggression is high, awareness of a camera being present may further escalate the event.[42] In these instances, it may be beneficial not to announce that a camera is present.

Another critical issue related to BWCs is the recording of non-involved third parties, witnesses, victims, or juveniles. The release of any juvenile law enforcement record, including a recording, is regulated in all U.S. states. All juvenile law enforcement records are considered confidential unless a juvenile offender is waived to adult court. If law enforcement video footage captures the image of a juvenile, the video footage must be redacted before the record can be released. Similarly, the identity of crime victims must be redacted from any requested video record. Regarding the identity of witnesses or complainants, generally the record should be redacted if there is a demonstrated reasonable probability that their identity would endanger them. Additional insight about laws that regulate BWC recordings can be viewed on the National Conference of State Legislatures website: https://www.ncsl.org/civil-and-criminal-justice/body-worn-camera-laws-database.

An often contentious policy issue for consideration involves when cameras should be activated. Some advocate for an "always on" approach,[43] while others, including the American Civil Liberties Union (ACLU), support an "only on" policy whenever a law enforcement officer is responding to a call for service or initiating a citizen contact.[44] The ACLU further recommends continuous recording until the end of the contact, while practitioners believe pausing the recording at times is necessary, especially when discussing sensitive investigative information or law enforcement tactics.[44] This is an unsettled issue that will continue to be debated among scholars and practitioners.

The Community Briefing

VRUOF incidents are powerful and can create strong emotional reactions from viewers. Often, incidents are recorded from multiple perspectives and civilian recordings may be live-streamed or uploaded to social media before evaluators or leaders can determine whether the force is objectively reasonable. Civilian video accounts that offer other useful perspectives may be incomplete, but law enforcement cannot control how the footage is distributed to the masses or public reactions to those videos.

Overexposure to incomplete video can negatively affect public perceptions of the incident. To counter any outcry or allegation of excessive or inappropriate force, law enforcement leaders are forced to release video footage before inquiries into reasonableness are complete. An effective way of demonstrating transparency is to create "community briefing" videos, which include relevant video footage of the UOF incident and a narrative that provides a general explanation of the incident. Timely release of UOF video recordings can provide a wider context of what happened. This will

76 Police Use of Force Through the Lens

also demonstrate transparency and help viewers overcome cognitive biases that may motivate adverse public reactions.[45] VRUOF footage that portrays procedurally just policing (e.g., treating individuals fairly, giving them the opportunity to voice their concerns) enhances community perceptions of the police and their actions.[46] These videos also provide law enforcement with an opportunity to provide another perspective, which may not otherwise be shown or available in recordings aired on social media or the news media. An examination of various community briefing videos reveals that they typically achieve the following:

- Professional production quality.
- Effective warning to viewers about what they are about to watch.
- Protection of identities of uninvolved people, juveniles, or victims
- Elimination of any personal details that would reveal protected identities by blurring images or garbling voices, and by obscuring home addresses or interiors that may reveal identity.
- Inclusion of factual content about the incident.
- Removes allusion to conclusions or objective reasonableness.
- Includes dispatch audio, BWC footage, dash camera footage, surveillance footage, etc.
- Syncs multiple camera perspectives so the footage can be viewed simultaneously.
- Includes a closing comment that the case is under investigation.

Good examples of community briefing videos can be viewed at the D.C. Metropolitan Police Department website: https://mpdc.dc.gov/page/community-briefing-videos.

Does Video Footage Speak for Itself?

Scott v Harris (2007) was the first case in front of SCOTUS where the justices reviewed video footage of a high-speed chase. Coweta County, Georgia, Deputy Tim Scott joined a vehicle pursuit of a speeding violator, 19-year-old Victor Harris. Instead of stopping, Harris sped away, at times at speeds greater than 85 miles per hour. Deputy Scott attempted to apply a pursuit intervention technique (PIT) maneuver, but the high speeds prevented its proper application. Instead, the deputy rammed Harris, which caused Harris to lose control, leave the roadway, and roll over multiple times. Harris suffered serious injuries and was left a quadriplegic. He filed suit alleging excessive force, claiming that Deputy Scott's actions equated to unjustified deadly force. The lower courts found in favor of Harris and the state appealed to SCOTUS, which agreed to hear the case.

The Camera Perspective **77**

Deputy Scott's dash cam footage became a key piece of evidence viewed by the justices, which depicted a dangerous, "Hollywood-style car chase of the most frightening sort, placing police officers and innocent bystanders alike at great risk of serious injury." In an 8–1 opinion in favor of Deputy Scott, the justices were so moved by the dash cam video footage that they said, "We are happy to allow the videotape to speak for itself" and that to believe otherwise was "visible fiction." The lower courts, according to the majority, "should have viewed the facts in the light depicted by the videotape." The force used by Deputy Scott to stop a dangerous motorist who threatened the lives of innocent bystanders did not violate the Fourth Amendment, even if it placed Harris at risk of serious injury or death.[47] Dash cam footage of this vehicle pursuit can still be viewed online as of this publication.

The Harris decision was embraced by law enforcement, while civil rights advocates believed the force used was excessive. Although there were contrasting views about the force used, the impact of the video footage that led to the majority opinion became an area of interest for researchers. Could the video really *speak for itself*?

Deputy Scott's video was shown to a diverse sample of 1350 Americans, and the majority agreed with SCOTUS. However, among the sample there were contrasting perspectives and perceptions along lines of demographics, cultural worldviews, and political ideologies.[48] One might conclude that video did not necessarily speak for itself. Our demographics, ethnicity, age, where we grew up, political and religious ideologies, interactions with police, and even the television shows or movies we have watched do shape our biases and how we view the world. These same biases influence how we perceive and interpret VRUOF. Mitigating the impact of our biases is necessary to most accurately determine if VRUOF is objectively reasonable. Mitigating the impact of our biases is discussed in the next chapter.

References

1. Wasserman, H. M. (2017). Recording of and by police: The good, the bad, and the ugly. Journal of Gender, Race & Justice, 20(3), 543–562.

2. Glasauer, S. & Shi, Z. (2021). The origin of Vierordt's law: The experimental protocol matters. PsyCh Journal, 10, 732–741. https://doi.org/10.1002/pchj.464

3. Babin, S., & Koslicki, W. (2017). Resilient communications project: Body worn camera perception study Phase 1 memorandum report. Department of Homeland Security, Science, and Technology Directorate. https://www.dhs.gov/sites/default/files/publications/971_OIC_AOS-17-1302_Body-Worn-Camera-Perception-Study-Phase-1_171117-508.pdf

4. Hung, V., Babin, S., & Coberly, J. (2016). A primer on body worn camera technologies. National Institute of Justice. Retrieved from https://www.ncjrs.gov/pdffiles1/nij/grants/250382.pdf

5. Axon (2020, July 29). Accurate video evidence tells another story in use of force case. https://www.axon.com/resources/accurate-video-evidence-tells-another-story-in-use-of-force-case

6. Wallentine, K., Scarry, L., & Fredericks, G. (2017). Should cops see body cam video before giving UOF statements? Force Science Institute. https://www.police1.com/police-products/body-cameras/articles/should-cops-see-body-cam-video-before-giving-use-of-force-statements-w0ZL3Oqq6z69wrNm/

7. Caruso, E. M., Burns, Z. C., & Converse, B. J. (2016). Slow motion increases perceived intent. PNAS, 113(33). https://doi.org/10.1073/pnas.1603865113

8. Hüttner, N., Sperl, L., & Schroeger, S. (2023). Slow motion bias: Exploring the relation between time overestimation and increased perceived intentionality. Perception, 52(2), 77–96. https://doi.org/10.1177/03010066221139943

9. Wojtach, W. T., Sung, K., Truong, S., & Purves, D. (2008). An empirical explanation of the flash-lag effect. PNAS, 105(42), 16338–16343. www.pnas.org/cgi/doi/10.1073/pnas.0808916105

10. SKYbrary (n.d.). Information processing. https://skybrary.aero/articles/information-processing

11. Wilson, D. (2016, Oct. 6). Inadvertent errors. Flight Safety Foundation. https://flightsafety.org/asw-article/inadvertent-errors/

12. Blake, D. M. (2015). Body worn cameras: Comparing human and device to ensure unbiased investigations. Law Enforcement Executive Research Forum, 15(4), 22–40. doi: 10.19151/LEEF.2015.1504c

13. Stoughton, S. W. (2018). Police body-worn cameras. North Carolina Law Review, 96, 1362–1424. Retrieved from http://amjudges.org/pdfs/2018%20Annual%20Meeting/Police-Body-Worn-Cameras.pdf

14. Friedersdorf, C. (2016, Feb. 1). The conspiracy to brutalize Derrick Price. The Atlantic. https://www.theatlantic.com/politics/archive/2016/02/the-conspiracy-to-brutalize-derrick-price/457134/

15. Magoc, E. (2016, Apr. 20). Judge calls Marion County case a "true tragedy" as he sentences former deputies to prison. NPR. https://www.wuft.org/news/2016/04/20/former-marion-county-deputies-sentenced-in-derrick-price-beating/#:~:text=Jesse%20Terrell%20is%20a%20free,Theirs%20was%20a%20unanimous%20decision.

16. Bailey, R. L., Read, G. L., Yan, Y. J. H., Liu, J., Makin, D. A., & Willits, D. (2021). Camera point-of-view exacerbates racial bias in viewers of police use of force videos. Journal of Communication, 71(2), 246–275

17. Tyler, T. (2003). Procedural justice, legitimacy, and the effective rule of law. Crime and Justice: A Review of Research, 30, 431–505

18. Williams, T., Thomas, J., Jacoby, S., & Cave, D. (2016, Apr. 1). Police body cameras: What do you see? New York Times. https://www.nytimes.com/interactive/2016/04/01/us/police-bodycam-video.htm

19. Geis, C. E., & Blake, D. M. (2015). Efficacy of police body cameras for evidentiary purposes: Fact or fallacy? The Police Chief, 83(5). Retrieved

from https://www.hptinstitute.com/wp-content/uploads/2014/01/Body-Cameras.pdf

20. Roenker, D. L., Cissell, G. M., Ball, K. K., Wadley, V. G., & Edwards, J. D. (2003). Speed-of-processing and driving simulator training result in improved driving performance. Human Factors, 45(2), 218–233. https://doi.org/10.1518/hfes.45.2.218.27241

21. Espenant, M., Murwanashyaka, J. N., Gagne, D. M., & Wollbaum, A. A. (2015). Scoping, technical, and operational evaluation of body worn video. Canadian Safety and Security Program (CSSP)-2014-TI-2031 final report. Defence Research and Development Canada. https://cradpdf.drdc-rddc.gc.ca/PDFS/unc199/p802456_A1b.pdf

22. Boivin, R., Gendron, A., Faubert, C., & Poulin, B. (2017). The body-worn camera perspective bias. Journal of Experimental Criminology, 13(1), 125–142.

23. Cornell Center for Materials Research (2016). Can humans ever see in the dark with no night vision glasses or other aids? https://www.ccmr.cornell.edu/faqs/can-humans-ever-see-in-the-dark-with-no-night-vision-glasses-or-other-aids/

24. Murray, N. P., Lewinski, W., Allen, C., Heidner, G. S., Albin, M. W., & Horn, R. (2024). The eyes have it! Functional field of view differences between visual search behavior and body-worn camera during a use of force response in active-duty police officers. Police Practice and Research, 25(4), 490-497. doi: 10.1080/15614263.2024.2328665

25. Greendale Police Department (2020). Mobile audio/video recording equipment. https://cms4files1.revize.com/villageofGreendalewi/9.03%20Mobile%20Audio%20Video%20Recording%20Equipment.pdf

26. Brucato, B. (2015). Policing made visible: Mobile technologies and the importance of point of view. Surveillance & Society, 13(3), 455–473.

27. Roche, S. P. (2017). Cops and cells: Theorizing and assessing the implications of smartphone surveillance for policing [Doctoral dissertation, State University of New York at Albany] (Order No. 10608099). Available from ProQuest Dissertations & Theses Global. (1947275055).

28. Brown, G. R. (2015). The blue line on thin ice: Police use of force modifications in the era of cameraphones and YouTube. British Journal of Criminology, 56, 293–312. doi: 10.1093/bjc/azv052.

29. Kopak, A. (2014). Lights, cameras, action: A mixed methods analysis of police perceptions of citizens who video record officers in the line of duty in the United States. International Journal of Criminal Justice Sciences, 9(2). Retrieved from https://www.sascv.org/ijcjs/pdfs/kopakijcjs2014vol9issue2.pdf

30. Sandhu, A., & Haggerty, K. D. (2017). Policing on camera. Theoretical Criminology. 21(1), 78–95. doi: 10.1177/1362480615622531

31. Parry, M. M. (2017). Watching the watchmen: How videos of police-citizen encounters influence individuals' perceptions of the police [Doctoral dissertation, Arizona State University] (Order No. 10276288). Available from ProQuest Dissertations & Theses Global. (1901795129).

32. Singh, A. (2017). Prolepticon: Anticipatory citizen surveillance of the police. Surveillance & Society, 15(5), 676–688. https://ojs.library.queensu.ca/index.php/surveillance-and-society/article/view/6418/6675

33. KKTV (2018, June 1). Colorado Springs to pay cameraman $41,000 after First Amendment audit of police. https://www.kktv.com/content/news/Colorado-Springs-to-pay-cameraman-41000-after-First-Amendment-audit-of-police-484291511.html

34. Hunter, J. (2018, Aug. 3). Investigation: 3 officers acted improperly against "First Amendment Auditor." Wisconsin Newspaper Association. https://wnanews.com/2018/08/03/first-amendment-auditor-case-discipline/

35. Phelps, A. (2012, Mar. 27). After a major First Amendment ruling, Boston police settle a cellphone recording lawsuit. NiemanLab. https://www.niemanlab.org/2012/03/after-a-major-first-amendment-ruling-boston-police-settle-a-cellphone-recording-lawsuit/

36. ACLU of IL v. Alvarez, No. 11-1286 (7th Cir. 2012). https://law.justia.com/cases/federal/appellate-courts/ca7/11-1286/11-1286-2012-05-08.html

37. Glik v. Cunniffe, 655 F.3d 78 (2011). https://casetext.com/case/glik-v-cunniffe

38. Wisconsin State Legislature, 968.31. Interception and disclosure of wire, electronic or oral communications. https://docs.legis.wisconsin.gov/statutes/statutes/968/31/2/b

39. Ariel, B. (2016). Police body cameras in large police departments. Journal of Criminal Law & Criminology, 106(4), 729–768.

40. Ariel, B., Sutherland, Al., Henstock, D., Young, J., Drover, P., Sykes, J., Megicks, S., & Henderson, R. (2016). "Contagious accountability": A global multisite randomized controlled trial on the effect of police body-worn cameras on citizen complaints against the police. Criminal Justice and Behavior, 44(2). doi: 10.1177/0093854816668218

41. Demir, M. (2023). Effect of awareness and notification of body-worn cameras on procedural justice, police legitimacy, cooperation, and compliance: Findings from a randomized controlled trial. Journal of Experimental Criminology, 19(2), 311–341. https://doi.org/10.1007/s11292-021-09487-6

42. Ariel, B., Sutherland, A., Henstock, D. Young, J., & Sosinski, G. (2018). The deterrence spectrum: Explaining why police body-worn cameras "work" or "backfire" in aggressive police–public encounters. Policing: A Journal of Policy and Practice, 12(1), 6–26. https://doi.org/10.1093/police/paw051

43. Coudert, F., Butin, D., & Le Metayer, D. (2015). Body-worn cameras for police accountability: Opportunities and risks. Computer Law & Security Review, 31(6), 749–762. https://doi.org/10.1016/j.clsr.2015.09.002

44. American Civil Liberties Union (ACLU) (2018). A model act for regulating the use of body worn cameras by law enforcement. Retrieved from https://www.aclu.org/other/model-act-regulating-use-wearable-body-cameras-law-enforcement

45. Mieth, T. D., Venger, O., & Lieberman, J. D. (2019). Police use of force and its video coverage: An experimental study of the impact of media source

and content on public perceptions. Journal of Criminal Justice, 60, 35–46. https://doi.org/10.1016/j.jcrimjus.2018.10.006

46. Roche, S. P., Fenimore, D. M., & Taylor, P. (2022). But did they get it "right"? Deadly force, body-worn camera footage, and hindsight bias. Policing: An International Journal, 45(4), 618–632. https://doi.org/10.1108/PIJPSM-09-2021-0126

47. Scott v. Harris, 550 U.S. 372 (2007)

48. Kahan, D. M., Hoffman, D. A., & Braman, D. (2009). Whose eyes are you going to believe? Scott v. Harris and the perils of cognitive illiberalism. Faculty Scholarship Series. Paper 97. http://digitalcommons.law.yale.edu/fss_papers/97

5

CAMERA FOOTAGE AND MITIGATING THE IMPACT OF BIAS

This chapter explores how various types of bias – a tendency, inclination, or prejudice toward or against something or someone – can influence how we perceive video-recorded use of force (VRUOF). Viewers of VRUOF, including experienced officers or experts, can be influenced by what they see and formulate conclusions about the reasonableness of force before all facts are known. To help arrive at the most accurate and objective conclusion about the reasonableness of VRUOF, viewers must therefore consciously suppress their biases accordingly. Further, the application of a specific type of bias, namely hindsight bias, to determine objective reasonableness is prohibited by the United States Supreme Court (SCOTUS). Hindsight bias is often demonstrated by viewers when their perspectives of a VRUOF incident are influenced by outcomes or facts not known to the officer at the time of the incident. More simply, people often believe "I knew it all along" after they discover what actually happened. The impact of heuristics and hindsight bias, as well as attribution bias, confirmation bias, camera perspective bias, and outcome bias, will be discussed, along with ways to mitigate or minimize their impact.

Heuristics: System 1 and System 2 Thinking

To accurately conclude whether VRUOF is objectively reasonable, aligns with policy and procedure, or is consistent with best practices requires viewers to consider all available information. Viewers must also consider alternative information. To date, one study has been conducted to examine the impact of bias when determining if force captured on body-worn

DOI: 10.4324/9781003538738-5

cameras (BWCs) is appropriate.[1] Other studies have examined how cognitive biases can affect the evaluation of criminal cases.[2] Findings suggest that BWC footage cannot entirely eliminate conflicts between what is seen on video and in an officer's report,[1] and that biases can adversely affect criminal case outcomes.[2] Although not specifically related to determining whether VRUOF is objectively reasonable or appropriate, these studies provide insight into how heuristics and biases can affect perceptions and interpretation of information about the appropriateness of an officer's actions.

When making decisions about the appropriateness of officer actions, evaluators may use heuristics, or cognitive shortcuts, to guide their judgment or conclusions. Heuristics can help guide decision-making when there is limited information or time, and in "fast and fugal" moments, may lead to accurate decisions or responses.[3] However, ignoring all available information or failing to consider other available information may lead to inaccurate judgments.[3] For example, an evaluator who views a complex VRUOF incident may, without considering all available information, conclude that the force used is appropriate, although more information (e.g., found within an officer's report) may create an alternative perspective. Any conclusion that fails to encompass all appropriate information would be inappropriate, incomplete, or inaccurate.

Heuristics helps us process stimuli, information, or actions by attuning to patterns, especially when making decisions in a complex environment.[2] When faced with decisions that must be made quickly, we rely upon the patterns created by our experiences to help make the correct decision. Officers often rely upon heuristics to make use-of-force (UOF) decisions[4] – a process that is learned or reinforced in training and through field experience. BWCs and dash cameras do not recognize an officer's ability to detect dangerous patterns of behavior that require eye or head scanning, and may justify a force response.[5]

UOF training often exposes officers to scenarios such as suspect actions, behaviors, or movements that require an appropriate response. This training can help teach officers to recognize dangerous patterns and make quick and, it is hoped, accurate force decisions. At the same time, the training may create inappropriate mental shortcuts that might be used under dynamic and stressful conditions.[6] While mental shortcuts can help officers make the right decisions, sometimes the wrong decision is reached, with tragic outcomes.

On September 4, 2014, former South Carolina State Trooper Sean Groubert stopped motorist Levar Jones in a gas station parking lot for not wearing a seatbelt. The traffic stop, recorded via dash cam, showed Jones exiting his vehicle and standing by the open driver's side door. Trooper

84 Police Use of Force Through the Lens

Groubert, before he is within camera view and likely standing near his open squad car door before walking up to speak with Jones, requested, "Can I see your license please?" Jones responded to this request by turning away from Trooper Groubert and reaching into the vehicle. Trooper Groubert then yelled, "Get out of the car, get out of the car!" while moving across the front of his squad within the camera field of view and firing a total of four rounds at Jones. Jones immediately came out of the open driver's side door, raised his empty hands straight up while backing away from the gunshots, and fell to the ground, out of camera view. Trooper Groubert commanded, "Get on the ground! Get on the ground!" Jones replied, "I just got my license! You said get my license! I got my license right here!"[7]

Next, Trooper Groubert approached Jones, ordered him to put his hands behind his back, and the ratcheting of applying handcuffs is heard. Jones asked, "What did I do sir?" and Trooper Groubert replied, "Are you hit?" Jones said, "I think so, I can't feel my leg. I don't know what happened. I just grabbed my license ... why did you shoot me?" Trooper Groubert explained, "Well you dove headfirst back into your car ... and you jumped back out ... and I'm telling you to get out of your car." "I'm sorry," Jones pleaded, "I didn't hear two words." No weapon was found inside Jones's vehicle. He had merely attempted to comply with Trooper Groubert's request for his driver's license. Thankfully, Jones survived, but will forever be affected by this tragic mistake. Online video recording of this shooting can still be viewed as of the time of writing.[7]

At his sentencing, Trooper Groubert admitted, "I realize now that I misread body language" – a misinterpretation that resulted in the mistaken use of deadly force.[8] If Jones had reached into the vehicle and obtained a weapon, the outcome or perception of reasonableness would likely have been different. What if Trooper Groubert had used a different approach? Instead of beginning the contact with "Can I see your license please," Trooper Groubert could have said, "The reason I stopped you is for not wearing a seatbelt ... do you have your driver's license with you?" This could have allowed for Jones to reply, "Yes, it is in my vehicle," and any movement or reaching into the vehicle could have been controlled or perceived as less threatening.

In Trooper Groubert's case, he likely made a "System 1" decision, which is an intuitive, automatic, and impulsive decision-making process based upon training or experience.[4] System 1 decisions and actions occur when we are forced to make quick conclusions that involve risk or danger, uncertainty, or emotion. These conclusions, based on incomplete information, often occur in UOF incidents.[9] Sometimes incorrect System 1 decisions may have dire consequences. System 1 errors are not unique to police work, and also occur in the medical community,[10] the airline industry,[11] and when driving our cars.[12] Mistakes like these may be avoided through scenario-based training that focuses on cognitive development (e.g., decision-making and problem solving) and not solely on techniques or skills.[13]

When evaluating VRUOF, we must consciously refrain from making any emotionally driven conclusions about the appropriateness of the force. VRUOF can have an emotional impact when viewing only the recording, which is potentially a limited objective reality and is not a complete picture of what occurred. Instead, evaluators should rely upon System 2 thinking, which is controlled, rational, systemic, and reflective.[4]

System 2 thinking can also help avoid the adverse effects of biases. Expert evaluators in the UOF have a large base of experience and training to draw upon, and may initially perceive the appropriateness of VRUOF before all information is available to them. Any conclusions about the appropriateness or reasonableness of force before all available information is known may lead evaluators to adverse cognitive and motivational biases.

Cognitive biases occur when evaluators do not process the full range of information available before they make a decision or conclusion, do not possess the cognitive capacity to make the decision, or fail to take the time necessary to make an informed decision.[14] Cognitive bias may also be driven by "recency bias," when perceptions about a VRUOF event are influenced by a recent similar event – although no two events are exactly the same.[9]

Motivational biases affect the evaluator who is invested in a specific outcome. Research on motivational bias among police investigators reveals they may treat information that is consistent or inconsistent with prior beliefs about a case differently, and are likely to disregard contrasting information that may threaten a desired conclusion.[15] When assessing VRUOF incidents, an evaluator with a self-serving desire to see the outcome of a case in favor or against an officer is likely to disregard information that may indicate an alternative conclusion.

When evaluating VRUOF, the appropriateness of these decisions must be considered in light of *all* circumstances faced by the officer, which cannot be deduced by video alone. Using cognitive shortcuts (i.e., System 1 thinking) to determine whether VRUOF is reasonable is inappropriate and may lead to inaccurate conclusions. Evaluators are not typically under time pressure or face the need to rapidly make decisions about the appropriateness of force. Evaluators must use higher-order thinking, or System 2 thinking, to help them arrive at more accurate conclusions, conduct thorough investigations or inquiries, and consider all available information to most accurately arrive at an objective conclusion.

86 Police Use of Force Through the Lens

Other biases, such as hindsight bias, outcome bias, confirmation bias, and attribution bias, along with how they are related to perceptions of officer performance and behavior, are described next.

Impact of Bias on Perceptions of Officer Performance and Behavior

> The "reasonableness" of a particular use of force must be judged from the perspective of a reasonable officer on the scene, rather than with the 20/20 vision of hindsight. (Graham v. Connor, 1989)

Biases are part of the human condition. A bias is prejudice in favor of one thing or another, including people or groups. Bias-based policing – where race, ethnicity, genders, socioeconomic status, sexual orientation, religion, background, age, or culture is the sole basis for taking action or enforcement – is unacceptable, unprofessional, and illegal. Perspectives about police are influenced by personal biases (e.g., positive or negative identification). This extends to the way we perceive video-recorded interactions.

When determining if VRUOF is reasonable, viewers must remember that video alone is not an objective, certain, and unambiguous display or view of reality.[16] As discussed earlier, video recordings can be misleading, incomplete, and inaccurate, while also emotionally impacting. For this reason, viewers may make judgments about reasonableness before considering all facts known to the officer at the time of the event. However, the video itself is inherently *more* objective and accurate than a police report,[1] which is influenced by human recollection, perception, and interpretation that may affirm or contradict what is seen on video.

Video recordings provide for easy application of hindsight bias or "Well, if that were me" conclusions that fail to consider all of what the individual officer may have experienced at the time of the event. People are also typically overconfident in their interpretations of what they see, and may disregard other evidence or perspectives contrary to initial interpretations.[17] This is especially true among experts,[18] who must consciously suppress biases and focus on objective examination of cases.[18] Experts may take cognitive shortcuts that allow them to quickly arrive at conclusions, but that may also cause them not to consider other information to best inform their decisions.[19] Efforts must therefore be made to avoid the impact of these shortcuts or biases when determining if force is objectively reasonable.

VRUOF incidents that contain content not known at the time of an incident can create an environment that is ripe for hindsight. For example, where officers believed a person was armed at the time, but video recordings later revealed the person was not armed, they might easily call into question their recollection or perception. Although the belief a weapon was present may have been reasonable, the fact that a weapon was *not* present would raise questions of misperception, deceitfulness, or flawed memory. However, if the same recording affirmed the officer's perception, we are then more likely to readily believe the officer's recollection or perception of the event. Therefore, the outcome of a VRUOF event will affect perception and beliefs about reasonableness. Outcome bias is just one example of the biases we will examine here.

To overcome the impact of bias, we must be consciously aware of how bias can impact perception. It is difficult to think critically if we are unaware of our biases. Unabated biases can easily lead to cognitive shortcuts that result in prejudgments, rash decisions, or error.[20] Viewers of VRUOF who naively believe that what we see enters our brain unfiltered and uninfluenced by our biases are sadly mistaken. These biases can also lead to false-positive conclusions (e.g., problematic retention and lack of accountability) or false-negative conclusions (e.g., problematic discipline and unlawful termination).

Hindsight Bias

Hindsight bias occurs when we view an event or action as more likely or predictable after it occurred.[21] When the outcome of an event is known, people commonly report the conclusion was "known all along." An officer never knows what the outcome of a force incident will be. However, viewers or evaluators of the recording always know the outcome, which in turn can influence how they perceive an officer's actions. For example, if an officer-involved shooting revealed the suspect had a facsimile gun, although the officer perceived a real gun, the threat posed by the suspect – in hindsight – would potentially be perceived as less significant. Hindsight bias can therefore lead to inappropriate decisions regarding the actions of others, especially in a legal context.[22]

The landmark case of Graham v. Connor (1989), discussed in Chapter 1, specifically prohibited the application of hindsight bias when determining whether an officer's UOF was objectively reasonable. Objective reasonableness does not necessarily mean the officer's perceptions were accurate, but rather reasonable from the perspective of the officer at the time of the event, not merely through the lens of a video camera. However, recordings are likely to produce hindsight bias, especially among novices (i.e., casual viewers) as well as those trained or experienced in police tactics, such as law enforcement managers, trainers, or experts, who may be tasked with determining if force is objectively reasonable.[20] These experienced reviewers may inappropriately view the video from their perspective – influenced by years of knowledge, training, and experience – versus the required "reasonable officer at the scene" perspective. Experienced reviewers should rely upon higher order cognitive processes (e.g., System 2 thinking) and apply the principles outlined in this work.

An evaluator who merely watches video of a police incident (e.g., UOF or a police vehicle pursuit) and arrives at a conclusion or "snap judgment" related to reasonableness without considering the officer's perceptions at the time of the event not only promotes erroneous interpretation, but also a rejection of conflicting perceptions and conclusions.[23] It is critical for reviewers to consider all available evidence before arriving at a conclusion, and to be consciously aware of the bias that recordings can cause.

Other types of bias that could influence an objectively reasonable conclusion are attribution bias, confirmation bias, and outcome bias. Attribution bias occurs when a law enforcement manager attributes certain officer traits, such as being "too" nice or not aggressive enough, to a UOF scenario.[23] For example, if an officer is known to be unskilled in applying tactics and is seen applying poor tactics, this attribute may be applied to the interpretation of a VRUOF incident and influence how the outcome is perceived by the manager.

Confirmation Bias

Confirmation bias occurs when an evaluator or viewer seeks out information that positively correlates with their preferred direction of the case.[23] For example, if a law enforcement manager has a preconceived hypothesis regarding the outcome of a VRUOF incident, they are more likely to seek out information to confirm the belief and disregard information that could undermine it,[24] regardless of its truthfulness or falsity.[25] They may be so certain that they cannot possibly be wrong, and will refuse to consider any other perspective. Confirmation bias about UOF is also influenced by our perceptions of the police. Officers, most likely in favor of the police, are more likely to seek out information that justifies the force, emphasizes the risk of not using force, and focuses on the moment force was used.[25] In contrast, citizens or casual viewers (some not in favor of the police) often focus on how the force could have been avoided and on the interactions leading up to the force.[26] Two different viewers with competing biases may watch the same video and arrive at different conclusions.

Outcome Bias

Outcome bias is evident when the judgment of a force incident is influenced by whether the outcome was positive or negative. The tendency to judge the appropriateness of an event after learning about the outcome (i.e., positive or negative) can have significant implications.[21] Outcome bias may cause a viewer to believe force was not justified because of a negative outcome (e.g., the suspect was seriously injured or killed), but may have concluded otherwise had the outcome been less adverse. Consider the following scenario.

An armed burglary suspect, a white adult male with a handgun, had fled the scene when police arrived. After a short foot chase that was captured on body camera, the suspect stopped running, got onto his knees, and put his arms up in the universal sign of surrender. The pursuing officer, somewhat winded from the sprint, stopped about 10 feet behind the suspect. The officer, believing the suspect was armed, pointed his service weapon at him and ordered, "Get on the ground, face first, lay down!" The suspect, with his back to the officer, quickly lowered his right hand to his front waistband, began to turn towards the officer, and said, "You will have to kill me!" Believing the suspect was reaching for a concealed handgun, the officer fired once, striking the suspect in the back, which caused him to fall and stop moving. Thankfully, the suspect survived, and a handgun was found in his front waistband. The VRUOF was later deemed objectively reasonable.

Would the perception of the force used have been different if the outcome were more adverse? For example, what if the suspect did not have a concealed handgun, but the officer believed he was armed, and the suspect died because of the shooting? Would the perception of the force used have been different even though the officer's perceptions were the same (i.e., he believed the suspect was armed and attempting to access a handgun when he was shot)? In both instances, the force would likely have been deemed objectively reasonable; but the outcomes were different, one more adverse than the other.

Camera Perspective Bias

Camera perspective bias is another phenomenon that viewers of VRUOF should be aware of. Camera perspective bias occurs when we attribute causality, or the reason for using the force, to the most salient person in camera view (i.e., focused within the frame), perhaps the suspect. This creates an illusory causation, and viewers tend to over-attribute the causation to the person they focused on during the recorded interaction.[27] This is yet another reason to seek out multiple camera views of VRUOF and consciously be aware of this potential bias. The single point of view caused by one BWC focused on a suspect does not allow the viewer to consider other officer actions (e.g., body language, relative positioning) that may contribute to the force used.

Reviewers and viewers of VRUOF must be aware of these biases and the potential impact they have upon perceptions of officers' UOF. This impact of bias is not unique to law enforcement evaluators. For example, biases can affect the decisions of forensic practitioners, especially when evaluating cases that involve complex, difficult, or high-stress situations.[28] Casual viewers must also be aware of their personal biases, which will affect how they perceive the appropriateness of VRUOF.

Mitigating Bias

Mitigating the impact of bias can be challenging, and there are no perfect methods to achieve it. We can help reduce our personal biases by working to reduce stereotypical perceptions of people who interact with police, increasing our cultural intelligence by interacting with people of different backgrounds, and viewing the world through a fair and equitable lens.[29] The following steps may help mitigate the impact of bias for evaluators of VRUOF:

- Acknowledge and be aware of your own biases.
- Consider the force incident from the officer's perspective at the time of the event.
- Consider using multiple independent reviewers, including people with different perspectives.
- Withhold judgment (first impressions are often wrong).
- Do not view video recordings before

  - reading all reports,
  - conducting or listening to officer interviews,
  - viewing supporting evidence (e.g., witness statements), and
  - consulting with internal or external experts (more on this later).

- Consider the totality of the circumstances from the beginning, middle, and end of the incident.
- Seek out all possible camera angles or recordings (e.g., BWC, dash camera, third-party recordings, surveillance footage).
- Examine the event in chronological order.
- Focus on the facts rather than "This is what I would have done" hindsight thinking.
- Consider alternative information and perspectives that may disprove your perspective.

To arrive at objective reasonableness most effectively, it is critical for evaluators to suppress biases, consider all accurate information, consider the input from others, make consistent decisions across procedures and practices, promote mechanisms to correct bad decisions, and arrive at conclusions ethically.[30] When decisions are unduly influenced by our biases, political objectives, or by predetermined narratives to sway a case in one direction or another, the outcomes will be inaccurate and fail to ensure procedurally fair conclusions. This runs contrary to our system of justice.

Failing to mitigate or reduce the impact of our biases may also cause us to ignore other information that may explain discrepancies between video recordings and an officer's report or recollection. Allowing our biases to influence conclusions or decision-making can result in inaccurate and adverse outcomes for officers and the people they are sworn to protect. When recordings of VRUOF events become evidence and part of civil or criminal litigation, we must ensure the video evidence can meet legal and judicial requirements. In the next chapter, we will examine how these recordings have been considered by the courts to ensure due process and justice.

References

1. Jones, K. A., Crozier, W.E., & Strange, D. (2017). Believing is seeing: Biased viewing of body-worn camera footage. Journal of Applied Research in Memory and Cognition, 6(4), 460–474. doi: 10.1016/j.jarmac.2017.07.007
2. Meterko, V., & Cooper, G. (2022). Cognitive biases in criminal case evaluation: A review of the research. *Journal of Police and Criminal Psychology*, 37, 101–122. https://doi.org/10.1007/s11896-020-09425-8
3. Halford, E. (2024). On the decision-making framework for policing: A proposal for improving police decision-making. International Journal of Law and Justice, 79. https://www.sciencedirect.com/science/article/pii/S1756061624000545
4. Hine, K. A., Porter, L. E., Westera, N. J., Alpert, G. P., & Allen, A. (2018). Exploring police use of force decision-making processes and impairments using a naturalistic decision-making approach. Criminal Justice & Behavior, 45(11), 1782–1801. https://doi.org/10.1177/0093854818789726
5. Murray, N. P., Lewinski, W., Allen, C. Heidner, G. S., Albin, M. W., & Horn, R. (2024). The eyes have it! Functional field of view differences between visual search behavior and body-worn camera during use of force response in active-duty police officers. Police Practice and Research, 25(4), 490–497. https://doi.org/10.1080/15614263.2024.2328664
6. Baldwin, S., Bennell, C., Blaskovits, B., Brown, A., Jenkins, B., Lawrence, C., McGale, H., Semple, T., & Andersen, J. P. (2022). A reasonable officer: Examining the relationships among stress, training, and performance in a highly realistic lethal force scenario. Frontiers in Psychology, 12, 759132. https://doi.org/10.3389/fpsyg.2021.759132

7. The State. (2014, September 25). Shooting at traffic stop by Trooper over seat belt violation [Video]. YouTube. https://www.youtube.com/watch?v=RBUUO_VFYMs

8. McLeod, H. (2017, Aug. 15). Ex-South Carolina trooper sent to prison for shooting unarmed black motorist. Reuters. https://www.reuters.com/article/idUSKCN1AV28I/

9. Mears, D. P., Craig, M. O., Stewart, E. A., & Warren, P. Y. (2017). Thinking fast, not slow: How cognitive biases may contribute to racial disparities in the use of force in police-citizen encounters. Journal of Criminal Justice, 53, 12–24. https://doi.org/10.1016/j.jcrimjus.2017.09.001

10. Tay, S. W., Ryan, P., & Ryan, C. A. (2016). Systems 1 and 2 thinking processes and cognitive reflection testing in medical students. Canadian Medical Education Journal, 7(2), e97–e103

11. Ali, S., & Sujarae, A. (2020). Human cognitive identification for generating safety requirements in safety critical systems. International Journal of Recent Technology and Engineering, 8(6), 5749–5758. https://www.ijrte.org/wp-content/uploads/papers/v8i6/F9598038620.pdf

12. Wickens, C. M., Toplak, M. E., & Wiesenthal, D. L. (2008). Cognitive failures as predictors of driving errors, lapses, and violations. Accident Analysis and Prevention, 40(3), 1223–1233. https://doi.org/10.1016/j.aap.2008.01.006

13. Cushion, C. (2022). Changing police personal safety training using scenario-based training: A critical analysis of the 'dilemmas of practice' impacting change. Frontiers in Education, 6. https://www.frontiersin.org/articles/10.3389/feduc.2021.796765/full

14. Bojke, L., Soares, M., Claxton, K., Colson, A., Fox, A., Jackson, C., Jankovic, D., Morton, A., Sharples, L., & Taylor, A. (2021). Developing a reference protocol for structured expert elicitation in health-care decision-making: A mixed-methods study. Health Technology Assessment, 25(37), 1–124. https://doi.org/10.3310/hta25370

15. Ask, K., & Granhag, P. A. (2007). Motivational bias in criminal investigators' judgements of witness reliability. Journal of Applied Social Psychology, 37(3), 561–591

16. Wasserman, H. M. (2017). Recording of and by police: The good, the bad, and the ugly. Journal of Gender, Race & Justice, 20(3), 543–562.

17. Gladwell, M. (2017). Blink: The power of thinking without thinking. London: Penguin.

18. Li, R., Smith, D. V., Clithero, J. A., Venkatraman, V., Carter, R. M., & Huettel, S. A. (2017). Reason's enemy is not emotion: Engagement of cognitive control networks explains biases in gain/loss framing. Journal of Neuroscience, 37(13), 3588–3598. https://doi.org/10.1523/JNEUROSCI.3486-16.2017

19. Hartigan, S., Brooks, M., Hartley, S., Miller, R. E., Santen, S. A., & Hemphill, R. R. (2020). Review of the basics of cognitive error in emergency medicine: Still no easy answers. Western Journal of Emergency Medicine, 21(6), 125–131. https://doi.org/10.5811/westjem.2020.7.47832

20. Boivin, R., Gendron, A., Faubert, C., & Poulin, B. (2017). The body-worn camera perspective bias. Journal of Experimental Criminology, 13(1), 125–142.
21. Wittlin, M. (2016). Hindsight evidence. Columbia Law Review, 116(5), 1323–1394.
22. Stoughton, S. W. (2018). Police body-worn cameras. North Carolina Law Review, 96, 1362–1424. Retrieved from http://amjudges.org/pdfs/2018%20 Annual%20Meeting/Police-Body-Worn-Cameras.pdf
23. Blake, D. M. (2017). Cognitive bias and use of force investigations. Investigative Sciences Journal, 9(3). Retrieved from https://pdfs.semantic scholar.org/f4bf/463f7d621b5efe502b2eda5a2e568730afd0.pdf
24. O'Brien, B. (2009). Prime suspect: An examination of factors that aggravate and counteract confirmation bias in criminal investigations. Psychology, Public Policy, and Law, 15(4), 315–334. https://doi.org/10.1037/a0017881
25. Elaad, E. (2022). Tunnel vision and confirmation bias among police investigators and laypeople in hypothetical criminal contexts. SAGE Open, 12(2). https://doi.org/10.1177/21582440221095022
26. Schlosser, M. D., Robbennolt, J. K., Blumberg, D. M., & Papazoglou, K. (2021). Confirmation bias: A barrier to community policing. Journal of Community Safety and Well Being, 6(4), 162–167. https://doi.org/10.35502/jcswb.219
27. Kalle, A (2019). Bias in video evidence: Implications for police body cameras. Applied Psychology in Criminal Justice, 15(2). https://dev.cjcenter.org/_files/apcj/15-2-2Kalle.pdf_1576689104.pdf
28. Kunkler, K. S., & Roy, T. (2023). Reducing the impact of cognitive bias in decision making: Practical actions for forensic science practitioners. Forensic Science International: Synergy, 7, 100341. https://doi.org/10.1016/j.fsisyn.2023.100341
29. Nordell, J. (2022). The end of bias: A beginning: how we eliminate unconscious bias and create a more just world. New York: Metropolitan.
30. Valkeapää, A., & Seppälä, T. (2014). Speed of decision-making as a procedural justice principle. Social Justice Research, 27(3), 305–321

6

COURTS AND VIDEO-RECORDED USE OF FORCE

Prior to the video camera era, police officer testimony was considered irreproachable, and any belief that an officer was not "inherently trustworthy" would have been unreasonable.[1] The dash camera era, from the early 1980s to 2005, gave a new glimpse into police work and, in some instances, revealed an ugly side of policing – ranging from inherent and, at times, expected violence to instances of officers lying on the witness stand. Today, in the body-worn camera (BWC) era, 2005 onward, we expect officers to be recording themselves with dash cameras and/or BWCs. Jurors also expect to see a video recording in the court room, favor BWC over testimony, and are skeptical of police if no video record is available.[2]

Video recordings of law enforcement officers provide various perspectives of an event, including how evidence was gathered. Video recordings can reveal how officers communicated with complainants, victims, witnesses, or suspects, and how they obtained documentary evidence or confessions. The officers' communications skills may be perceived as professional, rude, condescending, or coercive. Coercive communications with suspects may be interpreted as a violation of Fifth or Sixth Amendment rights. The video may also reveal how physical evidence was uncovered, where it was found, and even how it was collected. Improperly collected evidence may call into question its value or may cause a court to exclude it. When force is used, the recording can show how the force incident evolved, from the beginning and middle to the end, while showing previously unavailable perspectives of these events. These factors can influence perceptions of reasonableness. Camera recordings provide the courts with *more* evidence to consider in

DOI: 10.4324/9781003538738-6

the pursuit of truth and justice. How the evidence is used by the courts presents opportunities and challenges that are explored next.

Prosecutorial and Privacy Issues

Before BWCs, U.S. courts perceived great value in dash camera recordings. A 2004 study revealed that 91 percent of surveyed prosecutors used evidence from dash cameras in court, which increased case preparation time, but improved conviction and plea agreement rates and reduced time spent in court.[3] The same study outlined challenges associated with dash camera recordings: limited field of view; poor quality or lack of audio; poor video image quality; redacted recordings; availability of copies; recorded evidence that contradicted officer testimony; lack of equipment to show the evidence in court; and chain-of-custody issues.

Privacy concerns were also an issue addressed by the courts during the dash camera era. Carroll v. United States (1925) was used to support the use of dash camera recordings of police engaging in traffic enforcement that occurred in public spaces.[4] Carroll, which has been affirmed many times since, recognized that there is less expectation of privacy in an automobile versus a private residence, and therefore police recording in the public arena is acceptable. Years later, a 1984 Michigan Court of Appeals case, People v. Davis, upheld the use of undercover police following defendants and video recording their actions, deeming it was not a violation of the Fourth Amendment to video record evidence in public.[5] As previously discussed, BWCs create more significant privacy concerns, which must be addressed within policy and practice in keeping with state laws.

In 2016, a national survey by Merola et al. of criminal court prosecutors concerning the impact of BWCs revealed similar findings: BWCs improved the frequency of guilty verdicts; reduced the amount of time officers spend in court and the costs associated with officer court appearances; aided in witness preparation and memory recollection; increased the frequency or likelihood of plea bargains or convictions; improved Fourth Amendment compliance; and increased citizen trust of the court process.[6] According to those surveyed, some of the potential negative perceptions of BWCs in the courts included: a more burdensome discovery process due to the time it takes to view and redact problematic elements; sensitive or protected content (e.g., the identities of juvenile or non-involved people); inconsistent testimony that does not align with BWC recordings; court delays due to video evidence processing or review; and case dismissal due to missing recordings, failure to record, or technical problems.[6]

Other studies have affirmed Merola et al.'s findings. For example, Groff et al. (2018) found that BWC recordings make for more likely prosecution;[7] and Petersen et al. (2021) and White et al. (2021) reported that BWC recordings increase the likelihood of guilty pleas, convictions, and even exonerations.[8,9] A 2023 study provided a detailed quantitative and qualitative examination of BWC recordings and prosecutor experiences in Miami-Dade County, Florida.[10] Researchers discovered, in cases where BWC recordings are not used, common problems such as irrelevant camera angles, delayed activation, poor quality, difficulty or delay in obtaining BWC recordings, and time constraints with viewing them.[10] The longer it took for law enforcement to get BWC recordings to the prosecutor negatively affected usefulness of the video when making a charging decision.[10] BWC recordings were found to be more useful for trials, pre-trial motions, and when making charging decisions.[10]

Judicial Acceptance of Video Evidence

Like any piece of evidence, before video evidence is accepted by the courts, it must be deemed authentic and have probative value. Although other types of video evidence (e.g., surveillance recordings, video of crime scenes) have been accepted by courts, our focus will be on dash camera or BWC recordings.

Law enforcement officer-created video begins at the time of a contact. The recording may be started manually by the officer or automatically when it is activated by some event (e.g., activation of emergency lights, the removal of a weapon from a holster, or when in the presence of other activated cameras). During an incident, officers may manually stop a recording, turn off the microphone during sensitive discussions, or immediately turn it off if the recording is activated in a sensitive or First Amendment-protected area (such as a locker room or bathroom). At the end of an incident or when the recording is stopped, it can be saved or "tagged" as evidence, non-evidence, traffic stop, non-criminal offenses, training, or equipment check (such as when officers test their equipment at the beginning of a shift).

Most dash camera or BWC camera programs come with default tags, which can also be edited. Agencies may also create their own tags to meet specific needs (e.g., track BWC video for special task force activities). In addition, a report or incident number is often associated with the video recording, which can help match video records with report records, aiding retrieval. How BWC videos are tagged also determines how long they will be saved or retained. BWC video retention times typically align with evidence retention laws. For example, in Wisconsin, a BWC recording in non-criminal or non-evidentiary cases must be retained for a minimum of 120 days; in criminal cases, recordings must be retained until final disposition, including all appeals.[11] In instances where BWC recordings are related to *potential* criminal charges, the International Association of Chiefs of Police (IACP) recommends retaining them for at least one year after the statute of limitations has expired.[12]

Once the video has been saved and uploaded to the agency server or third-party storage location (e.g., a secure "cloud" location), it must remain in its original, unaltered, or authentic state. Restricting who can access, view, or edit (e.g., redact) uploaded or saved video helps prevent alteration. Enterprise programs such as Axon also track the identity of each person who accesses, views, or modifies video records.[13] In addition, dash camera and BWC programs use encryption to prevent unauthorized access, and cryptographic hash functions – i.e., message digest 5 (MD5) – to ensure authenticity.[14] The MD5 algorithm is the most widely used cryptographic hash function. When applied to a digital file, this function applies a 32-digit hexadecimal number.[15] The generated hash value uniquely identifies the original file, much like a vehicle identification number identifies a car. If the original file is altered or incomplete during an upload or download process, the hash value will change.[15] Furthermore, edits should be made to *copies* of the video rather than to the original file. This ensures the original video file remains untouched. Applying this cryptographic approach can help ensure dash camera or BWC video evidence is authentic when it is copied or transferred to the courts.

Video evidence will likely be used during prosecution if it has probative value. Any evidence relevant to a criminal case – whether it may prove or disprove facts, or be inculpatory or exculpatory – has probative value.[16] Evidence, including video recordings the prosecution intends to use during a criminal proceeding, must be shared with the defense via the discovery process. Adherence to video retention policies and practices, as well as documenting how evidence was transferred from law enforcement to the prosecutor's office, can help protect evidence integrity and authenticity, and therefore its probative value.

Probative video recordings that are not properly saved, or that are deleted or altered so as to be deemed inauthentic, may cause a criminal case to be dismissed. For example, in the case of Tennessee v. Angela M. Merriman (2013) a McMinnville, Tennessee, police officer arrested Merriman for driving under the influence, reckless driving, driving while suspended, and in violation of implied consent.[17] The dash camera recorded the incident, but it was not properly saved and was lost. The video recording may have contained exculpatory evidence that the defendant could have used at trial. The lower courts dismissed Merriman's case, citing the loss of the video recording, and the state appealed to the Tennessee Supreme Court. The Supreme Court agreed with the lower courts and upheld the dismissed

98 Police Use of Force Through the Lens

charges. Ensuring evidence is properly saved and preserved is therefore essential to fair jurisprudence.

Authenticating video evidence is achieved in one of two ways: "specific identification" or via the "chain of custody."[18] The Federal Rules of Evidence would support the authentication and identification of video evidence if an officer can testify to the accuracy of its content and relationship to the criminal case.[19] An officer would also be required to testify to the authenticity of "out of court" statements (e.g., statements made on the video record) to get them admitted into court. If an officer is not available or unable to testify to the authenticity of video, then it is unlikely to be admitted as evidence. A lack of authentication would amount to inadmissible hearsay, in violation of the Sixth Amendment confrontation clause. Video recordings cannot stand on their own and be played for a judge or jury without such authentication. For example, the justices in a 2023 California Supreme Court case (People v. Gray) said that a district judge erred by allowing a BWC recording of a witness to be accepted as her testimony after she refused to testify against the defendant, in violation of the Sixth Amendment confrontation clause.[20]

A valid chain of custody would include documentation of every person who handled the video evidence and what they did with it (e.g., redaction, splicing or parsing out recordings, creating copies for delivery to the prosecution, upload). A lack of testimony to identify video evidence or a broken chain of custody would likely prohibit the recording from being admitted during a criminal court proceeding.

Contemporary Case Law and Video Evidence

Since it viewed the dash camera recording from the Scott v. Harris (2007) case to help render its decision, SCOTUS and other courts have relied upon video recordings to draw more informed conclusions. We will discuss some of these court cases to help us further understand how dash camera and BWC recordings have been used by the courts.

The People v. Dontrae R. Gray (2023)[20]

The California Supreme Court ruled in this case that BWC recordings cannot replace witness testimony when a witness refuses to testify in court. The defendant, Dontrae Gray, was on probation and was accused of trying to kick in a residential door. Police arrested him behind the residence. The victim, Gray's girlfriend, gave police a verbal statement about the incident, which was recorded via BWC. The victim explained that Gray had forced himself into her residence and started "punching [her] everywhere," "stomping [her] out," and "tried to punch [her] approximately 20 times, mainly on her arms, and that she fell to the ground." Gray was arrested and charged with "inflicting corporal injury upon a person in dating relationship" and "residential burglary."

A few days later, the victim recanted her statement and did not appear to testify at Gray's criminal trial. The prosecution moved to admit the victim's BWC recorded statement as a "spontaneous statement" (exception to the hearsay rule), but the court ruled that her recorded statements were inadmissible (without her testimony) under the confrontation clause of the Sixth Amendment. The trial court then held a probation revocation hearing and admitted the victim's BWC recorded "spontaneous statement" without in-person testimony, citing the Sixth Amendment only applied to criminal trials and not probation revocation hearings. The court found that Gray had violated his probation conditions, and sentenced him to seven years' confinement. Gray appealed and the justices affirmed the lower court's rationale in both proceedings. Gray appealed again to the California Supreme Court and the justices reversed.

Spontaneous statements, which are typically utterances made spontaneously under stress or duress, may be admitted at a criminal proceeding without supporting testimony. However, the victim's statement in this case was not deemed "spontaneous"; and, without her testimony to support the authenticity of the BWC and provide the defense with an opportunity to cross-examine her, the recording should not have been admitted at either proceeding. In short, BWC recordings cannot take the place of victim or witness testimony in criminal or probation revocation proceedings.

Baxter v. Roberts (2021)[21]

In this civil rights case, dash camera and BWC recordings, as well as the court record, were relied upon by the appeals court to examine allegations that police lacked reasonable suspicion to stop the defendant, conduct an open-air "dog sniff" around a vehicle, and determine if force used was unreasonable. Michael Baxter's vehicle was stopped for swerving in its lane and "touching the lines on either side of the lane multiple times," which was confirmed via dash cam video. When the officer, wearing a BWC, made contact with Baxter, an open alcohol container was seen inside the vehicle, which supported the basis for extending the duration of the stop. The officer ordered Baxter out of the vehicle; he initially refused. After several commands, Baxter complied, but refused to hand over his car keys. The officer forcibly removed the keys from Baxter's hand, decentralized him to the ground, and handcuffed him. Baxter suffered a chipped tooth and

100 Police Use of Force Through the Lens

facial abrasions. He was charged with resisting an officer without violence. The appeals court found the "de minimis" force used was objectively reasonable. The police K-9 alerted to the driver's side door of the vehicle, but no drugs were found inside. The court also upheld the dog sniff, which did not unduly prolong the stop. Rather, according to the court, Baxter's actions prolonged the stop.

City of Topeka v. Murdock (2018)[22]

Willie Murdock was convicted of possession of drug paraphernalia and appealed his conviction to the Court of Appeals of Kansas. Murdock had been issued a municipal citation for possession of drug paraphernalia after Topeka, Kansas Police Officer Blassingame saw the paraphernalia in plain view while inside Murdock's apartment. Murdock argued that he did not give the officer consent to enter his apartment and, therefore, any plain view observations were unlawful. Officer Blassingame's BWC recording had been admitted at the municipal trial and was also viewed by the appeals court judges. The video contained the interaction between Murdock and Blassingame, which began with the officer knocking on Murdock's apartment door. When Murdock answered, he opened the door, and stepped into the hallway. The BWC recorded the following interaction.

Officer Blassingame asked Murdock if he was the only one in the apartment and Murdock said, "Yes." Blassingame asked if he could come into the apartment and talk with him; Murdock slightly shook his head back and forth, indicating, "No," and asked "Why?" Blassingame stated he needed to talk with Murdock about personal business and he would rather not do it in the hallway. Murdock then said either "Well, come on" or "Well, come in," stepped back into the apartment, and gave a slight wave. Blassingame did not step forward into the apartment until he saw this response from Murdock

Once inside the apartment, Officer Blassingame saw the drug paraphernalia in plain view, which was ultimately seized and supported the citation for possession of drug paraphernalia. The appeals court judges relied upon and cited the BWC video evidence to affirm that Officer Blassingame entered Murdock's apartment with consent and his plain view observation of the drug paraphernalia was valid.

Emmanuel Reyna v. The State of Texas (2017)[23]

Emmanuel Reyna was arrested and convicted for driving while intoxicated. On appeal, Reyna claimed that he was stopped without reasonable suspicion. The arresting officer, Austin Police Officer Marcos Johnson, recorded Reyna's driving behavior with his dash camera. In addition to Officer Johnson's testimony, the appeals court judges considered the dash camera video to help render their decision. Officer Johnson stopped Reyna for driving partially in a bike lane, which was designated with painted lines or markings on the roadway. The dash camera video showed Reyna's vehicle veering out of its lane and crossing over the painted line of the designated bike lane on at least two occasions. The video and Officer Johnson's testimony were considered by the appeals court judges. The court concluded that reasonable suspicion existed when Reyna was stopped, and his conviction was upheld.

United States v. Kitchenakow (2016)[24]

Ashley Kitchenakow had been indicted for involuntary manslaughter after she killed one person and caused serious bodily injury to another while operating a motor vehicle while intoxicated on the Menominee, Wisconsin, Indian Reservation. While in custody, Kitchenakow made incriminating statements in the presence of Menominee Tribal Officer Grignon (who was wearing a BWC) and Federal Bureau of Investigation (FBI) Special Agent Lynch (who was using a digital recording device). Kitchenakow filed a motion alleging that her statements were made in violation of her Miranda rights (the right to refuse to answer self-incriminating questions). In rendering its decision, the federal court judge relied upon testimony, the recordings, and transcripts. The judge wrote, citing the video, "In fact, the video recording shows that the defendant is the one who was interrogating Officer Grignon, as well as the Chief of the Menominee Tribal Police, both of whom she knew on a first-name basis." Therefore, any statements volunteered by Kitchenakow and not in response to questions asked by law enforcement were admissible. In this case, the BWC helped resolve a potential Miranda rights violation.

United States v. McKee (2016)[25]

Nelson McKee was indicted for murder and filed eight motions prior to trial, one of them to suppress statements he made to police. Officers responded to an emergency call from a citizen who reported that a woman was pounding on her door, and had apparently been stabbed. Officers found McKee's wife, Cheryl, on the floor of the caller's residence, bleeding from stab wounds. Officers went to McKee's home, where they saw fresh footprints in the snow and blood droplets leading to the door. Officers knocked on the door and McKee answered; their interactions with McKee were recorded with BWCs. McKee allowed officers to enter, and in plain view they saw two knives. One was bent, and the other had blood on it. Officers handcuffed and detained McKee, and then asked several public safety-related questions – e.g., Why is Cheryl bleeding?"; "Did she fall over again, or did something happen?"; "Why is there a bloody knife on the table?"; "Did you cut her, or did she cut herself?" At the same time, other officers cleared the residence, did not find anyone else inside, and rendered the scene safe.

However, questions and statements from police to McKee continued and were deemed to be outside of the public safety exception – e.g., "Cheryl's bleeding; I've got a knife with blood all over it; I've got you sitting next to it." "Nothing? Something happened, Nelson, she's over there bleeding." "I can't figure out what the [expletive] happened; I don't know if she got stabbed or cut herself. You're not being very helpful."

The court relied in part upon the BWC recording to allow the public safety questions to be admitted during trial, but the non-public safety questions (i.e., interrogatory) were not allowed at trial. The BWC recording helped the court parse out the questions related to public safety and those in violation of McKee's Miranda rights.

Fischer v. State (2008)[26]

In this case, a trooper stopped a suspected drunk driver and recorded the event with his dash camera and wireless microphone. After each standard field sobriety test (e.g., Horizontal Gaze Nystagmus, One-Leg-Stand, and Walk-and-Turn), the trooper returned to his squad car and narrated the observed clues of impairment into his microphone. At trial, the state introduced the trooper's narrative as a "speaking offense report," which the judge allowed. The appellant, John Fischer, pleaded "no contest" to the charge, appealed, and argued that the trooper's audio-recorded narrative should not have been permitted at trial because it amounted to hearsay and was not a "present sense impression," which is an exception to the hearsay rule. The "present sense impression" occurs when people make non-narrative, off-hand comments about an event with no motive related to criminal prosecution. The appellate court overturned the state court, and concluded that the audio-recorded statements should not have been admitted at trial. The state appealed to the Court of Criminal Appeals, which upheld the previous ruling.

The trooper's intentional and calculated audio-recorded evidentiary observations, which he knew would be used against the defendant in criminal court, were not "present sense impressions" and should not be allowed at trial. The trooper could testify under oath to his observations, which may be exactly what he recorded, and be subject to cross-examination.

A practical takeaway from this case is that officers could narrate observations (e.g., audio notes) for later use when report writing versus taking written notes in the field. However, audio notes should never replace good observation and written note taking.

These seven cases provide a glimpse into how the courts have used or permitted the use of dash camera or BWC recordings. Litigating these issues and others will evolve over time. It is imperative for law enforcement leaders, scholars, and practitioners to stay informed about how the courts use video recordings to help educate the criminal justice community and ensure just and fair outcomes.

Judicially accepted video-recorded use-of-force (VRUOF) incidents will not necessarily speak for themselves. Officers must testify to the authenticity of the video and explain their actions, including why force was necessary. Experts may be consulted to explain why there are discrepancies between video recordings and officer recollection or reporting. Experts may also offer insight into human factors that help explain officer actions or inactions, along with citizen actions that may or may not have influenced the extent of force used. Human factors science – which has been used in other high-risk industries to help improve performance, avoid errors, or explain why errors occur – can also help improve law enforcement outcomes. Human factors science and its impact upon VRUOF incidents are addressed in the next chapter.

References

1. Warren, J. M. (2018). Hidden in plain view: Juries and the implicit credibility given to police testimony. DePaul Journal for Social Justice, 11(2), Art. 5. https://via.library.depaul.edu/cgi/viewcontent.cgi?article=1167&context=jsj
2. Robertson, O. N., McCluskey, J. D., & Uchida, C. D. (2024). Body cameras and adjudication: Views of prosecutors and public defenders. Criminal Justice Review, 49(1), 15–29. https://doi.org/10.1177/073401 68221124458
3. U.S. Department of Justice (2004). The impact of video evidence on modern policing. Retrieved from http://www.theiacp.org/Portals/0/pdfs/WhatsNew/IACP%20In-Car%20Camera%20Report%202004.pdf
4. Carroll v. United States 267 U.S. 132 (1925). https://supreme.justia.com/cases/federal/us/267/132/
5. People v. Davis, 52 Mich. App. 59; 216 N.W. 2d440 (1984). https://www.casemine.com/judgement/us/59149070add7b0493457682a/amp
6. Merola, L. M., Lum, C., Koper, C. S., & Scherer, A. (2016). Body worn cameras and the courts: A national survey of state prosecutors. Report for

the Laura and John Arnold Foundation. Fairfax, VA: Center for Evidence-Based Crime Policy, George Mason University

7. Groff, E. R., Ward, J. T., & Wartell, J. (2018). The role of body-worn camera footage in the decision to file. Report for the Laura and John Arnold Foundation. Criminal Justice Department, Temple University

8. Petersen, K., Mouro, A., Papy, D., Castillo, N., & Ariel, B. (2021). Seeing is believing: The impact of body-worn cameras on court outcomes, a cluster-randomized controlled trial in Miami Beach. Journal of Experimental Criminology, 19, 191–211. https://doi.org/10.1007/s11292-021- 09479-6

9. White, M. D., Gaub, J. E., Malm, A., & Padilla, K. E. (2021). Implicate or exonerate? The impact of police body-worn cameras on the adjudication of drug and alcohol cases. Policing: A Journal of Policy and Practice, 15(2), 759–769

10. Petersen, K., Papy, D., Mouro, A., & Ariel, B. (2023). The usage and utility of body-worn camera footage in courts: A survey analysis of state prosecutors. Journal of Empirical Legal Studies, 20(3), 534–569

11. Wisconsin State Legislature (n.d.). Body cameras and law enforcement, Section (§§) 165.87. https://docs.legis.wisconsin.gov/statutes/statutes/165/87

12. International Association of Chiefs of Police (IACP) (2015). Model body worn camera policy for police: An aid for prosecutors. https://bja.ojp.gov/sites/g/files/xyckuh186/files/media/document/20150714-best-practices-bwc-model-policy-pceandcdaafoundation.pdf

13. Axon (2022). Axon evidence user and administrator reference guide. https://public.evidence.com/help/pdfs/latest/EVIDENCE.com+Administrator+Reference+Guide.pdf

14. U.S. Department of Homeland Security (2024). Body-worn video cameras with automatic activation capabilities. https://www.dhs.gov/sites/default/files/2024-02/24_02_29_st_bodyworncamerasmsr_1.pdf

15. Sagar, F. A. (2016). Cryptographic hashing functions – MD5. Indiana State University. https://cs.indstate.edu/~fsagar/doc/paper.pdf

16. Brady v. Maryland, 373 U.S. 83 (1963). https://supreme.justia.com/cases/federal/us/373/83/

17. State of Tennessee v. Angela M. Merriman, No. M2011-01682-SC-R11-CD (2013).

18. Hurley, G. (2016). Body-worn cameras and the courts. National Center for State Courts. https://bja.ojp.gov/sites/g/files/xyckuh186/files/bwc/pdfs/final-bwc-report.pdf

19. Office of the Law Revision Counsel. (n.d.). Federal Rules of Evidence. Article IX: Authentication and identification. Rule 901. Authenticating or identifying evidence. https://uscode.house.gov/view.xhtml?path=/prelim@title28/title28a/node230/article9&edition=prelim#:~:text=Rule%20901.,the%20proponent%20claims%20it%20is.

20. People v. Gray, S269237 (California Supreme Court, 2023). https://law.justia.com/cases/california/supreme-court/2023/s269237.html

21. Baxter v. Roberts, Case No. 5:19CV216-MCR/MJF (2021). https://casetext.com/case/baxter-v-roberts

22. City of Topeka v. Murdock, No. 116,213 (Court of Appeals of Kansas, 2018). https://caselaw.findlaw.com/court/ks-court-of-appeals/1915448.html
23. Emanuel Reyna v. The State of Texas, No. 03-16-00774-CR (2007). https://casetext.com/case/reyna-v-state-80
24. United States v. Ashley E. Kitchenakow, 149 F. Supp. 3d 1062 (E.D. Wis. 2016). https://casetext.com/case/united-states-v-kitchenakow-1
25. United States v. McKee, 157 F. Supp 3d 879 (D. Nev. 2016). https://casetext.com/case/united-states-v-mckee-20
26. Fischer v. State, 252 S.W.3d 375 (Tex. Crim. App. 2008). https://casetext.com/case/fischer-v-state-6

7

HUMAN FACTORS, MEMORY, AND VIDEO-RECORDED USE OF FORCE

The rapid implementation of body-worn cameras (BWCs) within law enforcement outpaced the necessary research about consistent processes, methods, and policies throughout the industry. There remains a lack of consistency about how BWCs should be used by officers in use-of-force (UOF) events, from how they enhance report writing to their role in improving job performance. This chapter explores the dichotomy that often exists between what an officer remembers about a video-recorded use-of-force (VRUOF) incident and what the video captured. Human factors research will be discussed to help explain the perceptual and cognitive distortions often experienced by officers involved in high-stress events. Human factors research and principles, applied to VRUOF, can help us better understand officer performance and affirm or reveal new methods to improve positive outcomes and reduce adverse events.

Much of the research related to the effects of perceptual and cognitive distortions has involved high-stress encounters that *simulated* rapidly evolving events where officers often had only seconds to act.[1,2,3] Perceptual or sensory distortions occur when there is a lack of agreement between how a stimulus would be commonly perceived versus and it was perceived, especially under stress.[4] Sensory distortions experienced by officers under high stress include vision narrowing, altered sense of time (i.e., slowing down or speeding up), and auditory exclusion.[1]

The more complex and stressful the environment, the more pronounced the perceptual distortions will be.[5] Similarly, the Graham v. Connor (1989) court also recognized the challenges of tense, uncertain, and rapidly evolving events, and how they might affect an officer's ability to make

DOI: 10.4324/9781003538738-7

accurate force decisions (see Chapter 1). These decisions include how much force to use, and what type is appropriate in a particular situation. Interviews with officers who have been involved in rapidly evolving and dangerous force events have reported similar phenomena.[5] A review of cognitive and perceptual distortions often experienced during UOF events can help inform and improve the interpretation or understanding of a VRUOF incident.

Human Factors and the Use of Force

Human factors science has been used extensively in various industries – such as health care, commercial aviation, and transportation – to improve performance and reduce error.[6] Unfortunately, law enforcement has not embraced human factors science to a great extent to improve police performance.[6] Human factors are interactions of people with other systems that apply theory, principles, data, and methods to help optimize employee well-being and overall agency performance.[7] Law enforcement agencies, or any organization comprising people, can benefit from human factors science to help improve performance. Human factors research should be embraced by the law enforcement industry to help improve outcomes and reduce adverse risk.

Human factors are derived from scientific data about how people perceive, think, and act, especially in complex work settings.[8] Human factors research, where applied to understanding officer performance under stress, may help explain performance or recollection. This is particularly true when there are conflicts between perceived reality and video recordings. Factors that affect officer performance are movement (i.e., of officer and suspect), time constraints, environment, perception, and decision-making. Well-documented human factors associated with officer UOF decisions are perceptual impairments, cognitive (i.e., memory) impairments, and physiological impairments that affect fine motor skills and performance due to the body's response to adrenaline.[9] Perceptual impairments related to tunnel vision, diminished sounds, and inattentive blindness, followed by memory distortions, will be discussed next.

Perceptual Distortions

A body of research about officers experiencing perceptual distortions in high-stress situations – e.g., critical incidents, officer-involved shooting (OIS) – are derived from qualitative interviews, questionnaires, or surveys of the officers involved. The body of knowledge about these perceptual distortions can help explain officer actions, perceptions, or recollections,

108 Police Use of Force Through the Lens

and better inform the calculation of reasonableness. A summary of the research is presented in Table 7.1.

In a 2022 study (conducted more recently than those in Table 7.1), 122 experienced police officers were exposed to a high-stress, complex, dynamic, and realistic lethal force scenario to help determine whether their performance was affected by training, years of experience, and stress reactivity.[10] Participants self-reported the perceptual and cognitive distortions they experienced during and after the scenario. Over 70 percent of the participants reported experiencing tunnel vision, heightened visual clarity, and diminished sound. Again, these self-reported phenomena occurred in simulated environments versus real-world force incidents, which are inherently more stressful. An earlier 1998 study reported that 90 percent of the officers surveyed (n = 348) experienced perceptual distortions; however there were differences in the rates of occurrence (displayed in Table 7.1).[11] This study is one of two that reported on officer memory loss after a critical incident, further supporting the expectation that discrepancies between what an officer remembers and what camera footage shows are expected.

Some have criticized the perceptual distortions research, citing methodological issues and "small" sample sizes.[12] It appears that the best way to measure or examine the existence of perceptual or cognitive distortions is to conduct qualitative research by interviewing officers who have been involved in high-stress force incidents *or* by exposing them to simulations and have them share their experiences. Qualitative researchers become satisfied after they have interviewed enough participants, when "data saturation" is met – meaning when all relevant information to best inform the main research question has been obtained. Sample sizes for some qualitative studies are usually below 50 (often between 20 and 30).[13]

The sample sizes in the research cited in Table 7.1 (between 63 and 348) appear adequate, and the findings across studies are relatively consistent. The studies that used structured interviews, such as Nielsen[14] and Klinger and Brunson,[1] demonstrated sound methodology. Campbell conducted a longitudinal survey along with follow-up interviews.[15] Solomon and Horn's research was a pilot study, and they recommended officers receive training about perceptual distortions that commonly occur during a critical incident, which will help ensure that what they may or have experienced is normal.[16] Lastly, Artwohl distributed a survey to her sample population; it was later returned by participants.[17] However, nearly two-thirds of those participants had experienced a critical incident within a few weeks of completing the survey. The recency between the critical incident and the survey about perceptual distortions may have generated more accurate responses. These research findings strongly suggest that

Human Factors, Memory, and Video-Recorded Use of Force   **109**

TABLE 7.1 Perceptual Distortion Research Summary

Perceptual Distortion	Nielsen (1981) n = 63	Campbell (1992) n = 92	Solomon & Horn (1986) n = 86	Honig & Roland (1998) n = 348	Klinger & Brunson (2009) n = 80	Artwohl (2008) n = 157	Mean (Avg.)
Slow Motion	63.5%	60%	67%	41%	56%	62%	349 (58%)
Diminished Sound	27.0%	76%	51%	51%	82%	84%	371 (62%)
Tunnel Vision	42.9%	80%	37%	45%	51%	79%	334 (56%)
Heightened Visual Detail	N/A	N/A	18%	41%	56%	71%	186 (47%)
Intensified Sound	N/A	N/A	18%	23%	20%	16%	77 (19%)
Memory Loss	N/A	N/A	N/A	22%	N/A	21%	–
Fast Motion	N/A	N/A	15%	20%	23%	17%	75 (19%)

110 Police Use of Force Through the Lens

officers experience various perceptual distortions during critical incidents, which will affect how they recall or remember video-recorded critical incidents.

Tunnel Vision and Inattentive Blindness

Cameras, especially BWCs, are often promoted as capable of capturing interactions from the officer's point of view. This is a misleading perspective, and it is erroneous to assume an officer perceived exactly what was depicted on camera.[18] As discussed in Chapter 4, cameras capture events from a particular angle or point of view, and may not necessarily reflect what the officer saw at the time of the event.[19] The camera view is also affected by mounting position (e.g., chest, lapel, head band, glasses, or collar).[20] A camera mounted on an officer's hat or glasses will provide a more complete view of an incident than shoulder or chest mounts, especially when an officer's arms are extended straight out in front of the body while pointing their firearm.[20] The extended arms tend to obstruct some of the camera view, which may prevent a reviewer from seeing what an officer may have seen.[20]

Cameras will record less, more, and differently than a human would see, all at the same time.[21] There may be a clear difference between what the officer may see and what the camera records.[19] The effective field of view of a video camera is wider than the human eye.[20,21,22] As a result, officers will sometimes see something outside the camera field of view – they turned their head but the camera remained stationary; or, conversely, the camera will record something the officer did not see.[21] Additionally, recordings of police using force likely capture more details than were visible or perceived by the officer at the time of the incident.[22]

Cameras do not perceive danger, detect threats, or respond to dangerous actions. Also, recall from Chapter 4 that the camera is merely a static observer, and has 20/20 vision that exceeds the human eye, especially when attempting to focus on multiple items at varying distances.[21] A camera does not suffer from these limitations, and can clearly see all objects within its field of view. The camera will "see" and record more of a force incident with much higher quality than an officer is capable of seeing[17] in normal and low-light conditions.[20]

While under the stress of a force event, vision can be compromised in three ways: reduced peripheral vision (i.e., tunnel vision), distance-only eyesight, and forced binocular vision.[23] Tunnel vision is one of the most commonly cited perceptual distortions experienced by officers during high-stress force events. Tunnel vision occurs when the eyes focus on the source of a threat with heightened visual detail (of the threat), and this "tunnel" focus on the single threat may cause officers to miss other potential threats immediately around them.[9,23] A phenomenon called the "weapon focus" effect may also explain why this occurs, whereby attention is drawn away from peripheral details and vision focuses on the threatening object.[24] The peripheral details then become of low importance and are often not recalled well.[25] Even eyewitnesses are affected by this "weapon-focused" effect. Eyewitnesses often have a decreased ability to give an accurate description of a suspect pointing a gun at them because they pay more attention to the gun versus other peripheral details, such as what the suspect looked like or was wearing.[26]

After a force incident, officers may not recall seeing actions that happened right in front of them, even though the camera recording clearly shows the action. A phenomenon known as "inattentional blindness" may further explain why this happens. Inattentional blindness occurs when individuals focus attention on one task while completely overlooking an object or other event occurring within their field of view or line of sight.[5,27,28,] The more cognitively demanding a task, the more likely inattentional blindness will occur.[29]

Most studies that have confirmed inattentional blindness have featured videos or computer displays that divide viewers' attention by asking them to count the passes of basketballs between two teams and measuring their (in)ability to see an unexpected stimulus, such as a gorilla, walking through and spending nine seconds in the frame.[28] The well-known "Invisible Gorilla" video that demonstrated the validity of the inattentive blindness or selective attention phenomenon revealed that half of the viewers missed the gorilla. The only cognitive stress viewers experienced was counting the basketball passes. Often, if the viewer saw the gorilla, they then lost track of the number of basketballs passed. These static studies involved little or no emotional stress, in contrast to the high stress officers often experience when engaged in UOF encounters.

Other studies with direct applications to law enforcement have also validated inattentive blindness.[5,28] One study revealed that 33 percent of law enforcement officers and 58 percent of law enforcement trainees missed a handgun in plain view on a dashboard during a traffic stop scenario.[28] In another study, nearly half of the law enforcement participants noticed unexpected objects in a video scenario of an active shooter event, which is consistent with other inattentional blindness research.[5] In a third study, participants in a simulated foot pursuit were instructed to follow a jogger and count the number of times they touched their hat. About one minute into the "pursuit" there was a staged fight slightly to the right of the jogging path. The fight victim was punched, kicked, and thrown to the

112 Police Use of Force Through the Lens

ground. During daylight hours, 40 percent of the participants did not see the fight. At night, only one-third of the participants saw the fight.[30]

Inattentive blindness and tunnel vision may help explain why officers report not seeing certain actions or have no memory of them, even though the actions in question are clearly displayed on video.

Auditory Exclusion

Perceptual distortions related to hearing or sounds are the other most frequently documented perceptual distortion reported by officers during stressful force encounters. A phenomenon similar to inattentive blindness is "auditory exclusion," which attempts to explain why an officer may not hear certain sounds or voices, even though they can be heard clearly on a video recording. Auditory exclusion or diminished hearing may also occur during stressful force encounters or, far less often, sounds may seem louder than normal.[1,23,31] Auditory exclusion can have a significant impact upon the review of VRUOF incidents, especially when incidents occur within one's range of sound but are not reported or recalled. Consider the following hypothetical scenario.

Two officers, one male and the other female, are involved in a high-risk encounter with an armed robbery suspect who is holding a handgun. During the encounter, the female officer realizes the handgun is a facsimile weapon and announces this to the male officer, which is clearly captured on the audio record. The male officer perceives a deadly force threat and shoots the armed robbery suspect. During the inquiry that follows, the male officer reports he never heard the female officer say it was a facsimile weapon. Auditory exclusion may explain why the male officer did not hear the female officer. The higher the level of perceived threat, the more likely auditory exclusion and other perceptual distortions will occur.

Slow-Motion Time

Officers involved in high-stress encounters have reported that their sense of time slowed at the most critical or threatening moments (e.g., just before or when firing their weapon or attempting to avoid being shot).[32] When humans are exposed to dangerous events, such as car crashes or armed robberies, many report the events passed in slow motion, as if time slowed down.[33] Why slow-motion time occurs is not known. It is theorized however that the amygdala – the part of the brain responsible for processing fearful or threatening stimuli – may foster increased duration (of time) judgments retroactively due to the rich and potentially secondary encoding of the memories.[34] Upon recollection of the threatening incident, such as an officer-involved shooting, an officer may erroneously interpret the event to have spanned a greater period of time.[35] This does not imply that the officer is being untruthful. Rather, the theory provides insight into why slow-motion time occurs and how stressful incidents are recalled.

Recollections of slow-motion time during critical incidents may create misperceptions between what an officer perceived during a VRUOF incident and the video record. For example, if an officer reports that slow-motion time occurred but the video recording reveals the violent actions occurred quickly, the officer may question the validity of their recollection. Also, an officer who reports slow-motion time during critical moments may cause reviewers to perceive that the officer had more time to act than they actually did, which could negatively impact perceptions of reasonableness.

Tunnel vision, auditory exclusion, and slow-motion time all affect how high-stress UOF encounters are encoded and later recalled. These perceptual distortions can also help us understand why there may be a difference between a video recording and what an officer remembers. It is not uncommon for memories of stressful or violent events to be hazy or distorted.[35] Memory distortions, memory loss, and recollection of VRUOF encounters are discussed next.

Memory Distortion and Memory Loss

Because the mind is not a mechanized recording device, memory may differ from what is captured on video.[32] One cannot play back a memory like a video record.[3] Memory does not work like a video recorder, and people do not encode or recall every aspect of an event perfectly.[25] Memory is also not linear; rather, it is entwined from events and experiences, stored in various areas of the brain tenuously connected one to another.[17] Memory is fallible at best and unreliable at worst.[25] Discrepancies between an officer's recollection of an incident and what is captured on video is likely.[37] Evaluators and viewers of VRUOF events should note that memory is often limited and inaccurate.

Officers who experience UOF or other high-stress events may experience impaired memory recall and impaired performance.[38,39] Even in simulated critical incidents involving physical exertion, officer memory recall accuracy has been impaired or reduced.[38] Memory of a UOF event may be incomplete, erroneous, disjointed, out of order, or inaccurate.[10,31,36,40] The more stress officers experience during an event, the less accurate their overall memory will be both after and during the incident.[23,31] Recollection of verbal information, such as what a suspect said and may have been heard on video, are less likely to be accurately recalled than suspect actions.[2] High stress during a UOF encounter can also make it difficult

114 Police Use of Force Through the Lens

for the mind to remember and implement stored behaviors; officers may appear on video making less than ideal tactical maneuvers or decisions and making errors.[5,23]

There is also a relationship between emotional stress and memory recall during an interview. Shortly after a force event, when stress levels are still high, memory is likely to be vague and disjointed.[35] However, when stress levels are closer to the baseline, a more coherent account of the force event, with additional details, will likely be obtained.[35] Research in this area also informs law enforcement leaders regarding best practices after a VRUOF event, such as an officer-involved shooting (OIS) or other critical incident, and the timing of interviews of involved officers.

If an interview is conducted immediately after a critical incident, a follow-up interview should be conducted within one to two sleep cycles, or the next 24 to 48 hours, with the expectation that new and potentially conflicting information may be reported. This is an expected part of the memory consolidation process and should not be assumed an indication of lying.[41] Memory consolidation is when a temporary, labile (or easily altered) memory is transformed into a more stable, long-lasting form.[42] Research within and outside of law enforcement affirms the connection between sleep and memory consolidation.[43] However, memory consolidation does not necessarily guarantee a more accurate report or statement.

It is noteworthy that are no absolute proven methods about the timing of interviews after a stressful, high-risk force encounter.[44] This gives way to contrasting perspectives. The International Association of Chiefs of Police (IACP) recommends that, after an OIS, interviews or questioning of the officers involved should be delayed by 48–72 hours to enhance memory recall[45] as this delay period may allow for adequate sleep or rest, which is associated with enhanced recall of critical events.[5,41,46] Evidence further suggests that deep-stage rapid eye movement (REM) sleep helps consolidate highly emotional or value-laden memories.[47] This research presumes the officer involved in a high-stress encounter actually got REM sleep before report writing or giving a statement.

There is no *ideal* amount of time that should elapse between the force incident and the officer interview. It is unclear how sleep and memory are correlated, but controlled studies, such as by Geiselman (2010), have revealed that sleep can improve memory recall.[46] More recently, Stepan et al. (2017) discovered that one sleep cycle improved the accuracy of memory.[48] A contrasting finding reported that officers had sharper recollections immediately after a threatening encounter than those who shared memories after a few days had passed.[49] It is noteworthy however that the research cited in support of sleep cycle(s) and memory improvement for officers involved in high-stress events did not directly address OIS events or other stressful force encounters.[50] Additionally, none of the studies related to this subject were able to exactly replicate the stress an officer would face during a real-world force encounter.

There is currently insufficient evidence to support the belief that having an officer wait 24 to 72 hours after an OIS or other high-stress force incident will lead to more *accurate* memory, statement, or reports.[51] A delayed interview may result in more memory recall but not necessarily more *accurate* recall. The *quantity* of recall does not necessarily mean or guarantee the recalled memories will be more accurate. Quantity does not necessarily mean more quality. Additionally, Hope (2016) cautions that extending the delay between a stressful event and an interview may cause some detail to be forgotten, and memory may become contaminated by exposure to post-event information (e.g., news media reports, information from other officers).[52] More recently, researchers discovered that the timing of interviews (immediately after the event and two days later) for participants involved in a live-action active shooter study did not influence their recall of the incident.[53] Although memory improvement and sleep appear well correlated, additional research in this area specific to high-stress officer encounters and the accuracy of reporting is necessary.

Viewing Camera Recordings and Memory

Will officers who view their camera recording of a UOF incident have better memory of the event or will their report be more accurate? There is no clear answer to this question. If officers watch video of their incident before giving a statement, it will likely result in a statement or report that is consistent with the video. However, there is no way to know what the officers remembered before watching the video and how it may have changed what they "remembered" or believed they had remembered. Since our brains do not encode memories as video recordings do, our recollections often have gaps, which may be filled by the video. These memory gaps may not have been truly retrieved, but may be adopted as a "memory" because they fill in what is missing.

Retrieval-induced forgetting (RIF) and misinformation-type effects are two specific phenomena that may be influenced by viewing video before recollecting what occurred. RIF is the act of remembering part of an event, which in turn may cause other aspects of the event to be forgotten.[54] For example, if officers view video of their force event, they risk forgetting and failing to document details they actually witnessed or experienced. The result is an incomplete or inaccurate memory.

Misinformation-type effects, such as claiming to have a memory seen on video when it was not encoded at the time of the incident, is another

116 Police Use of Force Through the Lens

risk of allowing video viewing before writing about force used. The video may promote deceit. For example, officers could claim they observed the suspect holding a gun (which was visible in the video). While not originally encoded into memory, this confabulation could become the basis for their lethal force decision.[55] Human factors research affirms that officers are likely to misremember important details of high-stress encounters, and so should avoid video viewing that may further complicate authentic and accurate reporting or recollection.

Video Recordings and Report Writing

> It is simply not plausible that an officer's account will always perfectly match a video recording. Therefore, as a consequence of memory distortion, an officer may accidentally include inaccurate, misleading information in their report – misinformation – that is, by necessity, not depicted in the BWC footage. (Jones et al., 2017)[36]

There are competing perspectives about allowing officers to watch VRUOF incidents before report writing or making a statement. The law enforcement sector supports video viewing before report writing because it will make reports more accurate, enhance credibility, and overcome defense attorney attacks about video and report mismatches. Police agency policy, like that of the Milwaukee, Wisconsin, Police Department, endorses watching video to maximize the effectiveness of officer report writing (Figure 7.1).[56] The Graham case emphasized that the officer's perception of the incident is a determining factor of reasonableness and that viewing video before report

---

Milwaukee, Wisconsin, Police Department (Policy 730)

...the use of Mobile Digital Video/Audio Recording (MDVR)...equipment shall be used in order to accomplish several objectives that include, but are not limited to:

• Maximized effectiveness of officer reporting, evidence collection, and court testimony.

...and can aid in remembering details of an event for the purposes of proper documentation in official written reports."

NOTE: Critical incident viewing is at direction/discretion of investigating agency or MPD administration.

FIGURE 7.1 Sample Police Department Policy: Watching Video before Report Writing

Source: City of Milwaukee (2024). Milwaukee Police Department. 730 – In-Car Camera Systems. https://city.milwaukee.gov/ImageLibrary/Groups/mpdAuthors/SOP/730-MOBILEDIGITALVIDEOAUDIORECORDINGEQUIPMENT1.pdf

writing may influence officer perceptions. Scholars believe watching video recordings before report writing is not an accurate reflection or memory of what occurred, but rather one influenced by video. This is an unsettled issue, and we will do our best propose some solutions.

Officers involved in a VRUOF event must complete a written report afterward that articulates and justifies their actions. In critical incidents, such as an OIS, officers typically do not complete a report, but rather provide a verbal statement to investigators. The question often raised is, should officers be allowed to view available video recordings (e.g., via body camera, dash cam, surveillance, or third-party cameras) before completing their report or providing a statement?

Some law enforcement agencies allow officers to watch video recordings of force incidents before writing their reports while others prohibit it. Law enforcement officers overwhelmingly support the viewing of available video recordings prior to report writing.[57] Unlike other types of video-recorded incidents, such as impaired driving cases, where officers review their video prior to writing reports to accurately document objective facts, the reporting of force incidents relies less on objective facts and more on the reasonableness of actions and perceptions at the time of the event. A review of the literature on this subject confirms the existing dichotomy.

A common argument in support of allowing officers to view available video recordings of force incidents prior to writing their reports or giving a statement is that reports or statements will be more accurate, complete, avoid inconsistencies, and improve the report writing process.[38,58,59,60] Accurate report writing and memory recall are especially important when officers are involved in significant force incidents, particularly deadly force. In a study conducted by Dawes et al. (2016), allowing officers to view video recordings before report writing led to the correction of important errors related to mis-sequencing, omitting force, verbal warnings given, subject compliance, and other important elements related to force used.[58] Errors or oversights such as these may diminish an officer's credibility or lead to successful claims of excessive force, dismissal of charges, termination of employment, and even criminal prosecution.[2,59]

Accurate and complete reports help verify whether or not the force used is consistent with policy and procedure, lawful, and objectively reasonable according to the standards set forth in Graham v. Connor (see Chapter 1). Allowing officers to view available video recordings before making statements or writing reports helps elicit accurate details to support an objectively reasonable conclusion.[61] The "encoding specificity principle" posits that memory is improved when information available at the time of encoding is also available at retrieval.[62] Visual cues (i.e., the content present on BWC or dash camera video) that overlap with features of a to-be-remembered event are advantageous for memory.[56] The video also serves as a type of memory prosthesis and helps people recall additional facts about a recorded event.[63] Therefore, allowing officers to watch their VRUOF video prior to report writing or giving a statement could be advantageous to memory and more accurate report writing.

Submitting an inaccurate report that is inconsistent with video records can result in challenges to an officer's credibility by defense attorneys, inaccurate court dispositions, and can slow an already overburdened court system.[59] At the same time, based upon what is already known about the fallibility of memory, inconsistencies between the report and the video record should be anticipated and expected. Furthermore, prosecutors or evaluators cannot automatically presume an officer lied or used bad judgment when the reported actions are not consistent with the video record.[2,38]

The Graham court is also cited to justify why officers should not review available video prior to report writing or providing a statement. The Graham court requires that all force used by law enforcement officers must be objectively reasonable from the perspective of the officer at the scene rather than with 20/20 hindsight. Emphasis is placed on the officer's perception at the time of the event from the perspective of a reasonable officer. With Graham in mind, researchers Grady et al. (2016), believe officers should not watch video recordings before report writing or giving a statement because it could bias memory against the original perception that prompted the force decision.[51] For example, in a high-stress, low-light situation, an officer may perceive the suspect is holding a gun; but the video may later reveal the suspect was taking a shooting stance or platform while holding a cell phone.

The original perception of a threat is not about whether the officer was right or wrong, but rather if the perception was reasonable. Allowing officers to view video recordings before report writing may then cause a conflict in original and post-event perception.[51] It may also permit officers to tailor their reports or statements to best fit the video and "justify" their actions, especially in questionable force incidents, or fabricate a report to create reasonable suspicion regarding an encounter.[38,60] If officers are permitted to watch video before report writing or providing a statement, it would then not be an accurate *recollection* of the encounter, but rather one influenced by the video recording.[57,60] Allowing a review of camera recordings prior to writing a report or making a statement will irrevocably alter an officer's perception of an incident, which may cause an omission of forensically useful information that is not visible in the video or provide information that was never encoded in memory.[2]

If officers are aware they can watch their video recordings any time before report writing, it may also promote "cognitive offloading," which occurs when people engage in methods to preserve cognitive resources.[64] For example, officers who rely on their BWC to remember or recall important details are practicing cognitive offloading. Officers engaged in cognitive offloading are also less likely to take notes or pay close attention because, they may believe, the important details will be captured on video. The problem with this approach becomes readily apparent when it is later discovered that the interaction was not recorded or that the camera failed to record, resulting in no documentation to help with recall. Camera recordings should never replace good notetaking, active listening, or paying close attention to what is occurring.

Another risk of cognitive offloading may be created by artificial intelligence (AI), which has been implemented in BWCs to draft police report narratives based upon auto-transcribed BWC audio.[65] These reports are created based upon what the BWC recorded and not necessarily what the officer noted or saw. If the officer failed to pay attention or take notes, then the report is the AI version. AI should not replace the importance of paying close attention to what is occurring. Failure to pay attention may also cause officers to miss things that the BWC also fails to capture.

This use of AI may help reduce the amount of time officers spend report writing and merely require them to review the narrative for accuracy, make any necessary edits or additions, and submit it. However, as we have just seen, in UOF cases, the AI-generated report may not be an accurate reflection of what the officer perceived or remembered about the incident. So should the officer involved in a force incident be allowed to review their AI-generated report before they write a narrative or provide a statement about what they recalled or perceived at the time of the event?

One recommended approach to address competing perspectives about allowing officers to watch video of their force encounters or AI-generated reports before report writing or recollecting their perceptions comprises a two-step process called "clean reporting."[66] This process advocates for an initial report based upon the officer's perception at the time of the event, without the aid of video, and then a second, supplemental, report which can be added to the case file to address any clarification or discrepancies that exist after the video is viewed.[66] This clean reporting method also provides reviewers and the courts with a record that captures what the officer recalled without the aid of video, and what recollections were enhanced, changed, or newly discovered from the video. This method can also help overcome claims that video was used to "aid" memory or used to make reports align more with the video versus what was actually recalled without video assistance.

120 Police Use of Force Through the Lens

A header or footer can also be added to reports that identifies whether or not video recordings were viewed before report writing and the potential impact. Footer language may include: *At the time of this report the officer did not have the opportunity to review any available recordings. The report relies solely upon the officer's memory, which may be incomplete, disjointed, or out of order.*

If officers then watch available video recordings that change or add to their recollection of the incident, they should add new details to their report and not edit the original narrative or statement. Immediately before the new content, the officer should identify the new narrative with a new statement or header. The statement could then read: *After viewing available [insert video that was reviewed], the following new memories of the incident are documented below.*

Officers should specifically identify the video(s) viewed. For example, they could write: "After viewing my body-worn camera recording ..." or "After viewing my body-worn camera recording and surveillance camera video ... ." All videos viewed that supported memory recall or influenced reporting should be identified. This method, along with the human factors science that we have discussed, should also be supported by agency policy and procedure.

Cameras, Human Factors, and Law Enforcement Policy and Procedure

Some may believe that applying human factors science to UOF incidents helps excuse or justify force. Others might believe that human factors science allows us to better explain why force used is objectively reasonable or why certain perceptual or cognitive distortions occur. Policing is a complex system wherein officers make critical human decisions, often with limited information or during rapidly evolving events that impact decision-making and actions.[67] Like other industries, law enforcement should leverage human factors science to reduce error, explain mistakes, improve performance, and improve the rigor of UOF investigations. When science, policy and procedure, industry best practices, training, video, and officer recollection and account of the event(s) are used to best inform objective reasonableness, we can arrive at more accurate, informed, and fair conclusions – even when outcomes are adverse. Officers are more likely to accept adverse findings (e.g., the force was not objectively reasonable) if they perceive fair processes or methods were used to reach the conclusion. Similarly, civilians, plaintiffs, defendants, or review boards are also more likely to support outcomes if they believe fair processes or methods were used.

Procedural justice (mentioned earlier in Chapter 4) supports policies, procedures, and consistent methods for making informed decisions. This would include decisions about the objective reasonableness of VRUOF. Evaluators who do not follow policies, procedures, or proper methods or arrive at conclusions too quickly may be viewed as procedurally unfair. In contrast, outcomes based upon methods perceived as aligning with organizational justice are more likely to be supported by officers.[68] A lack of policies or procedures related to the application of human factors to VRUOF is also inconsistent with organizational theory. The policies or procedures also serve as the basis, in part, for determining or explaining why an officer's actions are objectively reasonable. The lack of policy or procedure related explicitly to the application of human factors fails to support best practices advocated by procedural justice and organizational theorists. This deficit also prohibits evaluators from relying on established policies to explain objective reasonableness or arrive at conclusions by following consistent methods. It is recommended that a human factors statement within policy should specifically direct evaluators to consider perceptual impairments, cognitive (i.e., memory) impairments, and physiological impairments that affect fine motor skills under stress.

Unlike other high-stress and high-risk industries (such as aviation) that have readily adopted human factors in policy, law enforcement has been slow to do the same. However some agencies, such as the San Diego (California) Police Department (SDPD), do now consider human factors. For example, SDPD policy DP 1.49 recognizes the importance of human factors related to BWCs and video recordings, as expressed below:

> BWCs have a field of vision of either 75 degrees for the Flex or 130 degrees for the Axon. While human beings have a field of vision of 180 degrees, the human brain has a field of attention of 50-60 degrees. Under stress, this field can narrow down to a ½ degree. Stress also induces auditory exclusion and prevents the brain from analyzing and remembering all the stimuli that it takes in through the senses.
>
> Officers make decisions based on the totality of the human senses. An officer's recollection of specific details may be different than what is captured in digital evidence since BWCs only capture audio and video.[69]

The Graham decision also appears to advocate for human factors consideration. The justices ordered that evaluators must take into account "the fact that officers … make split-second judgments … in circumstances that are tense, uncertain, and rapidly evolving." Quick, intense, uncertain, and rapidly evolving UOF events are likely to create cognitive or perceptual distortions that will affect performance. Evaluators should be well trained in human factors that affect officer performance and decision-making. However, just as there is a lack of nationwide UOF standards in the U.S., there is also a lack of law enforcement industry and organizational commitment to using human factors for determining, in part, objective reasonableness.

Before dash cameras or BWCs are deployed in the field, sound policies and procedures that regulate their use must be implemented. Policy and procedure development should be a collaborative process between administrators and the officers who will be using the cameras. Involving those most affected by policy in the process is not a new concept. Goldstein (1967, p. 1135) wrote, "Law enforcement personnel are more likely to want to conform and are more likely to develop an ability to conform if they are made a part of the process for making important decisions affecting their function."[70]

Law enforcement *policy* and *procedure* are significantly different from one another. Camera policy identifies the standard, rule, application, or intention about the use of cameras. For example, a BWC policy statement may say: "Officers with properly functioning body-worn camera equipment shall record all events surrounding the contact, stop, detention, interview and arrest of suspected violators and maintain this recorded evidence for consideration in criminal prosecution."[71] Procedures provide detailed processes, steps, or any exceptions about camera use. Camera procedures should address the broad range of issues that we have discussed in this work. Law enforcement associations such as the IACP have published a model policy, "Body-Worn Cameras", which contains procedures for the use of BWCs (see the references section below).[72] Reviewing other published camera policies and procedures can help formulate policies and procedures that meet agency and community requirements. Camera policies and procedures are a balance between applying established industry and researched best practices to ensure adherence to legal requirements while meeting community expectations and agency needs. Once formulated, officers must be trained in the proper application of policy and procedure, along with camera technology use. A lack of policy or procedure will negatively affect BWC implementation and result in inconsistent use.

Early BWC implementation was often met with officer resistance. A 2018 study summarized that officers believed BWCs would invade their privacy rights, negatively impact officer safety, violate conditions of collective bargaining, and be used to "burn a cop."[73] Others reported that officers believe BWCs would be used to monitor them and were suspicious that management would go to great lengths to demonstrate transparency and maintain their own image.[74] Some officers expressed concern that the supervisor would use BWCs to "fish" for complaints and discipline them or "Monday morning quarterback" their performance (i.e., criticize or question it after the event).[75] These perceptions tend to change in favor of BWCs with field use; there is a new perception that the cameras will help reduce citizen complaints and maintain police–community relations, rather than foster unfair discipline.[76,77]

Of course, officers' trust or perception of their immediate supervisors will influence their perspectives about how BWCs may be used within the context of the officer–supervisor relationship. Leveraging BWC recordings to support an officer performance-based approach, consistent with an earlier recommendation in this book, may also help allay fears of inappropriate disciplinary use. Proper BWC implementation or roll-out may help improve officer acceptance and ensure the appropriate framework is in place for program success. Sound policy and procedure can also help overcome these adverse perceptions and practices.

As with any type of organizational change, those most affected should be involved in the change process. BWC policy development must be an inclusive process.[78] When implementing BWCs, agencies that are organizationally just are characterized by their soliciting of officer feedback before implementation and deployment.[75] Officers' input on policy development is important, and their perspective should be sought about the many issues we have discussed in this book, including (but not limited to) the following:

- Where cameras can be worn or mounted
- When cameras must be on
- When they can be turned off or paused
- Where they cannot record (e.g., in private bathrooms or locker rooms)
- When video can and cannot be used during report writing
- How recordings must be saved or uploaded.

There has also been some research to support the importance of appropriately regulating the discretionary use of BWCs. In addition to more consistent use of BWCs, the evidence suggests that BWCs tend to mediate or reduce the frequency of force when discretion of when to activate cameras is limited and there is high camera activation compliance.[79] Peer review of other agencies' BWC policies can also provide insight into these issues. In agencies where police unions exist, they should also be engaged during policy development and before implementation. Consideration must be given to how BWCs may affect contractual "working conditions" language. Police and fire commission members, civilian review boards, and community members should also be part of the planning and implementation process.

124 Police Use of Force Through the Lens

In 2015, the U.S. Department of Justice (DOJ), the Office of Justice Programs (OJP), and the Bureau of Justice Assistance (BJA) jointly launched a BWC policy implementation program, which has evolved into a training and technical assistance program to help with BWC initiatives. It recommends the following steps when implementing a BWC program:

- Have a plan – program goals, timelines for deployment, pilot tests; establish working, ensure legal compliance, and determine technology needs.
- Be flexible – anticipate that plans will change, and agencies will be required to adapt to unexpected changes or deviations from the initial plan.
- Engage internal stakeholders – those most impacted by BWC implementation, the officers, must be involved in policy development, pilot testing, and training development.
- Engage external stakeholders – engage community members, criminal justice partners (e.g., prosecutors, city leaders, and representative from local court systems).
- Provide training before field implementation.
- Engage with a research partner who can independently and rigorously assess the BWC program.
- Audit or review BWC footage to ensure policy compliance, evaluate performance, or identify training opportunities.[80]

Researchers evaluated the relationship between BWC integration and acceptance by following similar BJA recommendations within the Tempe, Arizona, Police Department and discovered strong integration and acceptance of BWCs among officers, citizens, and external stakeholders.[77] Although one study cannot ensure this process will promote similar results in other parts of the country, the findings are promising and support other well-established organizational change methods (e.g., Kotter, 2012).[81]

Other Human Factors Research

As in other high-risk industries, human factors research can help explain officer performance during high-stress encounters. The airline industry uses human factors research to explain why pilots make errors; the medical community uses human factors to explain medical errors; and the military has been using human factors research since 1941 to improve service member safety and field performance.[82,83] Internal experts within these industries can therefore help explain performance, from what a person did during a stressful moment to what they should do when faced with certain or similar high-risk scenarios.

Similarly, internal law enforcement experts, researchers, and academics can help explain relationships between human factors research and officer performance in intense, rapid, high-pressure, and dangerous situations. The research can also help officers determine appropriate and reasonable action when faced with certain hazards or threats. However, there are no degree-granting institutions that offer academic programs focused on creating or developing human factors experts to help reduce law enforcement error and improve performance. This is a need for the law enforcement sector to fulfill.

Human factors training for law enforcement is offered by private organizations such as the Force Science Institute (FSI) or the California Human Performance Training Institute. Although both entities offer such training, they are not degree-granting institutions, and their curricula are not accredited by traditional academic accrediting bodies such as the Higher Learning Commission (HLC). Academically accredited, degree-granting institutions could help fill this void by offering programs on human performance with an emphasis on improving officer performance.

The "Force Encounters Course" offered by Force Science is accredited by the International Association of Directors of Law Enforcement Standards and Training (IADLEST) and their National Certification Program (NCP), which is accepted in 37 U.S. states.[84,85] Courses certified by IADLEST are designed to count towards officers' mandatory in-service training requirements.[84] Industry-level certification or accreditation is not a requirement, and may not provide the same level of oversight or review required of college or university programs to remain legitimate degree-granting institutions. However, IADLEST makes great strides to offer legitimate training programs or services to law enforcement entities or academies to help ensure the curriculum follows industry best practices (e.g., academy certification, curriculum development, audit services, technical assistance).

Force Science is a renowned human factors research center that has conducted and published academic and peer-reviewed research to help improve officer performance or explain why errors occur. The organization and its principal researcher, Dr. William Lewinski, have made significant contributions to the human factors literature, which can help provide insight, improve VRUOF investigations, offer explanations, or be used to improve outcomes. A few other researchers, such as Chabris et al., have also conducted relevant research and added to the law enforcement human factors literature.[28] Appendix A at the end of this volume comprises a literature review of relevant human factors research and the main findings of the studies.

This chapter explored the science of human factors and how it may be used to explain officer performance, decision-making, and recollection of VRUOF events. Human factors science must be part of the objective reasonableness calculation. Ignoring the impact of human factors on officer performance during rapid, intense, or dangerous force incidents is a disservice to officers and would likely lead to inaccurate or incomplete conclusions. We owe it to our law enforcement officers, the people they are sworn to protect, and to our justice system to arrive at accurate assessments or conclusions about the appropriateness and level of force officers use.

Next, we will explore expert witness review, analysis, and reporting methods, topics typically absent from scholarly works. We will also reveal a researched method for reviewing VRUOF incidents that provides an opportunity for more objectively reasonable conclusions.

References

1. Klinger, D. A., & Brunson, R. K. (2009). Police officers' perceptual distortions during lethal force situations: Informing the reasonableness standard. Criminology & Public Policy, 8(1), 117–140. doi: 10.1111/j.1745-9133.2009.00537.x
2. Hartman, M., O'Neill, D. A., O'Neill, J., & Lewinski, W. (2017). Law enforcement memory of stressful events: Recall accuracy as a function of detail type. Law Enforcement Executive Forum, 17(3), 21–41
3. Hough, R. M. (2017). Mental chronometry and officer training. Law Enforcement Executive Forum, 17(2), 1–6
4. Hancock, P., Szalma, J., & Weaver, J. (2002, Dec.). The distortion of perceptual space-time under stress. Paper presented at the 23rd Army Science Conference, Orlando, FL.
5. Ross, D. L. (2013). Assessing lethal force liability decisions and human factors research. Law Enforcement Executive Research Forum, 13(2), 85–107. https://www.aele.org/Ross_Forum_2013-2.pdf
6. Blake, D. M. (2015). Body worn cameras: Comparing human and device to ensure unbiased investigations. Law Enforcement Executive Research Forum, 15(4). doi: 10.19151/LEEF.2015.1504c
7. Bone, D. H., Normore, A. H., & Javidi, M. (2015). Human factors in law enforcement leadership. FBI Law Enforcement Bulletin. Retrieved from https://leb.fbi.gov/articles/featured-articles/human-factors-in-law-enforcement-leadership
8. Human Factors and Ergonomics Society (2021). policy statement on reducing deadly force by law enforcement. https://www.hfes.org/Portals/0/HFES%20policy%20law%20enforcement%20-%20FINAL_1.pdf
9. Hine, K. A., Porter, L. E., Westera, N. J., Alpert, G. P., & Allen, A. (2018). Exploring police use of force decision-making processes and impairments using a naturalistic decision-making approach. Criminal Justice & Behavior, 20(10), 1–20. doi: 10.1177/0093854818789726

10. Baldwin, S., Bennell, C., Blaskovits, B., Brown, A., Jenkins, B., Lawrence, C., McGale, H., Semple, T., & Andersen, J. P. (2022). A reasonable officer: Examining the relationships among stress, training, and performance in a highly realistic lethal force scenario. Frontiers in Psychology, 12, 759132. https://doi.org/10.3389/fpsyg.2021.759132

11. Honig, A. L. & Roland, J. E. (1998). Shots fired; officer involved. The Police Chief. https://ovc.ojp.gov/sites/g/files/xyckuh226/files/media/document/int_police_involved_in_shooting-508.pdf

12. Novy, M. (2012). Cognitive distortions during law enforcement shooting. Activitas Nervosa Superior, 54. Retrieved from https://link.springer.com/article/10.1007/BF03379584

13. Marshall, B., Cardon, P., Poddar, A., & Fontenot, R. (2013). Does sample size matter in qualitative research? A review of qualitative interviews in IS research. Journal of Computer Information Systems, 54(1), 11–22. https://doi.org/10.1080/08874417.2013.11645667

14. Nielsen, E. D. (1981). The law enforcement officers use of deadly force and post-shooting trauma [Doctoral dissertation] (Order No. 8121983). University of Utah. Available from ProQuest One Academic. (303173382).

15. Campbell, J. H. (1992). A comparative analysis of the effects of post-shooting trauma on special agents of the Federal Bureau of Investigation [Doctoral dissertation] (Order No. 9233863). Michigan State University. Available from ProQuest One Academic. (304019914).

16. Solomon, R. M., & Horn, J. H. (1986). Post-shooting traumatic reactions: A pilot study. In: J. T. Reese & H. A. Goldstein, editors. Psychological services for law enforcement officers. Washington, DC: U.S. Government Printing Office

17. Artwohl, A. (2008). Perceptual and memory distortions during officer involved shootings. Americans for Effective Law Enforcement (AELE) Lethal and Less Lethal Force Workshop. http://www.aele.org/law/2008FPAUG/wb-19.pdf

18. Geis, C. E., & Blake, D. M. (2015). Efficacy of police body cameras for evidentiary purposes: Fact or fallacy? The Police Chief, 83(5). Retrieved from https://www.hptinstitute.com/wp-content/uploads/2014/01/Body-Cameras.pdf

19. Blake, D. M. (2015). Body worn cameras: Comparing human and device to ensure unbiased investigations. Law Enforcement Executive Research Forum, 15(4). doi: 10.19151/LEEF.2015.1504c

20. Suss, J., Raushel, A., Armijo, A., & White, B. (2018). Design considerations in the proliferation of police body-worn cameras. Ergonomics in Design, 26(3), 17–22. doi: 10.1177/1064804618757686.

21. Stoughton, S. W. (2018). Police body-worn cameras. North Carolina Law Review, 96, 1362–1424. Retrieved from http://amjudges.org/pdfs/2018%20Annual%20Meeting/Police-Body-Worn-Cameras.pdf

22. Boivin, R., Gendron, A., Faubert, C., & Poulin, B. (2017). The body-worn camera perspective bias. Journal of Experimental Criminology, 13(1), 125–142.

23. Andersen, J. P., & Gustafsberg, H. (2016). A training method to improve police use of force decision making: A randomized controlled trial. SAGE Open, 6(2). https://doi.org/10.1177/2158244016638708

24. Fawcett, J. M., Peace, K. A., & Greve, A. (2016). Looking down the barrel of a gun: What do we know about the weapon focus effect? Journal of Applied Research in Memory and Cognition, 5(7), 257–263

25. Lacy, J. W., & Stark, C. E. L. (2013). The neuroscience of memory: Implications for the courtroom. Nature Reviews Neuroscience, 14(9), 649–658. https://doi.org/10.1038/nrn3563

26. Kramer, T. H., Buckhout, R., & Eugenio, P. (1990). Weapon focus, arousal, and eyewitness memory: Attention must be paid. Law and Human Behavior, 14(2), 167–184. https://doi.org/10.1007/BF01062971

27. Hyman, I. E., & Thomas, A. (2018). Crime blindness: How selective attention and inattentional blindness can disrupt eyewitness awareness and memory. Policy Insights from the Behavioral and Brain Sciences, 5(2), 202–208. doi: 10.1177/2372732218786749

28. Simons, D. J., & Schlosser, M. D. (2017). Inattentional blindness for a gun during a simulated police vehicle stop. Cognitive Research: Principles and Implications, 2(1), 37. https://doi.org/10.1186/s41235-017-0074-3

29. Lee, G., O'Neil, J., & Houlihan, D. (2018). An examination of inattentional blindness in law enforcement in high-stress situations. Law Enforcement Executive Forum, 18(4), 38–48.

30. Chabris, C. F., Weinberger, A., Fontaine, M., & Simons, D. J. (2011). You do not talk about Fight Club if you do not notice Fight Club: Inattentional blindness for a simulated real-world assault. i-Perception, 2(2), 150–153. https://doi.org/10.1068/i0436

31. Sharps, M. (2017). Processing under pressure: Stress, memory and decision-making in law enforcement. Flushing, NY: Looseleaf Law Publications

32. Klinger, D. (2002). Police responses to officer-involved shootings: Executive summary. National Criminal Justice Reference Service. https://www.ojp.gov/pdffiles1/nij/grants/192285.pdf

33. Eagleman, D. M., Tse, P. U., Buonomano, D., Janssen, P., Nobre, A. C., & Holcombe, A. O. (2005). Time and the brain: How subjective time relates to neural time. Journal of Neuroscience, 25(45). doi: 10.1523/JNEUROSCI.3487-05.2005

34. Stetson, C., Fiesta, M. P., & Eagleman, D. M. (2007). Does time really slow down during a frightening event? PloS ONE, 2(12), e1295. https://doi.org/10.1371/journal.pone.0001295

35. Lacy, J. W., & Stark, C. E. L. (2013). The neuroscience of memory: Implications for the courtroom. Nature Reviews Neuroscience, 14(9), 649–658. doi: 10.1038/nrn3563

36. Howe, M. L., & Knott, L. M. (2015). The fallibility of memory in judicial processes: Lessons from the past and their modern consequences. Memory, 23(5), 633–656. https://doi.org/10.1080/09658211.2015.1010709

37. Jones, K. A., Crozier, W.E., & Strange, D. (2017). Believing is seeing: Biased viewing of body-worn camera footage. Journal of Applied Research in Memory and Cognition, 6(4), 460–474. doi: 10.1016/j.jarmac.2017.07.007

Human Factors, Memory, and Video-Recorded Use of Force **129**

38. Hope, L., Lewinski, W., Dixon, J., Blocksidge, D., & Gabbert, F. (2012). Witnesses in action: The effect of physical exertion on recall and recognition. Psychological Science, 23(4), 386–390. doi: 10.1177/0956797611431463

39. Phillips, S.W. (2018, Mar. 1). Eyes are not cameras: The importance of integrating perceptual distortions, misinformation, and false memories into the police body camera debate. Policing: A Journal of Policy and Practice, 12(1), 91–99. https://doi.org/10.1093/police/paw008

40. Lewinski, W. J., Dysterheft, J. L., Priem, M. M., & Pettitt, R. W. (2016). Police officers' actual vs. recalled path of travel in response to a threatening traffic stop scenario. Police Practice & Research, 17(1), 51–67

41. Honig, A., & Lewinski, W. J. (2008). A survey of the research on human factors related to lethal force encounters: Implications for law enforcement training, tactics, and testimony. Law Enforcement Executive Research Forum, 8(4). Retrieved from https://iletsbeiforumjournal.com/images/Issues/FreeIssues/ILEEF%202008-8.4.pdf

42. Squire, L. R., Genzel, L., Wixted, J. T., & Morris, R. G. (2015). Memory consolidation. Cold Spring Harbor Perspectives in Biology, 7(8), a021766. https://doi.org/10.1101/cshperspect.a021766

43. Payne, J. D., & Kensinger, E. A. (2018). Stress, sleep, and the selective consolidation of emotional memories. Current Opinion in Behavioral Sciences, 19, 36–43. https://samlab.nd.edu/assets/288068/payne_kensinger_2018.pdf

44. Alpert, G. P., Rivera, J., & Lott, L. (2012). Working toward the truth in officer-involved shootings. FBI Law Enforcement Bulletin. Retrieved from https://leb.fbi.gov/articles/featured-articles/working-toward-the-truth-in-offi cer-involved-shootings

45. International Association of Chiefs of Police (IACP) (2016). Officer-involved shooting guidelines: A guide for law enforcement leaders. Washington, DC: Office of Community Oriented Policing Services. Retrieved from https://www.theiacp.org/sites/default/files/2018-08/e051602754_Officer_Involved_v8.pdf

46. Geiselman, R. E. (2010). Rest and eyewitness memory recall. American Journal of Forensic Psychology, 28(2), 1–5. Retrieved from https://www.hptinstitute.com/wp-content/uploads/2014/01/Rest-Eyewitness-Memory-Recall-Geiselman.pdf

47. Genzel, L., Spoormaker, V. I., Konrad, B. N., & Dresler, M. (2015). The role of rapid eye movement sleep for amygdala-related memory processing. Neurobiology of Learning and Memory, 122, 110–121. doi: 10.1016/j.nlm.2015.01.008

48. Stepan, M. E., Dehnke, T. M., & Fenn, K. M. (2017). Sleep and eyewitness memory: Fewer false identifications after sleep when the target is absent from the lineup. PLoS One, 12(9), e0182907. https://doi.org/10.1371/jour nal.pone.0182907

49. Noble, J. J., & Alpert, G. P. (2013). Criminal interrogations of police officers after use-of-force incidents. FBI Law Enforcement Bulletin. Retrieved from https://leb.fbi.gov/articles/featured-articles/criminal-interrogations-of-pol ice-officers-after-use-of-force-incidents

50. McClure, K. A., McGuire, K. L., & Loftus, E. F. (2019). Officers' memory and stress in virtual lethal force scenarios: Implications for policy and training. Psychology, Crime, & Law. doi: 10.1080/1068316X.2019.1652748

51. Grady, R. H., Butler, B. J., & Loftus, E. F. (2016). What should happen after an officer-involved shooting? Memory concerns in police reporting procedures. Journal of Applied Research in Memory and Cognition, 5(3), 246–251. Retrieved from https://escholarship.org/uc/item/6mz8w7qd

52. Hope, L. (2016). Evaluating the effects of stress and fatigue on police officer response and recall: A challenge for research, training, practice, and policy. Journal of Applied Research in Memory and Cognition, 5(3), 239–245. Retrieved from https://www.ncjrs.gov/pdffiles1/nij/grants/184188.pdf

53. Schnell, C., Spencer, M. D., Mancik, A., Porter, L. E., Ready, J., & Alpert, G. P. (2022). Expanding research on investigations of officer-involved shootings: An experimental evaluation of question timing on police officers' memory recall. Criminal Justice and Behavior, 49(7), 1031–1049. https://doi.org/10.1177/00938548211035824

54. Anderson, M. C., Bjork, E. L. and Bjork, R. A. (2000). Retrieval-induced forgetting: evidence for a recall specific mechanism. Psychonomic Bulletin and Review, 7(3), 522–530.

55. Blaskovits, B., & Bennell, C. (2020). Exploring the potential impact of body worn cameras on memory in officer-involved critical incidents: A literature review. Journal of Police and Criminal Psychology, 35(3), 251–262. https://doi.org/10.1007/s11896-019-09354-1

56. Milwaukee Police Department (2024). Standard operating procedure: 730 – In-car camera systems. https://city.milwaukee.gov/ImageLibrary/Groups/mpd Authors/SOP/730-MOBILEDIGITALVIDEOAUDIORECORDINGEQU IPMENT1.pdf

57. Gramagila, J. A., & Phillips, S. W. (2017). Police officers' perceptions of body-worn cameras in Buffalo and Rochester. American Journal of Criminal Justice, 43, 313–328. doi: 10.1007/s12103-017-9403-99

58. Dawes, D., Heegaard, W. Brave, M. Paetow, G., Weston, B. & Ho, J. (2016). Body-worn cameras improve law enforcement officer report writing accuracy. Journal of Law Enforcement, 4(6). Retrieved from: http://jghcs.info/index.php/l/article/viewFile/410/355

59. Koen, M. C., Willis, J. J., & Mastrofski, S. D. (2018). The effects of body-worn cameras on police organization and practice: A theory-based analysis. Policing and Society, 29(8), 968–984. doi: 10.1080/10439463.2018.1467907

60. Otu, N. (2016). Police body cameras: Seeing may be believing. Salus Journal, 4(3), 49–64. Retrieved from http://scci.csu.edu.au/salusjournal/wp-content/uploads/sites/29/2016/11/Otu_Salus_Journal_Volume_4_Number_3_2016_pp_49-64.pdf

61. Lippman, G. E. (2017). Police body cameras part II: Will body cameras improve policing in Florida? The Florida Bar Journal. Retrieved from https://www.floridabar.org/news/tfb-journal/?durl=%2Fdivcom%2Fjn%2Fjnjournal01.nsf%2F8c9f13012b96736985256aa900624829%2F13382a1fc078bad38525814b0054f70c

Human Factors, Memory, and Video-Recorded Use of Force **131**

62. Tulving, E. (1983). Elements of episodic memory. Oxford: Oxford University Press
63. Hoisko, J. (2003). Early experiences of visual memory prosthesis of supporting episodic memory. International Journal of Human–Computer Interaction, 15(2), 209–230. https://citeseerx.ist.psu.edu/document?repid=rep1&type=pdf&doi=4e36fcab7f104aabde9c2d776bfa399ee7dd771d
64. Risko, E. F., & Gilbert, S. J. (2016). Cognitive offloading. Trends in Cognitive Sciences, 20(9): 676–688. https://doi.org/10.1016/j.tics.2016.07.002
65. Axon (2024, Apr. 23). Axon reimagines report writing with Draft One, a first-of-its kind AI-powered force multiplier for public safety. https://investor.axon.com/2024-04-23-Axon-reimagines-report-writing-with-Draft-One,-a-first-of-its-kind-AI-powered-force-multiplier-for-public-safety
66. Yu, H., & Bogen, M. (2017). The illusion of accuracy: How body-worn camera footage can distort evidence. Upturn: The Leadership Conference. Retrieved from https://www.upturn.org/static/reports/2017/the-illusion-of-accuracy/files/Upturn%20and%20LCCHR%20-%20The%20Illusion%20of%20Accuracy%20v.1.0.pdf
67. McFarlane, P., & Amin, A. (2021). Investigating fatal police shootings using the human factors analysis and classification framework (HFACS). Police Practice & Research, 22(7), 1777–1791. https://doi.org/10.1080/15614263.2021.1878893
68. Kyle, M. J., & White, D. R. (2017). The impact of law enforcement officer perceptions of organizational justice on their attitudes regarding body-worn cameras. Journal of Crime and Justice, 40(1), 68–83. https://doi.org/10.1080/0735648X.2016.1208885
69. San Diego Police Department (2021, Sept. 2). Procedure. 1.49 – Administration: Axon body worn cameras. https://www.sandiego.gov/sites/default/files/149-axonbodyworncameras.pdf
70. Goldstein, H. (1967). Police policy formation: A proposal for improving police performance. Michigan Law Review, 65(6), 1123–1146. https://repository.law.umich.edu/cgi/viewcontent.cgi?article=5782&context=mlr
71. Texas Commission on Law Enforcement (n.d.). Sample model policy on body-worn cameras. https://tcole.texas.gov/document/sample_1.pdf
72. International Association of Chiefs of Police (IACP) (2014). Model policy: Body-worn cameras. https://www.theiacp.org/sites/default/files/all/b/BodyWornCamerasPolicy.pdf
73. Huff, J., Katz, C. M., & Webb, V. J. (2018). Understanding police officer resistance to body-worn cameras. Policing: An International Journal, 41(4), 482–495. https://doi.org/10.1108/PIJPSM-03-2018-0038
74. Todak, N., & Gaub, J. E. (2019). Predictors of police body-worn camera acceptance: Digging deeper into officers' perceptions. Policing: An International Journal, 43(2), 299–313. doi: 10.1108/PIJPSM-06-2019-0085
75. Cochran, H., & Worden, R. E. (2023). Police culture and officers' receptivity to body-worn cameras: A panel study. Policing: An International Journal, 46(1), 24–39. https://doi.org/10.1108/PIJPSM-06-2022-0076
76. Goetschel, M., & Peha, J. M. (2017). Police perceptions of body-worn cameras. American Journal of Criminal Justice, 42, 698–726.

77. Snyder, J. A., Crow, M. S., & Smykla, J. O. (2019). Police officer and supervisor perceptions of body-worn cameras pre- and postimplementation: The importance of officer buy-in. Criminal Justice Review, 44(3), 322–338. https://doi.org/10.1177/0734016819846223

78. White, M. D., Todak, N., & Gaub, J. E. (2018). Examining body-worn camera integration and acceptance among police officers, citizens, and external stakeholders. Criminology & Public Policy, 17(3). doi: 10.1111/1745-9133.12376

79. Maskaly, J., Donner, C., Jennings, W. G., Ariel, B., & Sutherland, A. (2017). The effects of body-worn cameras (BWCs) on police and citizen outcomes: A state-of-the-art review. Policing: An International Journal, 40(4), 672–688. https://doi.org/10.1108/PIJPSM-03-2017-0032

80. Rodriguez, D. (n.d.). From the field: What have we learned from the first two years of providing training and technical assistance to police agencies implementing body-worn camera programs? Body-Worn Camera Training & Technical Assistance. https://bwctta.com/resources/commentary/view-what-have-we-learned-bwc-implementation-program-so-far

81. Kotter, J. P. (2012). Leading change. Boston, MA: Harvard Business Review Press

82. Brennan, P. A., Mitchell, D. A., Holmes, S., Plint, S., & Parry, D. (2016). Good people who try their best: Recognition of human factors and how to minimize error. British Journal of Oral and Maxillofacial Surgery, 54(1), 3–7. https://doi.org/10.1016/j.bjoms.2015.09.023

83. Tossell, C. C., Finomore, V. S., Endsley, M. R., Wickens, C. D., Bennett, W. R., Knott. B. A., & McClernon, C. K. (2016, Sept.). Human factors and the United States military: A 75-year partnership. Proceedings of the Human Factors and Ergonomics Society Annual Meeting, 60(1), 91–93 https://www.researchgate.net/publication/308182131_Human_Factors_and_the_United_States_Military_A_75-Year_Partnership

84. International Association of Directors of Law Enforcement Standards and Training (IADLEST) (n.d.). National Certification Program. https://iadlest-ncp.org/

85. Force Science (2023). Force encounters course. https://www.forcescience.com/training/force-encounters-course/

8

EXPERT REVIEW, ANALYSIS, AND REPORTING METHODS

Throughout this volume we have examined important concepts for helping determine whether video-recorded use-of-force (VRUOF) is objectively reasonable. Until now, no methods or best practices have been widely identified to most accurately do so. There are also no established best practices for expert review and reporting of VRUOF incidents. This chapter proposes a research-supported framework for examining VRUOF incidents, and puts forth expert review reporting methods to best determine and articulate if force is objectively reasonable.

Fortunately, most VRUOF incidents are not controversial and are relatively easy to evaluate. For example, if an officer is recorded using indecent or profane language that aggravated someone and was the proximate cause of force in a situation where force would otherwise have been unlikely, an evaluator would easily identify deficiencies in professional communications skills or other tactics. The more dynamic, intense, rapidly evolving, and threatening a VRUOF incident is – such as an officer-involved shooting (OIS) – the more challenging the analysis.

Although the use of video in law enforcement and other protective industries continues to increase, there are no industry standards or best practices about how to use video recordings to most accurately determine whether forced used is objectively reasonable. A review of 70 empirical studies about BWCs revealed that none of them examined the use of video recordings to determine objective reasonableness.[1] What methods should be used to properly analyze VRUOF incidents to arrive at an objectively reasonable conclusion most accurately? Recently, I set out to answer this question, and conducted a qualitative study with Northeast Wisconsin law

DOI: 10.4324/9781003538738-8

134 Police Use of Force Through the Lens

enforcement managers at the rank of sergeant or above, who are often tasked with video review of force incidents. A summary of the study follows. Many of the themes relate to the literature and concepts we have discussed thus far.

Qualitative Study – Proper Management of VRUOF Incidents

The study entitled *A Qualitative Study Exploring Proper Management of Video Recorded Use of Force Incidents* further affirmed that no standards or best practices exist on the use of video recordings to most accurately determine whether forced used is objectively reasonable.[2] Other findings of the study aligned with issues, challenges, advantages, and limitations of VRUOF recordings, some of which have been mentioned in this book; these are discussed in more detail next.

There exists a lack of training for law enforcement managers in the use of video to determine objective reasonableness. Only one-third of managers reported having some training in this area, although not specific to methods that should be used to most accurately determine if VRUOF is objectively reasonable. Others reported training in technical aspects, such as evidence collection and how to retrieve recorded video records. The lack of training specific to VRUOF and other related areas runs counter to what others have suggested for training law enforcement managers. Managers should be well trained in: the investigation of officer-involved shootings and other critical force incidents;[3,4] the influence of human performance factors that affect behavior under stress;[5] and the pros and cons of video recordings.[2] Appropriate training is also necessary to prevent erroneous interpretation of VRUOF and a rejection of conflicting perceptions or conclusions.[6]

There is also a lack of consistency among law enforcement managers about the order of viewing VRUOF to determine objective reasonableness most accurately. Much like the contrasting research about an officer viewing video footage before report writing or making a statement, perceptions about watching video first or reading an officer's report or interviewing them to determine the appropriateness of force are inconsistent. Some evaluators believed that watching the video first was appropriate, while others preferred to read an officer's report or conduct an interview before watching video.

Evaluators must approach the viewing of video with caution and cannot conclude the video is an objective reality. Video recordings of officers using force or apparently using force can be misleading and deceptive.[6,7] Video alone may cause an evaluator to conclude the force was appropriate when, in fact, it was not.[8] The opposite conclusion may also be drawn, that the force was inappropriate when it was not. The video cannot capture the officer's perception of the event, which must be considered when determining objective reasonableness. Police managers who watch video before speaking to the officer or reading a report fail to first learn about the officer's perception. Watching the video first is likely to unduly influence an evaluator's perspective before they can obtain the officer's perspective.[9]

The inconsistency about when an evaluator should watch video recordings also demonstrates the lack of knowledge, training, and methods. Video must be used in conjunction with the officer's human perception or account of the incident to help improve the fact-finding process and objective reasonableness determination.[10] In force incidents, the officer's original perception of the threat is critical to determining objective reasonableness. The original perception of a threat is not about whether or not the officer was right or wrong, but, instead, whether the perception was reasonable. The "clean reporting" format, discussed in Chapter 7, recommends an initial report based upon the officer's perception at the time of the event. A second, supplemental, report can be then added to the case file to address any clarification or discrepancies that exist after the video is viewed. None of the study participants recommended or alluded to the "clean reporting" format.

A lack of policy or procedures exists about how human factors should be part of the objectively reasonable analysis. Only one study participant said human factors were part of a policy or procedure, and none of them cited a specific policy or procedure requiring human factors to be part of the objectively reasonable analysis. Strong consideration must be given to human factors when managing VRUOF incidents to determine objective reasonableness.[11] The lack of sound policy and procedure about human factors would fail to support procedural justice.

There is also a lack of procedures about methods of applying human factors to VRUOF incidents. Any application of human factors to VRUOF incidents would also be influenced by the order of video viewing. For example, if the evaluator watched the force video before speaking with the officer, they are unlikely to discover any potential impact of human factors on the officer's perception, memory, or recollection, which is then a lost opportunity to gather the officer's perception first.

The study participants were also asked about methods they use to help ensure their perspectives are not adversely impacted by hindsight bias when reviewing VRUOF incidents. Participants who acknowledged the existence of bias provided insightful recommendations or methods they use to help mitigate the impact of bias. Some of the recommendations included: bringing in more than one internal person to get different perspectives; having external reviewers (e.g., certified instructors from a college or an officer

136 Police Use of Force Through the Lens

with another agency) evaluate the incident; acknowledging bias and withholding judgment until all facts are in; considering the event from the officer's perspective at the time of the incident; looking at the totality of the incident; and viewing the event in a chronological perspective from beginning, middle, to end.

These methods are consistent with the research on minimizing bias (discussed in Chapter 5). It is essential for evaluators to suppress biases, consider all accurate information, receive input from others (i.e., experts), make consistent decisions across procedures and practices, and arrive at conclusions ethically.[12] Although the participants cited appropriate methods for mitigating bias, none of their agencies had formal procedures or policies specifically for bias reduction. These methods may help reduce bias, but bias cannot be eliminated entirely.

Consistent with what we discussed earlier in this work, evaluators must be aware that the viewing of VRUOF is likely to produce hindsight bias, especially among those trained or experienced in police tactics, who may be tasked with determining if force is objectively reasonable.[9] All participants interviewed for this study were highly experienced and, therefore, video would likely influence bias. This finding also supports the importance of not watching video before speaking with officers or reading their reports to determine human perceptions of the incident. An evaluator who merely watches video of a police incident (e.g., use of force (UOF) or a police vehicle pursuit) and arrives at a conclusion about reasonableness without considering the officer's perceptions at the time of the event promotes erroneous interpretation and a rejection of conflicting perceptions and conclusions.[6] Hindsight bias can also lead to inappropriate decisions regarding the actions of others, especially in a legal context.[13]

Finally, various uses of video camera recordings were identified by the study participants, including training, learning why mistakes occurred during force incidents, resolving citizen complaints, and how different camera angles can provide alternative perspectives of the same event. This proactive use of video can help enhance officer training.[14] Participants also discussed how video could be used for training, along with developing training scenarios based upon the review of VRUOF incidents. The use of video for training is not a new concept and was expressed in a 2002 study conducted by the International Association of Chiefs of Police (IACP).[15] Dash camera recordings have been used for law enforcement training (e.g., the Constable Lunsford case outlined in Chapter 2), and contemporary video that offers various angles provides for more robust training opportunities.

BWCs offer a first-person view, which is more up-close and personal than dash cams. The BWC recording may reveal detail a dash cam cannot.

Expert Review, Analysis, and Reporting Methods **137**

For example, if a suspect seated in a car quickly points a gun at an officer standing alongside the open driver's side door, the BWC will likely capture this movement, while the dash cam would not. The BWC recording could be used to study the physiological actions of potentially armed suspects, which could help train officers to better recognize early warning signs or pre-attack movements, and thus take appropriate action to stop, avoid, mitigate, or de-escalate.

Sometimes officers make mistakes when making force-related decisions. Video recordings of officers making mistakes can be used to identify performance deficiencies, hold law enforcement officials accountable, and promote transparency.[4] When errors occur, evaluators should seek answers about why the mistakes happened. Evaluators should take into account the officer's years of experience, training, the nature of the incident, potential sequences that may be misleading or incomplete, and the officer's perception at the time of the event. These considerations are consistent with the literature. For example, evaluators should consider human factors (which impact perception),[5] be aware of the link between stress and impaired memory recall,[16,17] recognize that high-stress events can cause perceptual distortions (e.g., slow-motion time, auditory exclusion, and visual distortions) that may impact decision-making,[18] and that video can be misleading.[6] These well-documented factors may help provide insight into why officers make (or apparently make) mistakes during VRUOF encounters. The recording should be leveraged to improve officer performance, consistent with the video-recorded training methods discussed earlier.

Video recording is also used to resolve or investigate citizen complaints. The video may confirm the validity of a civilian complaint or exonerate officers accused of wrongdoing.[19,20] The video can also more efficiently clear up complaints, requiring supervisors to spend less time investigating them.[14] Consistent with the literature, participants discussed how video is used to investigate and resolve citizen complaints. Participants cited that complaints have been resolved and officers exonerated simply by watching videos. Additionally, camera recordings reduce the amount of time spent investigating citizen complaints, which can also equate to cost savings.

When evaluating VRUOF incidents, various camera angles can provide alternative or more complete perspectives of an incident. Different camera angles of the same event can also offer different perspectives. Video of the same event may come from BWCs, dash cams, surveillance cameras, traffic cameras, or civilians filming the incident. Multiple views of the same incident can also enhance context or provide additional insight.[21] One participant explained how BWCs and overhead surveillance camera recordings were able to piece together the events of an officer-involved

138 Police Use of Force Through the Lens

shooting, which helped provide an objectively reasonable conclusion. In another instance, dash cam recordings helped shed light on the officers' perspectives and provided a "bigger picture" of what occurred. Consistent with our earlier discussions, evaluators should diligently seek out multiple camera angles to obtain more accurate perspectives of critical incidents.

Not only did this study reveal what has been discussed thus far, but a thorough examination of the findings and an extensive analysis of the literature also helped identify methods that evaluators should follow when determining if VRUOF is objectively reasonable.

Method – Viewing and Analysis of VRUOF Incidents

Because VRUOF incidents are emotionally impacting and can easily fuel biases, any evaluator should resist the urge to view video first. The order of video viewing to determine objective reasonableness is important. Viewing the video first fails to take into consideration the officer's reasonable perception of the threat at the time of the incident, which is required by the Graham v. Connor (1989) decision (see Chapter 1). Only the officers themselves can report on their perceptions at the time of the event. Perception cannot be determined via video. The video cannot convey how human factors (e.g., slow-motion time, auditory exclusion, or inattentional blindness) or cognitive factors (e.g., memory deficits) affected the officer at the time of the incident and afterward. Furthermore, the video cannot show any perceptual distortions the officer may have experienced. The research therefore suggests that evaluators should speak to the officer first or read the officer's report before watching video.[2]

Some evaluators may be convinced that watching video before reading reports or speaking with the officers is acceptable. It is recognized that UOF investigations take time, especially OIS incidents, which are often investigated by another law enforcement entity. Also, demands for transparency, requests for information from news media outlets, and social media reports of VRUOF incidents may cause the leader or evaluator to view video before other information is available. In these instances, evaluators must remind themselves of the potential emotional impact video can have on them, along with camera limitations, as discussed earlier. Conclusions regarding the appropriateness or justification of force cannot typically be made by merely watching a video.

To date, there are no published methods related to systematic best practices that evaluators should follow when determining if VRUOF is objectively reasonable or aligns with policy, procedure, state standards, or industry best practices. Other research about the analysis of force via BWC

Expert Review, Analysis, and Reporting Methods **139**

recording has proposed coding strategies (as mentioned in Chapter 3) to help identify why force occurred and how force occurred.[22] An evaluator should be focused on one standard of analysis at a time, and not attempt to determine if the force used aligns with all perspectives. The proposed process also helps evaluators use controlled, rationale, systematic, and reflective System 2 decision-making, and help avoid System 1 thinking (see Chapter 5).

Based upon the literature discussed throughout this text and my original research (Knetzger, 2020),[2] what follows is a proposed method for evaluators to use when they are tasked with determining if VRUOF is objectively reasonable or aligns with policy, procedure, state standards, or industry best practices. This series of steps is presented with special acknowledgment to Seth Stoughton, Professor of Law at the University of South Carolina, who has presented on BWC UOF investigations, and whose work and feedback also influenced this proposed method.

Step 1 – Does video exist? From where?
Consider: Has all available video evidence been collected (e.g., BWC, dash cam, surveillance, third-party, or social media recordings)? What are the video frame rates, field of view, distance of recording, angle, and so forth?

Step 2 – Who has seen the video?
Consider: Who has seen the video (e.g., other officers, supervisors, trainers, etc.). Any potential evaluator who has seen the video before reviewing available reports may have a biased perspective that was unduly influenced by the video, and may not be in the best position to be an unbiased evaluator.

Step 3 – Read reports and all supporting documentation (e.g., witness statements, victim statements, suspect statements, etc.).
Ask: Are the officer perceptions objectively reasonable? Do they align with policy procedure, state standards, or industry best practices?

Step 4 – Watch all videos in "real time" with sound on and then off. Watching video with sound off allows the viewer to focus primarily on actions.
Determine: What is on the video? What is not on the video? Consider reasons.
Ask: Are the officer perceptions objectively reasonable? Do they align with policy, procedure, state standards, or industry best practices?

140 Police Use of Force Through the Lens

Step 5 – Are there discrepancies between video and officer reports? If so, why?
Ask: Did the officers view video before or after report writing?
Ask: What human factors may explain any discrepancies?

Step 6 – Watch videos in slow motion or conduct frame-by-frame analysis.
Ask: Are the officer perceptions objectively reasonable? Do they align with policy, procedure, state standards, or industry best practices?
Consider: Slow-motion time may create the inaccurate perception that officers had more time to act than they actually did. Frame-by-frame analysis provides additional insight into the objective reality – what really happened – and whether an officer's actions were reasonable in light of that reality.

Step 7 – Consider *all* evidence and come to a conclusion.
Ask: Is the force used objectively reasonable?
Ask: Does the force align with department policy or procedure?
Ask: Does the force align with applicable state, federal, or industry standards?

Step 8 – Collaborate with other expert(s) to confirm findings.
Consider: Collaborating with another expert or peer can further help ensure findings are valid and reliable, assuming appropriate methods, standards, and materials were used to reach an unbiased and objective conclusion.

There are no perfect methods or processes that will guarantee an evaluator will arrive at the most accurate conclusion about the reasonableness of force. There is also likely to be some debate about reading reports first and then watching video, or vice versa. Each perspective is addressed separately.

Watching Video First

Watching video first may cause viewers to make judgments about reasonableness before considering all facts known to the officer at the time of the event. Evaluators who watch video before speaking to the officer or reading reports fail to first learn about the officer's perception, which can never be completely obtained from the video. Watching the video first is likely to unduly influence an evaluator's perspective before they obtain the officer's perspective via their report or statement. Video will never

Expert Review, Analysis, and Reporting Methods **141**

portray the officer's perspective. The Jacob Blake shooting in Kenosha, Wisconsin, is a practical example that highlights some of these issues. This tragedy – for Blake, the officers involved, and the community – will have lifelong impact. Like other practical examples discussed in this book, we can also learn valuable lessons – including how incomplete video footage can influence perceptions, and how the lack of BWC footage may be a new "CSI effect," where a lack of video calls into question witness accounts.

On August 23, 2020, Jacob Blake had been involved in a disturbance with the mother of his children. She reported that Blake had the keys to her rental vehicle, and feared he would take the car and crash it. There was also a felony warrant for Blake's arrest. Officers encountered Blake outside, and the complainant told officers, "My kids are in the car," while trying to take it. Officers attempted to arrest Blake on the warrant, but he resisted. Blake was taken to the ground, but overcame the officers, who also deployed tasers to no avail. At some point during his resistance, Blake armed himself with a knife. With the knife in his left hand, Blake tried to enter the vehicle, and refused commands to drop the knife. Just before being shot, Blake twisted his body and knife towards an officer, who then fired seven rounds, four into Blake's back and three into his left side.[23]

A cell phone recorded video segments of this incident from outside a second-story residential window across the street. The officers were not wearing BWCs. The cell phone recorded the moments just before Blake was shot, but not the resistance and taser deployments. When viewing the video in real time, it is difficult to see Blake holding the knife. In addition, Blake's actions just before he was shot were obscured by the open driver's side door. Digital enhancement of the recording was required to show the open knife; unfortunately, this is not what was shown to the masses.

The incomplete and unclear video recording went viral and sparked protests and riots that decimated the city of Kenosha. Within 72 hours, well before all the facts and the officer's perceptions would be known, the following post to social media site X (formerly Twitter), attributed to the chief of the Albuquerque, New Mexico, Police Department (APD), was sent out:

> The senseless shooting of Jacob Blake once again shows why our community and communities across the nation are seeking justice and change. On behalf of APD, I offer my sympathy to Jacob Blake's family and his children who witnessed this disturbing act. I sincerely hope he makes a full recovery.[24]

142 Police Use of Force Through the Lens

However, the post was quickly taken down after it was discovered that it had been sent out by a representative, and without the chief's knowledge or approval. The chief followed up with:

> Earlier today, a statement was posted attributed to me that I had not prepared or approved. This was an error and will be addressed. With respect to the officer involved shooting in Wisconsin, I have faith in the justice system that the facts of the incident will ultimately be revealed and comments by me about that incident without all the facts would be premature and inappropriate.[24]

Regardless of who made the initial post, apparently the incomplete video recording was emotionally affecting enough that viewers or representatives of a police agency immediately drew conclusions about the appropriateness of the force used. A thorough investigation would later reveal that Blake's actions, confirmed with enhanced video and witness statements, created a reasonably perception of imminent risk of death or great bodily harm to the officer(s), and the use of deadly force was justified.[23]

The lack of BWC footage in this case may have also influenced initial perceptions. BWCs have prompted a new "CSI effect" where jurors – or casual viewers – expect to see BWC footage, and without it they are more likely to question the veracity of witness accounts.[25] No BWC footage resulted in less information for viewers to consider.

Not only could watching video first cause emotionally driven conclusions before all facts are known, but reviewers may also seek to affirm what they see on video within an officer's report and disregard alternative or conflicting information. How we perceive the appropriateness of video-recorded police actions are influenced by our demographics, cultural worldviews, and political ideologies.[26] We are more likely to be emotionally affected by what we see on video than what we read in a report. Reading text, such as an officer's report, intellectually engages the brain, while video is more visceral and emotionally affecting.[27,28] Emotionally driven decisions about the judgment of others can bias conclusions, and the attributed emotions can be difficult to set aside when reaching the conclusion – even when information that would suggest a different conclusion is presented.[29]

Reading the Officer's Report First

Similarly, when reviewers read an officer's report first, they may seek a video recording that affirms what they read in the report while disregarding discrepancies, inconsistencies, or missing content in the recording. While

Expert Review, Analysis, and Reporting Methods **143**

it is well documented in the literature that we should expect discrepancies between officer reports and video recordings, neither approach will eliminate this problem entirely. Reviewers must therefore consider the totality of the circumstances from the officer's perspective at the time of the incident.

The best solution to this dichotomy may be for two separate evaluators to use contrasting approaches (e.g., one watches video first while the other reads reports first) and compare outcomes. Alternatively, if only a single evaluator is available, then a contrasting iterative approach may be most the appropriate. For example, the evaluator could follow the steps outlined above and then reverse the order of video viewing or report reading and compare conclusions.

In 2017, researchers examined how misinformation within an officer's report is weighed against BWC recordings of the same event. In that study, the police report contained intentional misinformation (added by the researchers) that the suspect, upon whom force was used, was carrying a knife and attacked the officer. The video does not confirm or show the suspect was carrying a knife, and the extent of assaultive behavior against the officer is unclear. Viewers tended to give weight to the misleading content when they read the report first, even though it conflicted with a more objective source – the video. Viewers who had more favorable perspectives of the police tended to give more weight to the officer's report. However, participants who viewed both sources of evidence – the BWC video and the report – relied less on misinformation than those who only read the report. Video recordings do not entirely eliminate bias or perspectives about the appropriateness of force.[30]

In addition to following this proposed method, evaluators must also remember to consider the impact of bias on their perceptions. They would be well served by applying the bias mitigation suggestions discussed in Chapter 5. It is imperative for evaluators to not let hindsight and other biases affect their perceptions. I conclude that this recommended method will help evaluators arrive at accurate conclusions about the objective reasonableness of VRUOF. Once an evaluator has arrived at a conclusion about the reasonableness of VRUOF, they must explain their findings in writing. Expert analysis and reporting are discussed next.

Expert Analysis and Reporting

As discussed earlier, evaluators must be aware of the emotions video recordings can arouse because these emotions may influence their initial perceptions about the VRUOF. VRUOF incidents should be reviewed just

144 Police Use of Force Through the Lens

as they occurred: from beginning to end, with a focus on reading *all* officer, victim, witness, and suspect statements first.

Experts may be asked to consider whether VRUOF is justified from a constitutional, state, or policy and procedure perspective. The appropriate criteria must be used to help determine reasonableness. Appropriate criteria can be derived from industry standards, training or teaching curricula and manuals, state laws, federal laws, policies or procedures, and published research. Experts must focus on drawing conclusions that are free of bias and ensuring conclusions are supported by available criteria and facts of the case. Experts with track records of varied findings (e.g., who have determined that force is objectively reasonable and not objectively reasonable) can more likely establish examples of mitigating bias.

Expert opinions are often expressed in writing, but there is no published industry format. Experts often learn from others who have "been there," passing the knowledge down to the next generation of experts. A sample reporting format that can help experts articulate their methods and findings is outlined next.

Introduction and Front Matter

Include a cover page that identifies the appropriate court case number, police report number, defendant or plaintiff, and author of the report. Explain the method of review and that it was conducted in an objective, unbiased, and independent fashion. Outline qualifications to help readers recognize subject matter expertise (SME). Provide a list of material used during the analysis, including all reports and literature used to help formulate an opinion. Be prepared to support SME qualifications with a comprehensive curriculum vitae (CV).

Case Review or Facts of the Case

Summarize the facts of the case, from beginning (e.g., dispatch information), through the middle, to the end. Emphasize that all conclusions contained within the report are based upon the facts known at the time and subject to revision if new or additional information is provided. If multiple officers are involved in the incident, summarize the incident from each officer's perspective. The summary should include facts derived from officer reports, victim or witness statements, and available camera recordings. This portion of the report should not include any conclusions about the reasonableness of the force.

Analysis

Analyze the incident from the appropriate perspective: constitutional, agency policy or procedure, state standards, or industry best practices. Conclude if the VRUOF was objectively reasonable, consistent with Graham v. Connor. Apply the Graham standards, which were discussed in Chapter 1.

Determine whether the VRUOF was consistent with agency policy or procedure. Sometimes, agency policy can be more restrictive than constitutional or state standards. For example, we know from a constitutional perspective that an officer's pre-seizure conduct is not a factor when determining whether force used is objectively reasonable. If an officer used unprofessional, vulgar, or profane language prior to or during a justified force incident, it may be found objectively reasonable, but the language used may be a violation of department policy or procedure. Although a reviewer may conclude the force used was constitutional, they may also conclude there were violations of policy or procedure.

Determine whether the VRUOF was consistent with state standards or any defensive or arrest tactics curriculum. Some states, such as the Wisconsin Department of Justice Division of Training and Standards, publish statewide defensive and arrest tactics manuals and curricula. Any justified force used by a Wisconsin officer must be consistent with the curriculum. Peace Officer Standards and Training (POST), which is adopted by some states and federal law enforcement agencies, also includes defensive tactics curricula, providing further criteria for helping determine whether VRUOF is objectively reasonable.

Other literature that may be relied upon during analysis includes published and peer-reviewed studies (e.g., human factors research), previous and similar cases, or published industry materials (e.g., literature from an appropriate Department of Justice publication that supports the subject of analysis). All conclusions must be supported with appropriate criteria and literature.

In this portion of the report, it is also helpful to include any content to support opinions or conclusions – such as video-recorded screen captures, quotes from manuals, or specific criteria about the force being analyzed.

Conclusion

Expert evaluators must determine whether the VRUOF is objectively reasonable or justified from the appropriate perspective (e.g., constitutional, state standards, policy and procedure, and industry best practices). The

146 Police Use of Force Through the Lens

conclusion is typically brief, and clearly articulates the subject matter expert's position. A sample expert report is presented in Appendix B.

There are no perfect methods or processes for evaluators to use when determining whether VRUOF is objectively reasonable. The proposed methods recommended in this chapter are supported by empirical research and best practices, and have the potential to support more accurate outcomes. The information shared in this chapter and throughout this book can help law enforcement leaders, trainers, evaluators, and academics better understand how cameras can be leveraged to improve performance, more accurately evaluate the reasonableness of force, increase transparency, and promote accountability.

The limitations of cameras have also been highlighted. Video can be misleading or incomplete, and will never represent what an officer perceives at the time of the force incident. Perception can be reported only by the officer involved. In most cases, overreliance on video will create inaccurate perceptions about the reasonableness of force. When UOF incidents are examined, evaluators must first consider the officer's perspective before reviewing video, while consciously suppressing biases, to most accurately arrive at conclusions about the reasonableness of force.

To civilian readers, including police and fire commissioners and those affiliated with other supervisory bodies, I hope this book has provided additional insight about how video footage of officers using force can reveal more *or* less information, and sometimes generate more questions than answers. Although there are, and will be, more instances of officers engaging in obviously excessive force, these are not the norm. The vast majority of officers protecting your communities are ethical and honest men and women who never intend to use excessive force. During high-risk, dangerous, and violent rapidly evolving events, officers sometimes have seconds to evaluate, decide upon, and use the appropriate level of force. These decisions, under varying levels of stress and fear, are oftentimes correct but sometimes wrong.

When inappropriate levels of force are used, we should also consider whether the actions are a mistake of the heart (e.g., officers intended to use the correct level of force, but did not) or a mistake of the mind (e.g., they intentionally used excessive force). Officers who clearly and intentionally use excessive force must be held accountable, and video recordings can help promote that accountability. Nonetheless, mistakes of the heart must also be addressed, and video can provide more insight into why the mistake occurred. The "why" in turn can help guide accountability and provide insight into areas of individual and agency deficiencies.

We must continue to support the use of cameras in law enforcement and other protective industries, while realizing they will not magically improve service and outcomes. A camera is just another tool that an officer carries. It must be used appropriately, consistent with the concepts and considerations discussed in this book. Cameras are invaluable for most accurately determining whether VRUOF is objectively reasonable, which will undoubtedly lead to improved outcomes.

References

1. Lum, C., Stoltz, M., Koper, C. S., & Scherer, J.A. (2019) Research on body-worn cameras: What we know, what we need to know. Criminology & Public Policy, 18, 93–118. https://doi.org/10.1111/1745-9133.12412
2. Knetzger, M. R. (2020). A qualitative study exploring proper management of video-recorded law enforcement use of force incidents [Doctoral dissertation]. Colorado Technical University
3. Chapman, B. (2018). Body-worn cameras: What the evidence tells us. National Institute of Justice. Retrieved from https://www.nij.gov/journals/280/Pages/body-worn-cameras-what-evidence-tells-us.aspx
4. Lum, C., Koper, C. S., Merola, L. M., Scherer, A., & Reioux, A. (2015). Existing and ongoing body worn camera research: Knowledge gaps and opportunities. Report for the Laura and John Arnold Foundation. Fairfax, VA: Center for Evidence-Based Crime Policy, George Mason, University. Retrieved from https://cebcp.org/wp-content/technology/BodyWornCameraResearch.pdf
5. United States Department of Justice (2016). Officer-involved shootings: A guide for law enforcement leaders. Retrieved from https://www.theiacp.org/sites/default/files/2018-08/e051602754_Officer_Involved_v8.pdf
6. Stoughton, S. W. (2018). Police body-worn cameras. North Carolina Law Review, 96, 1362–1424. Retrieved from http://amjudges.org/pdfs/2018%20Annual%20Meeting/Police-Body-Worn-Cameras.pdf
7. Williams, T., Thomas, J., Jacoby, S., & Cave, D. (2016, Apr. 1). Police body cameras: what do you see? New York Times. Retrieved from https://www.nytimes.com/interactive/2016/04/01/us/police-bodycam-video.html
8. Turner, B. L., Caruso, E. M., Dilich, M. A., & Roese, N. J. (2018). Body camera footage leads to lower judgements of intent than dash camera footage. PNAS, 116(4), 1201–1206. doi: 10.1073/pnas.1805928116
9. Boivin, R., Gendron, A., Faubert, C., & Poulin, B. (2017). The body-worn camera perspective bias. Journal of Experimental Criminology, 13(1), 125–142.
10. Wasserman, H. M. (2017). Recording of and by police: The good, the bad, and the ugly. Journal of Gender, Race & Justice, 20(3), 543–562
11. Geis, C. E., & Blake, D. M. (2015). Efficacy of police body cameras for evidentiary purposes: Fact or fallacy? The Police Chief, 83(5). Retrieved from https://www.hptinstitute.com/wp-content/uploads/2014/01/Body-Cameras.pdf
12. Valkeapää, A., & Seppälä, T. (2014). Speed of decision-making as a procedural justice principle. Social Justice Research, 27(3), 305–321
13. Wittlin, M. (2016). Hindsight evidence. Columbia Law Review, 116(5), 1323–1394.

14. Edmonton Police Service (2015). Body worn video: Considering the evidence. Retrieved from https://www.edmontonpolice.ca/News/BWV
15. International Association of Chiefs of Police (IACP) (2002). Impact of video evidence on modern policing research and best practices from the IACP study on in-car cameras. Retrieved from https://www.bja.gov/bwc/pdfs/IACPIn-CarCameraReport.pdf.
16. Hope, L., Lewinski, W., Dixon, J., Blocksidge, D., & Gabbert, F. (2012). Witnesses in action: The effect of physical exertion on recall and recognition. Psychological Science, 23(4), 386–390. doi: 10.1177/0956797611431463
17. Phillips, S.W. (2018). Eyes are not cameras: The importance of integrating perceptual distortions, misinformation, and false memories into the police body camera debate. Policing: A Journal of Policy and Practice, 12(1), 91–99. https://doi.org/10.1093/police/paw008
18. Andersen, J. P., & Gustafsberg, H. (2016). A training method to improve police use of force decision making: A randomized controlled trial. SAGE Open, 6(2). https://doi.org/10.1177/2158244016638708
19. Jennings, W. G., Fridell, L. A., & Lynch, M. D. (2014). Cops and cameras: Officer perceptions of the use of body-worn cameras in law enforcement. Journal of Criminal Justice, 42(6), 549–556. doi: 10.1016/j.jcrimjus.2014.09.008
20. Koen, M. C., Willis, J. J., & Mastrofski, S. D. (2018). The effects of body-worn cameras on police organization and practice: A theory-based analysis. Policing and Society, 29(8), 968–984. doi: 10.1080/10439463.2018.1467907.
21. Suss., J., Raushel, A., Armijo, A., & White, B. (2018). Design considerations in the proliferation of police body-worn cameras. Ergonomics in Design, 26(3), 17–22. doi: 10.1177/1064804618757686.
22. Willits, D. W., & Makin, D. A. (2018). Show me what happened: Analyzing use of force through analysis of body-worn camera footage. Journal of Research in Crime and Delinquency, 55(1), 51–77.
23. City of Kenosha, District Attorney (n.d.). Report on the officer involved shooting of Jacob Blake. https://www.kenoshacounty.org/DocumentCenter/View/11827/Report-on-the-Officer-Involved-Shooting-of-Jacob-Blake
24. Laflin, N. (2020, Aug. 25). APD officers angry over tweet about Wisconsin shooting on APD's Twitter. https://www.koat.com/article/apd-officers-angry-over-tweet-about-wisconsin-shooting-on-apds-twitter/33799630
25. L'Hoiry, X., Santorso, S., & Harrison, K. (2024). Body-worn cameras and unintended consequences: A case study of a British police force. The Police Journal, 97(4), 658–675 https://doi.org/10.1177/0032258X231211177
26. Kahan, D. M., Hoffman, D. A., & Braman, D. (2009). Whose eyes are you going to believe? Scott v. Harris and the perils of cognitive illiberalism. Faculty Scholarship Series. Paper 97. http://digitalcommons.law.yale.edu/fss_papers/97
27. Sherwin, R. K. (2007). A manifesto for visual legal realism. Loyola of Los Angeles Law Review, 40, 719–744.

28. Irvine, S. (2015, Oct. 21). Why people respond to video more than text. Medium. https://medium.com/@stewartirvine/why-people-respond-to-video-more-than-text-14ec21d4b257#:~:text=We're%20evolutionarily%20adapted%20to,than%20we%20can%20process%20text

29. Lerner, J. S., Ye, L., Valdesolo, P., & Kassam, K. (2015). Emotion and decision making. Annual Review of Psychology, 66, 799–823. https://www.annualreviews.org/doi/10.1146/annurev-psych-010213-115043

30. Jones, K. A., Crozier, W.E., & Strange (2017). Believing is seeing: Biased viewing of body-worn camera footage. Journal of Applied Research in Memory and Cognition. doi: 10.1016/j.jarmac.2017.07.007

Appendix A

LAW ENFORCEMENT HUMAN FACTORS RESEARCH

The following offers a comprehensive summary of pertinent human factors research on officer UOF and the dynamics of high-stress encounters. The results of these studies can better inform objective, reasonable analysis, help explain officer performance under stress, improve training, and explain discrepancies between camera footage and human recollection as well as differences between camera perspective and human perspective.

Artwohl, A. (2008). Perceptual and Memory Distortions during Officer Involved Shootings. Americans for Effective Law Enforcement (AELE) Lethal and Less Lethal Force Workshop. http://www.aele.org/law/2008FPAUG/wb-19.pdf.

Key Findings: Self-reported perceptual and memory distortions experienced by officers involved in shootings. The most common distortions are diminished sound (84%), tunnel vision (79%), auto-pilot (acting without conscious thought, 74%), heightened visual clarity (71%), slow-motion time (62%), memory loss for part of the event (52%), and memory loss for some of own behavior (46%).

Blake, D. M. (2015). Body worn cameras: Comparing human and device to ensure unbiased investigations. *Law Enforcement Executive Research Forum, 15*(4). doi: 10.19151/LEEF.2015.1504c.

Key Findings: Police officers are human, and their inherent abilities do not surpass those of the rest of the populace. There will be variations between what an officer sees (or recalls) and what body-worn cameras (BWCs) record. The law enforcement industry should embrace human factors science and apply it to policy, procedures, training, and core practices.

Bone, D. H., Normore, A. H., & Javidi, M. (2015). Human factors in law enforcement leadership. *FBI Law Enforcement Bulletin.* Retrieved from https://leb.fbi.gov/articles/featured-articles/human-factors-in-law-enforcement-leadership.

Key Recommendations: Law enforcement leaders must focus on understanding how officers perform under stress and making thoughtful adjustments to certain critical activities to make their jobs safer. Leaders must promote officer wellness and physical conditioning, address combat fatigue, and recognize the perceptual distortions that officers experience under high-stress events.

Fawcett, J. M., Peace, K. A., & Greve, A. (2016). Looking down the barrel of a gun: What do we know about the weapon focus effect? *Journal of Applied Research in Memory and Cognition, 5*(7), 257–263.

Key Findings: When weapons are unexpected (e.g., a sudden assault), memory impairment is likely and recollection of key details, such as the description of a suspect, are likely to be inaccurate or incomplete.

Hartman, M., O'Neill, D. A., O'Neill, J., & Lewinski, W. (2017). Law enforcement memory of stressful events: Recall accuracy as a function of detail type. *Law Enforcement Executive Forum, 17*(3), 21–41.

Key Findings: Recall accuracy of officers involved in a video-recorded UOF event was better among officers who watched their video versus those who did not. This is expected. When officers watch video before completing a report, it is expected that their reports will be more aligned with the video. However, when officers watch video before report writing, we do not know what their original perceptions were and what was altered by video.

Hope, L. (2016). Evaluating the effects of stress and fatigue on police officer response and recall: A challenge for research, training, practice, and policy. *Journal of Applied Research in Memory and Cognition, 5*(3), 239–245. Retrieved from https://www.ncjrs.gov/pdffiles1/nij/grants/184188.pdf.

152 Appendix A: Law Enforcement Human Factors Research

Key Findings: Police officers are more fatigued than other occupational groups. Fatigue tends to increase anxiety and fearfulness while lowering an officer's ability to deal appropriately with complex stressful situations (e.g., UOF). Fatigued officers are also more prone to irritability and anger (often manifested via communications skills), and there are strong correlations between fatigue, excessive force, and accidents. (When UOF incidents occur, consider asking: How much sleep did the officer get before their shift? How many hours were they awake? How does shift work affect their sleep patterns?)

Honig, A., & Lewinski, W. J. (2008). A survey of the research on human factors related to lethal force encounters: Implications for law enforcement training, tactics, and testimony. *Law Enforcement Executive Research Forum*, 8(4). Retrieved from http://www.expertcop. com/Survey%20Research%20Human%20Factors%20Related%20 To%20Lethal%20Force%20Encounters.pdf.

Key Findings: A literature review of the human factors science that law enforcement officers may experience during lethal force encounters. The greater the trauma, the more likely there will be memory impairment and errors such as false negatives (failing to identify a weapon when one exists) and false positives (seeing a weapon when one does not exist). The brain is capable of attending to only one source of information at a time (e.g., selective attention) and may experience inattentional blindness and auditory exclusion. Tunnel vision or narrowing is common under stress (and officers will "miss" things that occur right in front of them, although present on BWCs or dash cameras). "Retrograde amnesia" refers to the loss of memory for events that occur up to two minutes prior to a traumatic event. "Hyper amnesia" refers to the fact that memory for emotionally charged events tends to improve over time (peripheral or unimportant details are often not encoded while central details, such as perceived threat, are encoded). Information processing takes four times longer than the actual time to respond. Human factors must be considered when evaluating performance.

Klinger, D. A., & Brunson, R. K. (2009). Police officers' perceptual distortions during lethal force situations: Informing the reasonableness standard. *Criminology & Public Policy*, 8(1), 117–140. doi: 10.1111/ j.1745-9133.2009.00537.x.

Key Findings: The single most common perceptual distortion during lethal force encounters is diminished sound, followed by tunnel vision, heightened sense of visual detail, and slow-motion time.

Lee, G., O'Neil, J., & Houlihan, D. (2018). An examination of inattentional blindness in law enforcement in high-stress situations. *Law Enforcement Executive Forum, 18*(4), 38–48.

Key Findings: Based upon an active shooter scenario, the researchers confirmed the existence of inattentional blindness – the inability to visually detect an unexpected stimulus while attending to a task or situation. About 45 percent of the study participants noticed an unusual item or individual, other than the victims (55 percent missed the unexpected stimulus). This detection rate fits with previous literature that suggests about half of participants would be expected to notice an unexpected stimulus when not under a high cognitive load. Under a low cognitive load, participants detected unusual or unexpected items at a higher rate. The higher the cognitive load, the more likely an officer is to miss unexpected or unimportant stimuli within their field of view.

Lewinski, W. J. (2008). The attention study: A study on the presence of selective attention in firearms officers. *Law Enforcement Executive Forum, 89*(6), 107–138. https://www.iletsbeiforumjournal.com/images/Issues/FreeIssues/ILEEF%202008-8.6.pdf.

Key Findings: Based on a particular scenario, this confirmed the existence of inattentional blindness, especially regarding things or details the officers are not focused on. Conferring among officers after a deadly force incident is likely to improve recollection and accuracy of reports. Selective attention and inattentional blindness or tunnel vision/hearing was apparent in every officer except one. Those officers who wrote reports provided about two-thirds less information than those who were interviewed, but the constables who wrote reports made significantly fewer errors than those who were interviewed. Although explored in the study, it is not recommended that officers are interviewed after an emotionally charged deadly-force or high-stress incident, and conferring before report writing or providing a statement is commonly prohibited.

Lewinski, W. J., Dysterheft, J. L., Priem, M. M., & Pettitt, R. W. (2016). Police officers' actual vs. recalled path of travel in response to a threatening traffic stop scenario. *Police Practice & Research, 17*(1), 51–67.

Key Findings: The aim of the study was to examine the average amount of error produced when trying to accurately recall a movement path from a high-stress situation. The experiment confirmed or supported previous research that demonstrated a large amount of error may be anticipated

154 Appendix A: Law Enforcement Human Factors Research

related to spatial details or recalling movement and location during high-stress events.

Lewinski, W. J., & Redmann, C. (2009). New developments in understanding the behavioral science factors in the "stop shooting" response. *Law Enforcement Executive Research Forum, 9*(4), 35–54. https://www.iletsbeiforumjournal.com/images/Issues/FreeIssues/ILEEF%202009-9.4.pdf.

Key Findings: Based on the "Tempe study," which involved pulling a trigger rapidly during a green light and stopping upon seeing a red light, it takes approximately 0.25 seconds. Just as it takes time to start an action (i.e., reactionary gap), so it takes time to stop an action. This 0.25-second gap between the decision to stop shooting and the signal to stop reaching the index finger typically results in one or two more rounds being fired.

Lewinski, W. J., Seefeldt, D. A., Redmann, C., Gonin, M., Sargent, S., Dysterheft, J., & Thiem, P. (2016). The speed of a prone subject. *Law Enforcement Executive Forum, 16*(1), 70–83. https://doi-org.proxy.cecybrary.com/10.19151/leef.2016.1601f.

Key Findings: Depending upon where the weapon is concealed underneath the body of a prone armed assailant, they can remove the weapon and fire one round in 0.52 to 0.77 seconds (from an officer's approach from the feet, at a 45-degree angle to the left or right of the feet, or the head). The fastest draw and fire was from under the chest to the target. Based upon prior research, it takes an officer an average of 0.37 to 0.56 seconds to perceive the threat and initiate action. Officers may be able to reduce the reactionary gap by assessing before moving in to initiate contact.

McClure, K. A., McGuire, K. L., & Loftus, E. F. (2019). Officers' memory and stress in virtual lethal force scenarios: Implications for policy and training. *Psychology, Crime, & Law.* doi: 10.1080/1068316X.2019.1652748.

Key Findings: Information about the perpetrator description was remembered better than information about events, suggesting officers attend to and define the central event relevant to a perpetrator – i.e., that which poses the greatest threat. Increased stress leads to less accurate memory. Memory or recall under high stress or emotion is subject to misinformation.

Phillips, S. W. (2018, Mar. 1). Eyes are not cameras: The importance of integrating perceptual distortions, misinformation, and false memories into the police body camera debate. *Policing: A Journal of Policy and Practice, 12*(1), 91–99. https://doi.org/10.1093/police/paw008.

Key Recommendations: The assumptions that officers who experienced a high-stress force incident can recall details that align frame by frame with video recordings of the incident are empirically unsupported. BWCs and dash cameras can improve many aspects of policing, including (but not limited to) training, developing scenarios, evaluating officer performance, and improving public perception. Police managers, leaders, and district attorneys cannot automatically assume that police officers lied, used bad judgment, or "went rogue" when their actions do not align with video footage. Perceptual distortions, misinformation, and false memories must become part of the "reasonable officer" standard or analysis articulated by the United States Supreme Court in Graham v. Connor (1989).

Ross, D. L. (2013). Assessing lethal force liability decisions and human factors research. *Law Enforcement Executive Research Forum, 13*(2), 85–107. https://www.aele.org/Ross_Forum_2013-2.pdf.

Key Findings: This document contains a thorough overview of the impact of human factors when assessing lethal force liability decisions. Human factors must be part of the objectively reasonable analysis.

Simons, D. J., & Schlosser, M. D. (2017). Inattentional blindness for a gun during a simulated police vehicle stop. *Cognitive Research: Principles and Implications, 2*(1), 37. https://doi.org/10.1186/s41235-017-0074-3.

Key Findings: When completing a routine vehicle stop scenario, both police trainees and experienced patrol officers (trained to look for and assess threats) frequently failed to notice a gun placed conspicuously on the passenger side dashboard. Although experienced officers were more likely than trainees to notice the gun, one-third of them missed it and proceeded to cite the driver. Nearly two-thirds of the trainees missed the gun. Less cognitive energy used by experienced offers regarding what to say, where to stand, and what steps to take versus inexperienced officers using more cognitive energy to accomplish the same task is a potential explanation. This study is the first to demonstrate robust inattentional blindness for an object of direct relevance to participants and their actions in a naturalistic situation.

Appendix B

SAMPLE EXPERT WITNESS REPORT

DT:

TO:

FR: Expert Witness Name

RE: Use-of-force (UOF) review, Case

The following documents were used for this review and analysis:

- All written documents, completed forms, and photographs within case 20-000000.
- Front dash camera footage from squad 58 (Officer Jones)
- Front dash camera footage from squad 62 (Officer Smith)
- Wisconsin Department of Justice Law Enforcement Standards Board (WI DOJ LESB) (2017). Defensive and Arrest Tactics: A Training Guide for Law Enforcement Officers. Madison, WI: DOJ.
- Wisconsin Department of Justice Law Enforcement Standards Board (WI DOJ LESB) (2014). Professional Communication: A Training Guide for Law Enforcement Officers. Madison, WI: DOJ.
- Any City Police Department (2019). Policy 300: Use of Force (Issued 02/15/2019).

NOTE: The report file also contains a cell phone video that captured all or some portion of this force incident. The cell phone video footage was not available to the reviewer at the time of this review and analysis. All other

158 Appendix B: Sample Expert Witness Report

resources used as part of the analysis are listed at the end of the report in the references section.

Request for Review

On Wednesday, September 2, 2020, at 10:56 a.m., I received an email from Lt. A. requesting a "Use of Force Instructor Review" of case 20-000000. The email text read, *"Jim will you review the use of force on 20-000000. This was a resistive subject that Jones used focused strikes on and what he deemed a headlock. There is video of the incident on Jones's front camera. Please look over the details, use of force summary and the video, then let me know your analysis. Thanks A."*

Case Review

Dispatch Information

On Monday, August 24, 2020 at 9:25 a.m., Officer Smith (1C3) and Officer Jones (1C2) were dispatched to a Family Services Day Treatment Center, 100 S. Irwin Avenue (CAD Record Number) for a teenager who had left on foot. The notes indicated it was the "Same juv as earlier." The earlier call (CAD Record Number) involved a "Child out of control ... threatening staff ...p hysical and verbal," named Steven H. (15 years old). In this previous call, Officer Smith entered notes indicating Steven was de-escalated and escorted back inside. Officers frequently respond to this "Day Treatment" facility, which is for youth (ages 7 to 18) who exhibit severe emotional or behavioral issues, including aggression.

While en route to the return call, dispatch notes further indicated staff were following Steven through some back yards and he was then coming at staff with a weapon. Officer Smith arrived on scene (9:28:09) and reported, "he is in a manhole cover." Ten seconds later, dispatch notes indicate, "M (male) had some sort of pole." At 9:29:27, Officer Jones reported, "Fighting W/juvenile male." Twenty-two seconds later, the communications center received a call back from the complainant advising, "Officers need back up ... still physically fighting officers. Both officers are tackling the male now. They are trying to handcuff male now. Had hit an officer with a metal rod."

Review of Details – Officer Smith

Officer Smith's report outlines the nature of the call, consistent with the dispatch notes, and he references the previous call where he de-escalated

Steven and escorted him back inside. Officer Smith initially responded in non-emergency mode but changed to emergency mode when staff reported Steven coming at them with a weapon.

Upon arrival, Officer Smith reported seeing Steven standing inside an uncovered sewer. As Officer Smith exited his squad, Steven quickly walked or ran away. Steven did not obey this lawful order and continued. Steven picked up a metal pole or pipe from the ground. Steven lifted the metal pipe in an overhand motion, like he was going to swing it like a baseball bat. Steven ran at Officer Smith with the metal pole over his head like he was going to hit him with it. As Steven was approximately 10 feet away, Officer Smith attempted to access his taser (a less lethal option against a potentially lethal weapon – a metal pole). Steven was able to rapidly close the 10-foot distance and Officer Smith was unable to successfully remove his taser. Steven swung the metal pole at Officer Smith's head, striking him near the head or neck area. Officer Smith "bear-hugged" Steven and decentralized him to the ground. Officer Smith landed on top of Steven, who was on his back. Steven's active and violent resistance continued by grabbing Officer Smith's testicles and biting his head and ears.

Steven then disarmed Officer Smith by obtaining his taser. Steven pressed the front of the taser against Officer Smith's left shoulder (believed to be an attempt to activate the taser and further injure or incapacitate Officer Smith). Steven was able to get back onto his feet. Officer Smith fought for control of the taser and was able to get it from Steven's grasp and throw it toward the curb and away from Steven. Officer Smith continued his attempt to control and get Steven into custody but was unable to. Officer Smith held Steven in another bear hug and pushed him against the squad car. Officer Smith told Steven to "calm down and to stop." Steven replied, "No, (expletive) you!" Steven continued to bite at Officer Smith's ear and neck area. Officer Smith decentralized Steven back onto the ground.

Officer Jones then arrived on scene. Officer Smith controlled Steven's legs while Officer Jones used active countermeasures (i.e., protective alternatives) against Steven, which he had "no reaction" to. Eventually, Officer Smith and Officer Jones were able to take Steven into custody.

Review of Dash Cam Video – Officer Smith

The majority of this UOF incident occurs off camera. There is no sound associated with the footage. When Officer Smith arrives on scene (09:27:48), Steven is standing inside the sewer. Steven stepped out of the sewer, looked at the squad car, and walked from left to right through and out of the frame, and pulled up his pants (09:27:50). Officer Smith

160 Appendix B: Sample Expert Witness Report

ran from the left to right, through the frame (09:27:55). At 09:28:10, a set of feet are visible in the lower right corner of the frame. This is likely the first time Officer Smith decentralized Steven after attacking Officer Smith with the metal pipe. During this struggle, Steven disarmed Officer Smith from his taser. The feet on the ground appear in the frame until 09:28:19. At 09:28:32, Officer Smith's sunglasses slide across the ground from right to left in the frame. At 09:28:35, Steven entered the right side of the frame, holding Officer Smith's taser in his right hand. Officer Smith was now behind Steven attempting to grab the taser from Steven. Officer Smith was able to get the taser and threw it towards the curb (09:28:37).

Review of Details – Officer Jones

Officer Jones also mentioned the previous call with Steven and, while en route to the scene, dispatch reported Steven had a weapon. Upon arrival, Officer Jones saw Officer Smith standing and fighting with Steven. Officer Jones saw Officer Smith decentralize Steven. Officer Jones saw Officer Smith on top of Steven, but believed something was wrong because Officer Smith was not performing any active countermeasures. When Officer Jones ran up to assist, Officer Smith said, "I am done, you need to take him," indicating officer injury or exhaustion.

Officer Jones tried to move Officer Smith out of the way to get to a more advantageous position. Steven rolled onto one side, which exposed the back of his head. Officer Jones applied strong side forearm strikes to the back of Steven's head because it was the only target area available. The strong side forearm strikes appeared to have no effect and Steven continued to violently resist or continued his assaultive behavior. Steven was able to get into a more advantageous position onto his hands and knees. Officer Jones applied a strong side knee strike to Steven's rib cage and another strong side forearm strike to the back of Steven's head. Both strikes appeared to have little or no effect. Officer Jones delivered another strong side knee strike to Steven's rib cage, two or three forearm strikes to the middle of Steven's back, and yet another strong side knee strike. These active countermeasures, intended to create temporary dysfunction and stop active resistance or violence did not appear effective. In response and along with Officer Jones's physical positioning at the time, he applied a "headlock" on Steven, which allowed Officer Jones to control Steven on the ground. Officer Jones maintained the "headlock" and told Steven to stop resisting and put his hands behind his back. Steven replied, "No, f### you!" Officer Jones described feeling Officer Smith struggle to get Steven handcuffed. At the same time, Officer Jones reported feeling active resistance from Steven. Once Steven was handcuffed and controlled, Officer Jones released the headlock and controlled Steven's head with his hands and inside of his thighs.

Steven made a statement that he could not breathe. Officer Jones released head control, allowed Steven to turn his head to the side, and controlled him with three-point ground stabilization. Steven said, "That's better" (related to being able to breathe).

Review of Dash Cam Video – Officer Jones

Officer Jones's dash camera captured Steven's continued active resistance, Officer Jones's use of force, and Officer Smith's attempt to control Steven. Officer Jones arrived in the area at approximately 09:29:08 and Officer Smith and Steven were in the distance, standing along the passenger side of Officer Smith's marked squad. Officer Smith decentralized Steven to the ground, which is the second decentralization documented in Officer Smith's report. When Officer Jones arrived, Officer Smith was on top of Steven in a ground defense position, inside his guard. Officer Smith's chest rested on top of Steven, Officer Smith's head was turned to his right, and his right hand was planted on the pavement (09:29:17). Steven then used his left arm to encircle the back of Officer Smith's head and neck (09:29:18).

Officer Jones ran to assist Officer Smith. Officer Jones shoved Officer Smith, which created some space in between Officer Smith and Steven. This also caused Steven to roll to his right and onto his stomach, which – if Steven stayed on the ground and stopped resisting – is a more advantageous position for officers. Officer Jones applied strong side forearm strikes near the upper back and head of Steven (09:29:24). Officer Jones and Officer Smith struggled to keep Steven on the ground. Officer Smith wrapped his arms around Steven's waist in an attempt to keep Steven down. Officer Smith attempted to keep Steven on the ground by using his bodyweight on Steven's upper torso. Steven was able to push himself up with two arms into a push-up position and effectively counter the attempts by both officers to control him (09:29:29). Officer Jones applied a strong side knee strike to Steven's right side and another strong side forearm strike to Steven's upper back and head area. Neither strike stopped Steven's resistance, and he continued to attempt a position of advantage by pushing up with his hands and knees. Officer Jones applied another strong side knee strike to Steven's right side, which did not stop Steven's active resistance (09:29:36).

Part of the force incident moved off frame left. Officer Jones can partially be seen applying elbow strikes to Steven's back and another strong side knee strike. This is also captured on Officer Smith's dash camera and mentioned above. None of these focused strikes appeared to stop Steven

162 Appendix B: Sample Expert Witness Report

and he continued to actively resist. The force incident moved back into the frame and Officer Jones applied the "headlock" he reported while obtaining side-mount control (09:29:49). Officer Jones maintained the "headlock" and side control until Officer Smith was able to apply handcuffs and gain control of Steven (09:30:26).

Officer Jones moved to the top of Steven's head and maintained control of Steven's head with his hands and thighs. During the side control, Steven's head was turned right, which would assist his ability to continually breathe. Officer Jones and Officer Smith maintained ground stabilization of Steven until Sgt. Johnson arrived on scene (09:32:06). Stabilization and control of Steven were taken over by Officer G. Raines and Off. T. Thomas. Sgt. Johnson retrieved the "wrap," which is used to safely control violently resistive subjects, and it is eventually applied to Steven.

For the purposes of this review and analysis, the reviewer stopped watching this dash cam footage at the 09:33:00. Also, contained in the footage was the metal pipe, lying on the middle of the roadway (approximately 10 feet away from the force incident), that Steven used to attack Officer Smith.

Review of Details – Officer Santiago

Officer Santiago interviewed Steven at St. Vincent Hospital and obtained an audio recording and signed written statement from him. Within the statement, Steven said he takes medication for anger and took it as prescribed on the day of this incident. Before the police arrived, Steven had become angry because he was told he would not receive any "points" for the day because he was grounded over the weekend. Steven punched a couple of walls inside the building, walked outside, and intentionally scraped his arm against a brick wall because he wanted to feel pain. Steven went back inside the day treatment building to apologize to staff but became angry again when the issue of no points was discussed. Steven left the building.

A female staff member named Jodi began to follow Steven. Steven found and picked up a metal pole. Steven walked towards Jody and said, "Jodi, this is your fault." Jodi said she would leave Steven alone. Steven replied, "No, you're getting this" (referring to being attacked with the metal pole). While Jodi walked away, Steven caught up to her quickly, and Jodi began yelling for help. Steven was thinking about hitting Jodi but did not. Steven put the metal pole into a "small sewer" and took the iron grate off another one and climbed inside.

When Officer Smith arrived on scene, Steven walked away and got the metal pipe. Steven walked towards Officer Smith with the metal pipe, held it above his head, swung it, and struck the officer with it. Officer Smith took Steven to the ground. Steven grabbed Officer Smith's "nuts" and "squeezed/pinched" them. Steven pulled Officer Smith's taser from its holster and attempted to "tase" Officer Smith but could not figure out how it worked. Steven continued "resisting the officer" until a second officer (Officer Jones) arrived, and the "physical altercation" continued. Steven admitted hearing an officer(s) command him to put his hands behind his back and he replied, "No!" Steven continued to resist until he was placed in the "wrap" device.

Steven's signed written statement is consistent with what Officer Santiago reported. In addition, Steven mentioned the "headlock" that Officer Jones applied. While in the "headlock," Steven reported, "I couldn't breathe and felt like I was going to die." Although Steven reported this "feeling," when told to put his hands behind his back he continued to resist and said, "No." Steven also admits, "I was fighting back the whole time because I did not want to be tased or put in handcuffs."

Review of Written Witness Statements

Reviewer Note: It is well documented in research literature that eyewitness recollection is often inaccurate or incomplete. Lack of eyewitness accuracy is not typically because witnesses are lying or being deceitful but are simply mistaken. Therefore, it is not uncommon for eyewitness accounts to conflict with written police accounts or video records.

Witness M. reported the following: Before police arrived, he saw Steven with what he described as a "bamboo stick" chasing after a white female who was yelling for help. It is believed the "bamboo stick" was the metal pipe Steven used to attack Officer Smith. He saw Steven drop the "stick," lift off a manhole cover, and climb inside the manhole. He saw Steven standing inside the manhole with his head sticking out. When Officer Smith arrived, he heard Officer Smith tell Steven to, "Stop!" Steven ignored Officer Smith and Steven picked up his "stick" (i.e., the metal pipe). Officer Smith backed away from Steven. Steven ran at Officer Smith and swung (the "stick") at Officer Smith, who "blocked the strike with his right forearm." Officer Smith pulled out his taser and Steven took it out of Officer Smith's hand. Steven threw the taser onto a driveway in the area. Steven began punching Officer Smith in the head. Officer Smith wrestled Steven to the ground and two officers took Steven into custody.

Witness G. reported the following: Before police arrived, he also saw Steven lift the cover of the manhole and climb inside it. When Officer Smith arrived, he saw Officer Smith tell Steven to stop. Steven ran away from Officer Smith. Steven picked up a "large stick." It is believed the

164 Appendix B: Sample Expert Witness Report

"large stick" was the metal pipe Steven used to attack Officer Smith. He heard Officer Smith yell at Steven to put the "stick" down. Steven then hit one of Officer Smith's arms with the "stick." Officer Smith and Steven began to fight and fell onto the street. At one point, he saw Officer Smith take out his taser and Steven took it and threw it. Officer Smith and Steven continued to fight. Another officer arrived on scene, and both were able to get Steven handcuffed.

Witness H. reported the following: From inside her residence, she heard a female yelling for help. She looked outside and saw Steven with a "metal rod" raised up like he wanted to hit someone. She also saw Steven attempting to get inside a sewer. When Officer Smith arrived on scene, Steven got out of the sewer holding the "metal rod" and walked away from Officer Smith. Officer Smith told Steven to, "Stop!" and Steven struck Officer Smith with the metal rod. Officer Smith lunged at the male and was able to get him to the ground. She possibly heard Officer Smith telling Steven to "Stop resisting!" When Officer Jones arrived, she saw him use his forearm to strike Steven's back. She described Steven as continually "combative" towards officers, "(an) officer had to sit on the male to keep him down," and "he was still kicking his legs as the officer was sitting on it."

Witness K. reported the following: She and a co-worker, Jody, had exited the "Family Services" building to monitor where Steven was going. She saw Steven jump over a fence to the east. She followed Steven while he was walking north on S. Irwin Avenue towards E. Mason Street. She saw Steven lower his pants and urinate on the street. She temporarily lost sight of Steven and found him again on Chicago Street and S. Irwin Avenue where he was being restrained on the ground by two police officers. Steven continued to resist officers while they gave him verbal commands.

Analysis

Any use-of-force (UOF) analysis must include an examination of State DOJ defensive and arrest tactics standards, policy and procedure, and an application of constitutional standards. The analysis is followed by a conclusion about the force used in this incident.

Defensive and Arrests Tactics (DAAT) Standards

Wisconsin law enforcement officers are permitted to use force when it is needed to achieve control of resistive subjects, to detain persons reasonably suspected of criminal behavior, make lawful arrests, to defend themselves

Appendix B: Sample Expert Witness Report **165**

or others, and to prevent escape (WI DOJ LESB, 2017). All five standards existed in this force incident. Officer Smith and Officer Jones encountered a resistive subject who was suspected of criminal behavior, had threatened to attack another person with a metal pipe or pole, had attacked Officer Smith, and attempted to escape.

Any force used by a law enforcement officer must fall into one of the following categories:

- A trained technique
- A dynamic application of a trained technique (i.e. not quite the classroom model, but as close as possible under the circumstances)
- A technique not trained, but justifiable under the circumstances (WI DOJ LESB, 2017).

The force options available to Wisconsin law enforcement officers include presence; dialogue; control alternatives, such as decentralizations, taser, or O.C. spray (to overcome passive resistance, active resistance, or their threats); protective alternatives, such as hand strikes, knee strikes, leg strikes, or brachial stun (to overcome continued resistance, assaultive behavior, or their threats, and temporarily disrupt an assault or continued resistance); and deadly force (to stop imminent behavior likely to cause great bodily harm or death) (WI DOJ LESB, 2017). It is not required for law enforcement officers to progress through force options in a sequential manner (WI DOJ LESB, 2017). Rather, law enforcement officers are authorized to use the amount and level of force reasonably necessary to control a subject and must always maintain a position of advantage (WI DOJ LESB, 2017). Force is not a 50/50 proposition, and the subject determines the level of force officers must use to establish control (WI DOJ LESB, 2017). When force is not effective, an officer may disengage or escalate to a higher level of force (WI DOJ LESB, 2017). Once control is achieved, officers must reduce the level of force to that needed to gain control and ensure appropriate follow-thru considerations (WI DOJ LESB, 2017).

The DAAT manual also discusses "special circumstances." Special circumstances are factors or situations which may justify a rapid escalation force or selection of higher force options. Some of the special circumstances that existed in this case include reasonable perception of the threat, special knowledge of the subject, sudden assault, the subject's ability to escalate force rapidly, and injury or exhaustion.

Deadly force is authorized against an individual who has caused or imminently threatens to cause death or great bodily harm to a law enforcement officer or another person. This assaultive behavior by Steven,

166 Appendix B: Sample Expert Witness Report

specifically the attack with a metal pole towards the head of Officer Smith, could have created a reasonable perception that deadly force was necessary or justified.

In addition to "stand up" defensive and arrest techniques, the DAAT system also contains ground fighting or ground defense techniques to protect officers and control subjects on the ground. The "Inside Guard Defense and Escape" technique includes a move that traps the arm of the subject along their head while the officer encircles the subject's neck or head to help achieve control. This technique can be used to help roll the subject onto their back and for the officer to gain side control and obtain a position of advantage.

The force used by Officers Smith and Jones comprised both trained techniques and dynamic applications of trained techniques. For example, Officer Smith used a "bear hug" as part of a decentralization and Officer Jones applied focus strikes to "other" target areas along with a "headlock" with ground side control, which ultimately allowed for both officers to gain control. A "headlock" is not specifically mentioned or defined in the DAAT system. A dictionary definition of a "headlock" is "a hold in which a wrestler encircles an opponent's head with one arm" (Merriam-Webster, 2020). A "headlock" is not a choke or a lateral vascular neck restraint. A choke occurs when a person encircles the front of the neck of another person and applies pressure to the windpipe, which can restrict breathing. A lateral vascular neck restraint applies pressure to the lateral (i.e. sides) of the neck and applies pressure, which interrupts oxygenated blood flow to the brain and results in unconsciousness. Officer Jones did not apply a choke or a lateral vascular neck restraint. The "headlock" Officer Jones applied is like the side-control techniques demonstrated in the above-mentioned DAAT ground defense video.

When Officer Smith was attacked with the metal pole, he attempted to disengage by creating distance, while moving backwards, as Steven attacked forwards. The estimated distance was 10 feet, which could be rapidly closed by Steven. Officer Smith attempted to use a less-lethal taser against a potentially lethal metal pole. Officer Smith showed great restraint by not escalating to deadly force, which could have been an option in this instance. The metal pole, in the hands of a violent, emotionally disturbed person, could have been perceived to imminently cause great bodily harm or death to Officer Smith, had it hit him on the head.

The protective alternatives (i.e. focused strikes) used by Officer Jones were intended to temporarily disrupt Steven's assaultive behavior or continued resistance. Officer Jones reported the strikes were ineffective. The video depicts the focus strikes, which in fact do appear ineffective.

When the strikes are applied, Steven continues to resist and gains a position of advantage by being on "all fours" (i.e. knees and hands pushing off the ground). Consistent with DAAT training, the application of an ineffective option permits a law enforcement officer to disengage or escalate (i.e. try a different force option). Officer Jones was able to gain control by applying a "headlock" and ground defense side control (discussed above).

The Professional Communications Skills (PCS) manual explains that emotionally disturbed people (EDP) can sometimes react violently and unpredictably (WI DOJ LESB, 2014). The PCS manual also indicates some EDPs can be difficult to control because the chemicals, endorphins, and adrenaline in their systems, as well as the fact that they often feel very focused and determined, can make them very strong (WI DOJ LESB, 2014). Steven was attending a day treatment program and took medication for anger management. Steven's behavior was consistent with being an EDP. In addition to being violently aggressive towards uniformed law enforcement officers, Steven had also lifted an iron sewer grate up and off the hole to climb into it. Based upon this reviewer's experience, an iron sewer grate weighs at least 100 pounds. Officer Smith and Officer Jones used force on Steven – an EDP – who exhibited a focus and determination to assault law enforcement officers or escape. The focused strikes used by Officer Jones appeared ineffective. Officer Jones did not obtain control of Steven until he applied the side headlock and maintained side control until Officer Smith could apply handcuffs.

Officer Smith reported "exhaustion" as an officer/subject factor on the use of force report form. This is also supported by written reports and video footage. The DAAT manual indicates, "If you don't achieve control in the first 20 seconds of a fight, you are likely to quickly run out of energy" (WI DOJ LESB, 2017, p. 28). By the time Officer Jones arrived on scene, Officer Smith had been attempting to achieve control for at least 90 seconds, likely a significant contributor toward exhaustion. Steven's assaultive behavior began with a sudden assault with a weapon (i.e. the metal pole). Steven also demonstrated an ability to quickly escalate violence and assaultive behavior, including disarming Officer Smith from his taser and attempting to discharge the taser into Officer Smith's shoulder. Officer Smith also possessed some special knowledge about Steven, such as being a patient at a day treatment facility with a history of anger management issues, which became apparent via his violent and assaultive behavior upon Officer Smith. These facts further demonstrate the restraint shown by Officer Smith by not resorting to deadly force and further justify the force options used by Officer Smith and Officer Jones.

168 Appendix B: Sample Expert Witness Report

The force applied by Officer Smith and Officer Jones to safely control Steven was consistent with their DAAT training.

Policy and Procedure

Any City Policy 300 regulates UOF by Any City officers. This policy adopts the standards outlined in Wisconsin's DAAT system (discussed above). Section 300.3 incorporates the language outlined in Graham v. Connor (1989), which is discussed below. This same section also recognizes, "Officers may find it more reasonable to improvise their response to rapidly unfolding conditions that they are confronting." This sentence is also consistent with the DAAT concept of "not trained by justified" and "dynamic application of trained techniques." Officer Smith improvised his response when he conducted modified decentralizations. Officer Jones applied a modified headlock and side-mount to control Steven. Their force applications are consistent with policy.

In addition to the factors outlined in Graham (1989) to help determine the reasonableness of force, Any City policy outlines 17 other factors used to determine the reasonableness of force. The Any City policy factors applicable to this case are listed below and related to this force incident.

- Immediacy and severity of the threat to officers or others.
  - Steven demonstrated an immediate and potentially severe threat to Officer Smith when he attacked him with a metal pole. Prior to Officer Smith's arrival, Steven had also threatened to attack a female staff member with the metal pole. The assaultive behavior upon Officer Smith was sudden and aggressive, which exposed Officer Smith to considerable danger.
- The conduct of the individual being confronted, as reasonably perceived by the officer at the time.
  - The perceptions of Steven's violent actions reported by Officer Smith and Officer Jones are reasonable and supported by their written accounts, eyewitness accounts, and video footage.
- Officer/subject factors (age, size, relative strength, skill level, injuries sustained, level of exhaustion or fatigue, the number of officers available vs. subjects).
  - Officer Smith and Officer Jones are experienced and physically fit officers who were larger and stronger than Steven. Officer Jones is a SWAT officer. However, Steven's emotional disturbance and mental illness, along with his focus and determination to assault with a

Appendix B: Sample Expert Witness Report **169**

potentially deadly weapon and physical resistance, allowed him to nearly overcome the attempts of both officers to safely get him into custody. Officer Smith also reported exhaustion, which is supported with video footage and nearly rendered him ineffective. Officer Smith's exhaustion merely allowed him to hold onto Steven as Officer Jones applied reasonable force to control Steven.

- Subject's mental state or capacity.
  - Please read the reviewer's previous comments related to Steven's emotional state.
- Proximity of weapons or dangerous improvised devices.
  - Not only was a weapon (i.e. metal pole) in close proximity to Steven, but he also obtained the weapon and violently assaulted Officer Smith with it. Steven then disarmed Officer Smith from his taser and attempted to deploy it against one of Officer Smith's shoulders, which may have incapacitated him. Officer Smith struggled to regain control of the taser and, when he did, he threw it out of Steven's reach to prevent it from being used against him.
- The availability of other options and their possible effectiveness.
  - When assaulted by Steven with the metal pole, Officer Smith attempted to use a less lethal taser against a potentially lethal weapon. Officer Smith then increased the force to protective alternatives and ground fighting techniques in an attempt to control Steven. Officer Jones applied protective alternatives, which were ineffective, until he applied a "headlock" with side control. Lesser force options were not reasonable because they were ineffective. Had Steven's violent resistance escalated further, other increased force options, up to and including deadly force, may have been justified. Once the force options resulted in control, Officer Smith and Officer Jones de-escalated to three-point ground stabilization until replaced by responding officers.
- Seriousness of the suspected offense or reason for contact with the individual.
  - The seriousness of the offense and reason for the contact with Steven is outlined above.
- Training and experience of the officer(s).
  - Please see comments above under *officer/subject factors*.
- Potential for injury to officers, suspects and others.
  - Please see comments above under *immediacy and severity of the threat to officers or others* and *proximity of weapons or dangerous improvised devices*.

170 Appendix B: Sample Expert Witness Report

- Whether the person appears to be resisting, attempting to evade arrest by flight or is attacking the officer.
  - Please see comments above under *immediacy and severity of the threat to officers or others* and *proximity of weapons or dangerous improvised devices.*
- The risk and reasonably foreseeable consequences of escape.
  - Prior to Officer Smith's arrival, Steven had demonstrated his intent, by words and actions, to assault a female staff member with the metal pole. Officer Smith had previously interacted with Steven on this same date and was aware of his "anger management" reasons for being in day treatment. Based upon Steven's documented words and actions, it is foreseeable to conclude he would pose a threat of harm to others.
- The apparent need for immediate control of the subject or a prompt resolution of the situation.
  - Steven's assaultive behavior upon Officer Smith determined the need for immediate control. Steven's assaultive behavior determined the force response by Officer Smith and Officer Jones. Steven's continued and violent resistance lasted more than 90 seconds, which further supported the need for immediate control before both officers were exhausted and no longer effective.
- Whether the conduct of the individual being confronted no longer reasonably appears to pose an imminent threat to the officer or others.
  - Once Steven's conduct no longer posed an imminent threat to Officer Smith or Officer Jones, they disengaged or de-escalated to three-point ground stabilization and maintained it until relieved by other officers.
- Prior contacts with the subject or awareness of any propensity for violence.
  - See comments outlined above about Steven's propensity for violence.

Based upon this reviewer's analysis of the entire case, the force options used by Officer Smith and Officer Jones are consistent with Any City Policy 300 – Use of Force.

Constitutional

Graham v. Connor (1989) is the landmark case that provides law enforcement officers with guidance on the reasonable application of law enforcement UOF. The Graham court outlined three factors to be considered when determining the reasonableness of force:

- The severity of the alleged offense.
- Whether the suspect poses an imminent threat to the safety of officers or others.
- Whether the suspect is actively resisting or attempting to evade arrest by flight.

Reasonableness must be judged from the perspective of a reasonable officer at the scene rather than with the 20/20 vision of hindsight. Reasonableness must also consider the totality of the circumstances available to the officer at the time.

Officer Smith was dispatched to a day treatment center where Steven had been "coming at staff with a weapon." Although the type of weapon was not mentioned in the dispatch notes, upon Officer Smith's arrival, it was quickly discovered to be a metal pole. Steven then attacked Officer Smith with the metal pole by swinging it at his head. This type of attack had the potential to cause great bodily harm or death. The actions by Steven posed an imminent threat to the safety of Officer Smith (and others before Officer Smith's arrival). Once decentralized by Officer Smith, Steven continued his violent and active resistance, including disarming Officer Smith from his taser. Steven then attempted to deploy the taser into Officer Smith's shoulder, but he was unable to successfully arm the weapon. Officer Smith wrestled the taser away from Steven and threw it out of his reach. Steven continued to violently resist and was decentralized again. Steven bit Officer Smith's ear and face, while encircling the back of his head while on the ground. Although Officer Smith had an advantageous ground position (i.e. a mounted ground position), his exhaustion, coupled with Steven's continued violent and active resistance, justified the applied force options (outlined above). When Officer Jones arrived on scene, Officer Smith made him aware of his exhaustion. Officer Jones applied protective alternatives to stop Steven's violent and active resistance. The protective alternatives were not apparently effective. Officer Smith, apparently exhausted, merely held onto Steven's torso while Officer Jones attempted to obtain control. Control was not obtained until Officer Jones applied a headlock and attained side-mount control, which allowed Officer Smith to handcuff Steven.

Based upon the totality of the circumstances and this reviewer's examination of all the aforementioned materials and facts, the force options used by Officer Smith and Officer Jones are objectively reasonable, consistent with Graham v. Connor (1989).

Conclusion

Based upon this reviewer's analysis of the above-mentioned case files, the force used by Officer Smith and Officer Jones is constitutional and objectively reasonable, consistent with DAAT training principles, and consistent with Any City Policy 300 – Use of Force.

References

Graham v Connor (1989), 490 U.S. 386 (1989).

Merriam-Webster (2020). Headlock. https://www.merriam-webster.com/diction ary/headlock.

Wisconsin Department of Justice Law Enforcement Standards Board (2014). Professional Communications Skills: A Training Guide for Law Enforcement and Jail Officers. Madison, WI.

Wisconsin Department of Justice Law Enforcement Standards Board (2017). Defensive and Arrest Tactics: A Training Guide for Law Enforcement and Jail Officers. Madison, WI.

Sincerely,

SME, D.M., M.P.A.
Doctor of Criminal Justice Management
State of Wisconsin Unified Tactical Trainer

INDEX

accountability, contagious 74
active countermeasures 20–21
attribution bias: definition of 88
auditors, First Amendment 72–3
auditory exclusion 112–13, 121
Axon enterprise program 97, 121

bias: mitigating 90, 136, 144
binocular vision, forced 110
Blake, Jacob 141
body-worn cameras (BWCs):
    benefits of 95–6; challenges
    in court proceedings
    95, 118; limitations of 89; officer
    performance 45–9; optimal
    clarity 65; policies regarding 56–7;
    privacy concerns with 95; and
    Rialto, CA Police Department 44;
    storage of recordings 55–6, 99; and
    UOF frequency 23–4
Bureau of Justice Assistance 124

C.O.P.S. Office, U.S. Department of
    Justice 39
California Human Performance
    Training Institute 125
Carroll v United States 95
clean reporting process 119, 135
cognitive biases 76, 83;
    definition of, 85
cognitive offloading 119

community briefing videos 75–6
confrontation clause, Sixth
    Amendment 98
contagious accountability 74
countermeasures: active 20–1

dash camera recordings: policies 43–4;
    privacy concerns with 95
deadly force: UOF continuum 21; and
    Fourth Amendment 4
deceptive intensity 69
delayed interview: memory recall 115
dialogue: UOF continuum 21
distance-only eyesight 110

emotional stress: memory recall 114
encoding specificity principle 117–8
expert opinions in writing: 144–6;
    sample format for 157–172
eyesight: distance-only 110

First Amendment auditors 72–3
Fischer v State 102
flash-lag effect 66
force outcomes; improved 13
Force Science Institute 125
forced binocular vision 110
forgetting: retrieval-induced 115

Galbraith, Officer R. H. 29
Glick Test 8, 10

174 Index

Graham Factors 14
Graham v Connor 5–8, 87, 106, 117, 138, 145

hearing, diminished *see* auditory exclusion
high-speed chase: first recorded 29
hindsight bias: definition of 82; minimizing 11; and objective reasonableness; on the part of evaluators 135–6
Holliday, George 32
human factors: considerations and objective reasonableness 120–2; definition of 107; and misremembering 116; and UOF decisions 107
Hurlburt, Sergeant Nelson 29–30

inattentional blindness: definition of 111
intensity: deceptive 69
International Association of Directors of Law Enforcement Standards and Training 125
international performance resilience and efficiency program 13
"Intervention Options" system 21–2
interview of officer after incident for optimal recall 114
iREP *see* international performance resilience and efficiency program

Johnson v Glick 8
justice, procedural 69, 74, 121, 135

King, Rodney 32–3, 71

Lewinski, Dr. William 125
Louima, Abner 9
Lunsford, Constable Darrell 33–4

memory recall: delayed interview 115; emotional stress 114; sleep 114; impaired 113–14
Modern Mechanix Magazine 29
Mothers Against Drunk Driving 30, 39
motivational biases 85

National Conference of State Legislatures 75
National District Attorney's Association 42

objective reasonableness 87, 90; and hindsight bias, 82; human factors considerations 122; standard 2, 10, 11, 14, 15
objectively reasonable UOF: steps for assessing 139–40; uniform standards 19
officer recollection v video recording 91, 103, 108, 113, 115, 119, 135, 140

passive countermeasures 21
Peace Officer Standards and Training 145
Peel, Sir Robert 16–17
People v Davis 95
perceptual distortions 107–8
peripheral vision, reduced *see* tunnel vision
physiological impairments 107, 121
Popular Mechanics Magazine 29
presence: UOF Continuum 20–1
procedural justice 69, 74, 121, 135

racial profiling: definition of 53
report writing and viewing video: recommended order 116–20; for evaluation 140
reporting process, clean 119, 135
retention of video evidence 96–7
retrieval-induced forgetting: definition of 115
Rialto, CA Police Department 34, 39
RIF *see* retrieval-induced forgetting

Scott v Harris 76, 98
sensory distortions 106
Sit-D *see* Situational decision-making
situational decision making 13
Sixth Amendment confrontation clause 98
sleep: memory recall 114
sousveillance 32, 71–2
Surgenor, Officer Bob 30–1
Systemic Social Event Modeling 49

tactics system: Wisconsin unified 15–6
Tennessee v Garner 2–4
Thompson, George 18
Time: perceived in slow motion 112–3
tunnel vision 108–10, 112

unified tactics system, Wisconsin 15–16
United Kingdom Police and Crime Standards Directorate 44

use of force (UOF): and fake or facsimile guns 15; frequency of 1, 18; and law enforcement training 12–13; and use of body-worn cameras 23

Verbal Judo 18
video evidence: judicial acceptance 118; as present sense impression 102; as spontaneous statement 99; authentication of 98; in lieu of testimony 98–9; retention of 96–7
video recording vs officer recollection 91, 103, 108, 113, 115, 119, 135, 140

video review: and artificial intelligence 119, 150; influence of slow motion upon 66; Natural Language Systems 50; officer performance 50–1; perception of distance upon 67
video viewing and report writing, recommended order 116–20
videos: community briefing 75–6
Vierordt's Law 65
Vision: forced binocular 110

weapon focus effect 111
Wisconsin unified tactics system 15–16

Printed in the United States
by Baker & Taylor Publisher Services